WEEKEND Adventures

FOR CITY-WEARY PEOPLE

CAROUSEL PRESS

OVERNIGHT TRIPS IN NORTHERN CALIFORNIA

CAROLE TERWILLIGER MEYERS

Other books by Carole Terwilliger Meyers:

*How to Organize a Babysitting Cooperative and Get Some **Free** Time Away From the Kids*

Eating Out With the Kids in San Francisco and the Bay Area

Getting in the Spirit, Annual Bay Area Christmas Events

One in the series: *Weekend Adventures for City-Weary People: Overnight Trips in the U.S.A.*
Copyright © 1984 by Carole Terwilliger Meyers

Library of Congress Catalog Card Number: 83-26139
ISBN: 0-917120-07-8
Printed in the United States of America

first printing, April 1984

10 9 8 7 6 5 4 3 2 1

Additional copies of *Weekend Adventures for City-Weary People* may be ordered by mail. See order form on p. 231.

CAROUSEL PRESS
P.O. Box 6061
Albany, CA 94706

for Gene

CREDITS

Typesetting and layout: Richard Ellington

Cover illustration and design: Ron Chan

Printing: Braun-Brumfield, Inc.

Photos:

page 12: Roaring Camp & Big Trees Narrow-Gauge Railroad

page 16: Marriott's Great America

page 18: Winchester Mystery House

pages 23, 25, 30, 43, 44, 45, 47, 50, 62, 78, 82, 83, 91, 102, 114, 119, 139, 157, 162, 192: California Department of Parks and Recreation

page 32: Jerry Lebeck, Monterey Peninsula Visitors & Convention Bureau

page 34: Pete Amos, California Department of Parks and Recreation

page 52: Theodore Osmundson, California Department of Parks and Recreation

page 54: John Kaestner, California Department of Parks and Recreation

page 61: King Merrill Associates, Solvang Business Association

pages 64, 73, 76, 98, 104, 108, 223: Redwood Empire Association

pages 68, 86: Ansel Adams, Redwood Empire Association

page 79: Eureka Inn

pages 120, 141, 149, 154: Larry Paynter, California Department of Parks and Recreation

pages 122, 127, 203, 204: Yosemite Park and Curry Company

page 125: John Michael Flint, Oakwood Lake

pages 130, 206: John M. Giosso, San Francisco Recreation and Park Department

page 136: Patt Gilman Public Relations

page 143: 39th District Agricultural Association

pages 164, 174, 182, 183: Greater Reno Chamber of Commerce

page 170: Travel Systems Ltd.

page 176: Northstar

page 179: Boreal

pages 184, 187: John F. Reginato, Shasta-Cascade Wonderland Association

page 196: Bob Everson, Alpine Meadows

page 197: Vance Fox, Northstar

page 200: Royal Gorge Nordic Ski Resort

page 212: Shasta-Cascade Wonderland Association

page 215: Dick Linford, ECHO

page 216: Wilderness Adventures

page 218: Shasta Llamas

page 221: Stone Witch Expeditions

TABLE OF CONTENTS

Due to inflation, many of the prices quoted in this book will be out of date before the book is even published. Specific prices are mentioned only to give you an approximate idea of what to expect. Phone numbers and addresses are listed so that you may call or write to determine current rates. All establishments listed in this book are mentioned to alert the reader to their existence; they are in no way endorsed by the author or publisher.

INTRODUCTION

It is quite frustrating to discover an area's main attractions after you have left. Most travelers don't take the time to collect and read all the brochures and books which would alert them to these facilities. This book is designed so that the reader can quickly determine what is of special interest in the area being visited. Phone numbers and addresses necessary for obtaining further information are included. With the aid of this book, a person can more easily plan trips and get the most out of a weekend away.

PLANNING TRIPS

- Write or call the Chamber of Commerce or Visitors Bureau in the area you plan to visit. Ask to be sent all pertinent literature. If traveling with children, ask for specific recommendations for families.

- Have children help pick a destination and plan the trip. Do some research together. Look at maps. (You may want to consider joining the **California State Automobile Association,** which offers excellent maps and services to members.) Create a flexible agenda. Plan to allow sufficient travel time between destinations so that you can make spontaneous exploration stops along the way.

- Hang up on a wall a detailed map of California. Use colored pushpins or flags to mark places you have visited. Children especially enjoy doing this.

- Make advance reservations at motels and campgrounds to avoid disappointment and a frantic, last-minute search for anything—and the possibility of finding nothing. Reservations sometimes save you money as well. Inexpensive rooms often are reserved first, leaving the expensive (albeit usually more luxurious) rooms for last-minute arrivals. Always ask for a written confirmation. Take it along as proof of your reservation. If you must cancel, do so as soon as possible. A complete refund is usually given with at least 48 hours notice.

> **Carole's Law of the Road:** The tendency to get sick increases in direct proportion to the approach of a trip. This is even more likely if you've paid a non-refundable deposit on accommodations.

- Take along sleeping bags for kids. Children are often allowed to sleep on the floor of your room at no charge. If you want to do this, inquire ahead of time about the lodging's policy.

- If you require a crib, reserve one at the time you make your room reservation. Otherwise, you may find none available when you arrive. Or purchase a portable crib to use when traveling. *Childcraft* (800/631-5652) sells a particularly nice one made of fabric and wood for approximately $100. A pattern for making a similar one appears on p. 182 of the May 1983 issue of *Sunset* magazine.

- Remember to take along traveler's checks or adequate cash. Surprisingly, some lodging and dining facilities will not accept out-of-town checks or credit cards.

- Make a checklist of all the items you need to gather or buy for your trip. For instance, if you are going to a beach or river area in the summer, you will want to consider taking along the following items:

swimsuits	sand toys
towels	inner tubes
suntan lotion	sandals/tennis shoes
beach blanket	air mattress
back rest	balls
sun umbrella	

And remember that if you do forget something, most of the destinations mentioned in this book are near a store where you can buy emergency replacements.

- Plan to start the trip early in the morning. Packing the night before helps. Plan to arrive at your destination early in the day to allow time to relax.

- When you arrive, reread the appropriate sections in this book to familiarize yourself with local facilities. Also, check the yellow pages in the telephone book for further information on things to do:

babysitting services	bicycle rentals
horseback riding/ stables	public swimming pools/ plunges
restaurants	skating rinks

Check, too, the local newspapers and tourist guides for current special events and activities.

TRAVELING WITH CHILDREN

Helpful Hints in the Car

Traveling anywhere in a car with children can be a trying experience for everyone concerned. Even short trips can be exhausting and can leave everyone in real *need* of a vacation. (Do you know where I can purchase the kind of taxi that has bulletproof, soundproof glass separating the parents from the kids—I mean the driver from the passenger?) If you can't leave the kids home or are in one of those moods where you really want to take them along, here are some suggestions on how to make a family car trip a more pleasurable experience.

- California residents are required by law to use a car seat for children under age 5 or weighing less than 40 pounds. For detailed information on the importance of car seats and brand recommendations, refer to *Consumer Reports* at your library. A fabric pad/liner makes the seat easier to clean and protects the child from the danger of hot plastic. Use seat belts for older children.

- Use a luggage rack to handle trunk overflow. For comfort, leave as much space as possible in the passenger section.

- Take along blankets and pillows for napping. Towels make good covers for hot carseats and can be used in countless other ways (rolled up as a pillow, to mop up spills, etc.)

- Keep a first-aid kit in your trunk. Fill it with:

bandages	children's aspirin
antiseptic	thermometer
safety pins	scissors
tweezers	adhesive tape
a roller bandage	gauze pads
q-tips	soap

washcloth   flashlight
a few dimes for emergency phone calls
These items will fit inside a large, empty coffee can.

- For clean-ups, pack pre-moistened towels or a damp wash-cloth in a plastic bag.

- Keep a package of medium-sized plastic bags in your car's trunk. These are handy for many things: holding messy items such as bibs, diapers, and wet bathing suits; holding items children collect; etc.

- Use a shoebag, hung on the back of the front seat or on the car door, to store games and miscellaneous items.

- Pack a supply of non-messy snacks for the road. Some ideas:

fruit rolls	dried apple rings
raisins	granola bars
cheese	apples
animal crackers	bananas
fig newtons	small boxes of dry cereal
small cans of juice, straws	

- For a long trip keep an ice chest stocked with milk, drinks, fruit, and other nutritious but perishable foods.

- Keep a good travel game book in the glove compartment.

- Consider packing only water for drinks. When spilled, it isn't sticky. A fun idea is to recycle commercial plastic containers which resemble lemons and limes. Empty the citrus juice, remove the insert (an ice pick helps), rinse, and fill with water. Children can then squirt drinks into their mouths with a minimum of mess and bother. Another idea is to give each child their own small thermos of water.

- Make disposable bibs by using an old *sweater guard* to hold a table napkin around the baby's neck.

- Purchase a molded plastic bib to use when dining. It is especially wonderful for catching ice cream drips. All you have to do to clean it is wipe or rinse.

- Have a few wrapped presents on hand to use for distracting children during restless times. Select items which are good additions to the goodie bag (see p. 6).

- Make a rest stop every few hours. This is a good time to eat, enjoy a sightseeing sidetrip, or let children run off some pent-up energy at a park.

- Picnic when possible. After the cramped experience of a car ride, a restaurant can sometimes feel too confining. Gas station attendants can be helpful in providing directions to a local park with a playground.

- Avoid eating in drive-ins. It is usually messy to eat in the car and it offers no chance to stretch, even though it does save time.

- A quick, inexpensive breakfast stop at a donut shop can help you get on the road fast.

- Buy gas in small quantities. Never fill the tank unless you are driving in desolate areas. This will require you to stop more frequently, giving passengers time to stretch, get drinks, and visit the restroom.

- Adults can take turns driving. The nondriving adult can sit in the back seat with one (two, three . . .) child while the other child sits in the front seat with the driver. This helps keep squabbles to a minimum and also gives the back-seat parent and child a chance to spend some time together. And, even though many adults will not jump at the chance to sit in the back seat, most children will jump at the chance to sit in the front seat.

- When traveling with a baby, consider purchasing a bottle warmer which plugs into the car's cigarette lighter. Also, removable screens for the car's windows keep the sun off baby and out of his/her eyes.

- For a baby no longer on formula but still on a bottle, try putting 1/3 cup (2 2/3 oz.) of powdered milk in a baby bottle. When milk is needed, add water to make 8 oz. and shake. This eliminates the need for refrigeration and is handy any time you are away from home.

- Turn your children into navigators. Give each his own map and then let each determine how far it is to the next town, etc. Give them a wide felt-tip pen to trace the route as you go.

- Provide each child with a notepad to use as a trip diary. Encourage them to make entries each day. Older children can do this alone. For younger children, you can write down what they dictate. Have crayons available for them to illustrate with. If you have an instant print camera, let each child take a few pictures each day to illustrate the diary.

- An inexpensive souvenir is postcards. Let your children select a few at each destination. They could also be used to illustrate their diaries. Or they can be kept as a collection, held together with a rubber band. Children could also write diary entries on the back of their postcards and keep a postcard diary.

- To help get all your gear from the car to the beach, consider using a molded plastic sled (borrowed from your winter checklist). Pack everything in the sled and drag it along the sand to your spot. Filled with a little water, it also makes a great place for a baby to splash and play safely.

- Try the **mad bag/glad bag** trick. Give each child a bag filled with nickels or dimes at the beginning of the trip. Mom and dad begin the trip with an empty bag. When a child has been deemed naughty, he must give up a coin to the parents' bag. If you are a liberated parent, you can let it work the other way too. Any coins left in the child's bag at the end of the trip are his to keep.

- Older children can make good use of a portable tape recorder. My family has found that it is especially fun to listen to prerecorded story tapes together. But when a child turns on the music in our car, he also puts on earphones.

- Travel in a motorcycle with a sidebucket. Daddy and one kid sit on the cycle, mommy and another sit in the bucket. This may be a very unsafe and inconvenient form of travel, but you won't hear a word.

THE GOODIE BAG

A good way to keep children occupied and happy on a car trip is to provide each with his own goodie bag. For the bag itself you might use an old purse, a back pack, a small basket, a shopping bag, a small suitcase, a plastic bucket, or a covered metal cake pan. Whichever container you choose, be sure to have a separate one for each child and try to fill them with the same items (or equivalent items if their interests differ). A flat, hard container makes a good foundation for writing and coloring. Things you might put inside include:

pads of paper	small scraps of
scotch tape	colored paper
colored pencils/	gummed paper shapes
felt pens	or stickers
midget cars	magic slate
finger puppets	eraser
little people toys	magnetic puzzles,
story books	chess, checkers
car games	sewing cards
workbooks	magnifying glass
pencil box	photo viewer toy
blunt scissors	small chalkboard
card games	and chalk
crayons	felt board and shapes
coloring books	glue stick
pipe cleaners	etch-a-sketch toy
snap-lock plastic	sponge puzzle
beads	plastic bags to
paper dolls	hold collectibles

The items you choose to put in the goodie bag will depend on your child's age. Be sure to keep the bag stocked and ready to go, and keep your eyes open for new items to unveil on future trips. For younger children, don't forget to bring along their lovies—teddy bear, blanket, etc.

I think you will find the goodie bag so useful that you will begin using it in other ways—on a rainy day, when your children are sick, when you leave them with a babysitter, and maybe even when you dine out in a restaurant

Picnic Goodie Bag

I usually prefer to just stop at a delicatessen for picnic fare. To help make our picnics more comfortable, I always keep in the trunk of my car: a picnic blanket, a day pack (for those picnic spots that require a hike to reach), and a plastic pull-string bag stocked with paper plates, cups, napkins, plastic eating utensils, straws, a can opener, and a corkscrew.

Musical Goodie Bag

For family fun by the campfire or fireplace, pack a musical goodie bag. The following inexpensive items can be purchased in most music shops:

slide whistle	plastic flute
kazoo	whistle
small tambourine	wooden rhythm blocks
jew's-harp	ratchet
gongs	rasps
bells	harmonica
cymbals	

Beach Play Goodie Bag

Many of these items can be gathered from your kitchen. Remember to avoid glass. I prefer to store them all in one big plastic bucket and save them especially for trips to the water.

spray bottle	bucket
spatula	funnel
scoop	cookie cutters
pastry brush	strainer
plastic cups	pancake turner
measuring spoons	

CONDOMINIUMS

Condominiums are a good choice for family lodging, especially when the stay is for longer than a weekend. And, though prices are not inexpensive, they are usually competitive with motels, and the condos offer additional space in the form of extra bedrooms, a living room, and kitchen. Vacation money can be stretched by making use of the kitchen to prepare breakfast and put together a picnic lunch. Barbecues are often available for cooking the evening meal. Occasional meals out then become more affordable.

Many condo complexes offer shared recreational facilities such as a pool, jacuzzi, and tennis courts as well as amenities such as laundry facilities and fireplaces. In the winter, packages with nearby ski resorts are often available.

The reservation numbers listed in this book are usually for an owners' rental service. Because maid service and office expenses have to be covered, the units cost more than if you rented directly from the owner. If you like staying in condos, be alert for advertised units. You'll save money that way.

GUIDELINES
FOR INTERPRETING THIS BOOK

This book is organized by geographical area. Each chapter has the following subsections:

Chamber of Commerce or Visitors Bureau: address, phone number.

Annual Events: where to get further information. Listings are in chronological order.

A Little Background: historical and general background information about the area; what kinds of activities to expect.

Getting There: other than car transportation; scenic driving routes.

Route: the quickest, easiest driving route; starting point is San Francisco.

Stops Along the Way: noteworthy places to stop for meals or sight-seeing.

Where to Stay: a select sampling of lodging facilities listed alphabetically and, when available, including the following information: name, address, toll-free 800 reservations number, area code and phone number, price range per night for two people/four people (see price code below), months closed, special facilities. Private baths are generally in all rooms unless otherwise stated. A ♥ before a listing indicates a "for adults only" establishment.

$ = under $45
$$ = $45–$65
$$$ = $65–$100
$$$+ = over $100

In 1982 the nation-wide average for a motel room was $39, a hotel room $58.

Where to Eat: a selective sampling of worthwhile restaurants listed alphabetically and, when available, including the following information: name, address, phone, meals served, days open, availability of highchairs, booster seats, children's portions; price range (see price code below), reservations status, credit cards accepted (see code below). Always call to confirm any information, as it frequently changes.

$ = inexpensive. Dinner for one adult might cost up to $10.

$$ = moderate. Dinner for one adult might cost from $10 to $15.

$$$ = expensive. Dinner for one adult might cost from $15 to $25.

Projected costs are based on dinner prices and are exclusive of drinks, dessert, tax, and tip.

Credit Cards: AE = American Express
CB = Carte Blanche
DC = Diners Club
MC = MasterCard
V = Visa, BankAmericard

What to Do: activities and sights in the area which are of special interest, listed alphabetically. Some of these facilities are closed on major holidays. Always call first to verify hours.

Side Trips: areas of special interest which are close by.

SANTA CRUZ MOUNTAINS

San Lorenzo Valley Chamber of Commerce
Boulder Creek 95006
408/338-4093

- *A LITTLE BACKGROUND*
Hidden in a dense redwood forest, this once-popular resort
area is now a little frayed around the edges. Motels and cabins,
many relics from a heyday that is long past, are generally far
from luxurious. Still, the abundance of trees, trails, and swimming holes as well as reasonable prices make it a choice destination for bargain-hunting vacationers.

- *ROUTE*
Located approximately 70 miles south of San Francisco. Take
Hwy 280 to Hwy 84 to Hwy 35 to Hwy 9.

- *WHERE TO STAY*
  Ben Lomond Hylton Motel, *9733 Hwy 9, Ben Lomond 95005, 408/336-
  5643; 2/$; pool; TVs; continental breakfast.* These motel rooms and
  cottages are shaded by tall redwoods on the banks of the San Lorenzo River.
  Griffin's Resort Motel, *5250 Hwy 9, Felton 95018, 408/335-4412; 2/$;
  some kitchens and fireplaces; TVs.* These cabins are located on the
  river across from Henry Cowell State Park.

11

Jaye's Timberlane Resort, *8705 Hwy 9, Ben Lomond 95005, 408/336-5479; 2/$, 4/$$; some fireplaces; kitchens, TVs; pool; cribs; two-night minimum in summer.* These modern cabins are scattered among the redwoods.

Merrybrook Lodge, *Big Basin Hwy (P.O. Box 845), Boulder Creek 95006, 408/338-6813; 2/$; closed Nov–April; some kitchens and fireplaces; TVs; 7-night minimum in cottages July & Aug.* These cabins and motel units are tucked in the redwoods; some overlook a creek.

■ *WHERE TO EAT*

Scopazzi's Inn, *Big Basin Way, Boulder Creek, 408/338-4444; lunch and dinner W–Sun; highchairs, booster seats, children's portions; reservations suggested; $$; AE, MC, V.* Italian fare is served in the casual atmosphere of this spacious, rustic 1904 mountain lodge. Menu choices include Italian items like cannelloni, veal scaloppine, and lamb chops Toscana as well as prime rib, fried prawns, and pepper steak flambé.

■ *WHAT TO DO*

Big Basin Redwoods State Park, *Big Basin, 408/338-6132.* California's

oldest state park, Big Basin features a Nature Lodge with exhibits and over 50 miles of hiking trails. Self-guiding Redwood Trail leads to interesting redwoods like the Animal Tree and the Chimney Tree. Campsites are available.

Covered Bridge, *off Graham Hill Rd., Felton.* Built over the San Lorenzo River in 1892, this creaky redwood bridge can still be walked on and is now a State Historical Landmark. Measuring 34 feet high, it is the tallest bridge of its kind in the U.S.

Henry Cowell Redwoods State Park, *Felton, 408/335-4598.* A number of trails lead through the park's redwood groves. Campsites are available.

Highlands County Park, *8500 Hwy 9, Ben Lomond, 408/336-8551; daily 9am–dusk, pool spring and summer 12:30–5pm; parking fee; pool, adults $1, 16 and under 75¢.* The grounds of this old estate have been transformed into a park with pool, playground, picnic tables, and nature trails leading to a sandy river beach.

Loch Lomond Recreation Area, *on Zayante Rd. 8 miles north of Felton, 408/335-7424; March–Sept daily 6am–sunset; $2.50/car.* Fishing, boating (rentals are available), and picnicking (barbecue facilities are available) are the main activities here. Swimming is not permitted.

Roaring Camp & Big Trees Narrow-gauge Railroad, *Graham Hill Rd., Felton, 408/335-4484; daily, call for schedule; adults $7.50, 3–15 $5.* This six-mile, hour-long train ride winds through virgin redwoods and crosses over several spectacular trestles. A stop is made at Bear Mountain, where riders may disembark for a picnic or hike and then return on a later train. An outdoor chuckwagon barbecue restaurant operates near the depot on weekends from noon to 3pm May through October. Bring along tidbits for the hungry ducks in the lake. Also bring sweaters. Though this area enjoys basically warm to hot weather in the summer, it can get chilly on the train ride.

SWIMMING HOLES:

Ben Lomond County Park, *Mill St., Ben Lomond, 408/336-9962; daily in summer; free.* A sandy beach and rope swing accent the good river swimming. Shaded picnic tables with barbecue facilities are available.

Boulder Creek Park, *Middleton Ave. east of Hwy 9, Boulder Creek; free.* This swimming hole has both shallow and deep areas and a sandy beach. Picnic tables and barbecue facilities are in a shady area.

LOS GATOS

Los Gatos Chamber of Commerce
5 Montebello Way
Los Gatos 95030
408/354-9300

■ *A LITTLE BACKGROUND*
Tucked in the lush, green Santa Cruz mountains, Los Gatos is known for its many antique shops.

■ *ROUTE*
Located approximately 60 miles south of San Francisco. Take Hwy 101 to Hwy 17 to the Los Gatos exit.

■ *WHERE TO STAY*

Los Gatos Garden Inn Motel, *46 E. Main St., 95030, 408/354-6446; 2/$$, 4/$$$+; some kitchens; pool; TVs; continental breakfast; three-night minimum on kitchen units.* These rustic Spanish bungalows offer quiet rooms and a location just two blocks from Old Town.

Los Gatos Lodge, *50 Saratoga Ave., 95030, 408/354-3300; 2/$$; some kitchens; pool, whirlpool; tennis courts; TVs; cribs; dining facilities.* This modern motel is located on attractive, spacious grounds. A putting green and lawn games are available to guests.

Saratoga Hostel, *15808 Sanborn Rd., Saratoga 95070, 408/867-3993.* These cottages are located in a redwood grove in the foothills of the Santa Cruz mountains. See also p. 219.

■ *WHERE TO EAT*

Mimi's, *in Old Town, 408/354-5511; breakfast and lunch daily, weekend brunch; highchairs, booster seats; reservations suggested; $; MC, V.* Anytime is a good time to dine outside among the hanging geraniums at Mimi's, but I think the best time is at breakfast when apple pancakes and strawberry waffles are on the menu. Exotic coffees, ice cream sundaes, and rich pastries are house specialties.

♥ **Mountain Charley's,** *15 N. Santa Cruz, 408/354-2510, call for hours and current music schedule.* This exceptional bar is a place you'll want to know about if you're in town and get thirsty. A live band and long communal tables make a visit to this jumping, gigantic saloon an exciting experience. Age minimum 21.

Noodle Palace, *140 N. Santa Cruz Ave., 408/354-0555; lunch and dinner daily; highchairs, booster seats, children's portions; no reservations;*

$$; MC, V. The huge dining area in this barn-like building is furnished with antiques. Diners choose from seven spaghetti sauces served over oodles of noodles. Ravioli, baked chicken, and roast beef are also on the menu. Dinners are served with salad and bread. Another part of the restaurant is devoted to Chinese Mandarin cuisine. Italian and Chinese food served in the same restaurant *is* an odd combination, but both are favored by children, making this a good dining choice for young families.

Pedro's, *316 N. Santa Cruz Ave., 408/354-7570; lunch and dinner daily, Sun brunch; highchairs, booster seats; no reservations; $$; MC, V.* This popular restaurant features an authentic Mexican decor and huge servings of tasty Mexican dishes. Unusual menu items include chimichangas (deep-fried flour tortillas filled with spicy shredded beef and topped with guacamole and sour cream), quesadillas (large flour tortillas filled with Jack cheese and topped with guacamole and sour cream), and—the house specialty—a crab enchilada. There is often a wait to get in. Some people pass the time sipping Margaritas and munching cornchips and salsa outside on the patio or in the cozy bar.

■ *WHAT TO DO IN TOWN*

Los Gatos Museum, *4 Tait St., 408/354-2646; Tu–Sun 10am–4pm; free.* Housed in a Spanish-style building, this small museum features exhibits on local history, science, and contemporary fine arts.

Novitiate Winery, *300 College Ave., 408/354-6471; tasting daily 10am–5pm; tours M–F 1:30 & 2:30pm, Sat 11am & 1pm; free.* Jesuit cellarmasters hand-cultivate the grape harvest at this renowned winery. Part of the harvest is still used to make sacramental wine. A picnic area is available.

Old Town, *50 University Ave., 408/354-5432; M–W & Sat 10am–6pm, Thur & F to 9pm, Sun noon–5pm.* Once the town elementary school, this attractive complex is now a series of interesting shops and restaurants. Free entertainment is often scheduled in the outdoor amphitheater.

PARKS:

Oak Meadow Park, *off Blossom Hill Rd.* This 12-acre park has picnic facilities, baseball diamonds, hiking trails, and a well-equipped playground with a *real* fire engine and airplane to climb on. **Billy Jones Wildcat Railroad,** a miniature steam locomotive, operates daily in summer, weekends in the spring and fall.

Vasona Lake County Park, *off Blossom Hill Rd.* This 175-acre park is dominated by a huge reservoir where you can rent canoes and sailboats, feed hungry ducks and seagulls, and fish—not to mention use the barbecue facilities and playground and visit the **Youth Science Institute.**

■ *WHAT TO DO NEARBY*

Garrod Farms Riding Stables, *22600 Mt. Eden Rd., Saratoga, 408/867-9527; daily 8:30am–4:30pm; $10/hour.* Ponies are available for young children to ride; an adult must walk them with a lead rope.

Hakone Japanese Garden, *21000 Big Basin Way, Saratoga, 408/867-3438*

x50; M–F 10am–5pm; Sat & Sun 11am–5pm; free. Now a city park, this garden was originally constructed by private interests to typify a mid-17th century Zen garden. It includes a Japanese-style house built without nails or adhesives, a pond stocked with Koi, and an authentic Tea Ceremony room.

Marriott's Great America, *on Great America Pkwy off Hwy 101 or Hwy 237, Santa Clara, 408/988-1800; call for schedule; $11.95, under 3 free.* There's no question about it: the thrill rides here are spectacular. The three roller coasters are great shocking fun. Then there are the Yankee Clipper and Logger's Run flume rides, the double-decker carousel, and the Sky Whirl—the world's first triple-arm Ferris wheel. Kid Kingdom features special rides and activities for children under 12.

Paul Masson Vineyards, *13150 Saratoga Ave., Saratoga, 408/725-4270; tours and tasting daily 10am–4pm; free.* Audio wands guide visitors through a tour of the champagne cellar. A large collection of antique wine glasses is on display.

Rosicrucian Egyptian Museum, *Park Ave./Naglee, San Jose, 408/287-9171; Sat–M noon–4:45 pm, Tu–F 9am–4:45pm; free.* Collection highlights include mummies, fine jewelry, and a full-size reproduction of a 4,000-year-old rock tomb—the only such tomb in the United States. The surrounding buildings and grounds are stunning; an adjacent Planetarium presents shows daily at 2pm.

Villa Montalvo, *Montalvo Rd./Hwy 9, Saratoga, 408/867-3421; arboretum: daily 9am–5pm, free; gallery: Tu–Sun 1–4pm; adults 50¢, under 19 free.* This majestic Mediterranean-style estate was once the summer home of U.S. senator James Phelan. Now it is the county center for fine arts and also serves as a bird sanctuary. Self-guided nature trails wind through the 175-acre estate gardens. Theatrical events are staged in the natural outdoor amphitheater and Carriage House Theater; call 408/249-8330 for information.

Winchester Mystery House, *525 S. Winchester Blvd., San Jose, 408/247-2101; daily 9am–4:30pm; adults $7.95, 6-12 $4.95, under 6 free.* As the story goes, Sarah Winchester, heir to the $20 million Winchester rifle fortune, believed that to make amends for a past wrongdoing she had to build additions to her home continuously, 24 hours a day. Her eccentric ideas resulted in some unusual features: asymmetrical rooms, narrow passageways, zigzag staircases, and doors opening into empty shafts. The tour takes in 110 rooms and more than 200 steps and covers almost a mile. (See photo page 18.)

Winchester Mystery House

COAST SOUTH

■ *WHERE TO STAY*

Montara Lighthouse Hostel, *on Hwy 1,* **25** *miles south of San Francisco,* *(P.O. Box 737), Montara 94037, 415/728-7177.* This restored 1875 lighthouse is now the cliffside setting for a picturesque retreat. Lodging is in a modern duplex—formerly the lightkeeper's quarters. Facilities include two kitchens, a laundry, a private beach, an outdoor hot tub, and bicycle rentals. See also p. 219.

San Benito House, *Main St./Mill (Route 1, Box 4A), Half Moon Bay 94019,* **35** *miles south of San Francisco, 415/726-3425; 2/$-$$; some shared baths; one suite with TV and kitchen; sauna; continental breakfast; dining facilities.* The upstairs rooms feature solid walls, high ceilings, and bathrooms with old-fashioned tubs. The charmingly decorated downstairs dining room features country-French cuisine made with fresh local produce and seafood. The kitchen is famous for its delicious French pastries. Make reservations when you book your room, as this cozy restaurant is also very popular with locals. The lively Western-style saloon also on the premises is the perfect spot for a nightcap.

Pigeon Point Lighthouse Hostel, *on Hwy 1,* **50** *miles south of San Francisco (P.O. Box 477), Pescadero 94060, 415/879-0633.* Built in 1871, this scenic lighthouse is the second tallest in the U.S. and now houses visitors in modern bungalows. Excellent tidepools are located just to the north. See also p. 219.

19

■ *WHAT TO DO*

Nearby activities include whale-watching expeditions (**Oceanic Society** trips leave from Princeton-By-The-Sea, 415/775-6880; reservations necessary), tide pooling (**Fitzgerald Marine Reserve**, 415/728-3584), horseback riding and hayrides (**Sea Horse Ranch** 415/726-2362, **Friendly Acres** 415/726-9871), and tours to see the elephant seals (**Año Nuevo State Reserve**, 415/879-0227, 879-0228; Dec–March, reservations necessary). Visiting the nearby beaches in summer and pumpkin fields in autumn are also popular activities.

SANTA CRUZ

Santa Cruz County Convention & Visitors Center
P.O. Box 1476
(Church/Center Sts.)
Santa Cruz 95061
408/423-6927

■ *A LITTLE BACKGROUND*

Santa Cruz has long been a popular summer beach resort and is close enough to San Francisco to consider visiting for just the day. The weather is reliably clear and sunny, and the beach features fine sand and a gentle surf.

■ *ROUTE*

Located approximately 80 miles south of San Francisco. Take Hwy 101 to Hwy 17, or Hwy 1 all the way.

■ *WHERE TO STAY*

Casa Blanca Motel, *101 Main St., 95060, 408/423-1570; 2/$-$$$, 4/$$-$$$; some kitchens, fireplaces, and ocean views; TVs, cribs; dining facilities.* Located across the street from the beach, this converted 1918 mansion features spacious, nicely decorated rooms. More modern rooms are available in the 1950s annex. Dinners and Sunday brunch are served in an adjoining restaurant.

Dream Inn, *175 W. Cliff Dr., 95060, 800/662-3838, 408/426-4330; 2-4/$$$; pool; ocean views, TVs; cribs; dining facilities; children under 12 stay free in parents' room.* Located right on the beach, each room in this huge hotel has a private balcony overlooking the beach and ocean.

Ocean Echo Motel & Cottages, *401 Johans Beach Dr., 95062, 408/475-8381; 2/$$-$$$, 4/$$$; some kitchens and ocean views; TVs; cribs.* Located a few miles south of the Boardwalk, these units are on a private beach.

Other. Many more motels are located in the area surrounding the Boardwalk, including some inexpensive ones dating from the 1930s.

■ *WHERE TO STAY NEARBY*

Pajaro Dunes, *2661 Beach Rd., Watsonville 95706, 408/722-9201; 2/$$$-$$$+, 4/$$$+; kitchens, fireplaces; some ocean views and TVs; 19 tennis courts; cribs; two-night minimum.* Facilities in this complex of condominiums and homes include bicycle rentals and a small parcourse.

■ *WHERE TO EAT*

Cooper House Restaurant, *110 Cooper St., 408/429-1414; breakfast, lunch, and dinner daily; highchairs and booster seats; no reservations outside; $$; MC, V.* Enjoying a meal on the patio here is a pleasant way to while away a sunny afternoon. Live jazz, fresh air, happy people, and good food (soups, salads, fresh seafood) make the experience memorable. Dinner is more formal and is served only inside, in the candle-lit dining room. The restored Cooper House building, the town courthouse circa 1895, houses a variety of shops including a very good candy/nut concession and a shop specializing in rainbow items.

The Crow's Nest, *2218 E. Cliff Dr., 408/476-4560; lunch and dinner daily; $$; MC, V.* Dine outdoors, protected by a glass windbreaker, and watch the yachts come and go from the Santa Cruz Yacht Harbor. Steak, seafood, and an oyster and salad bar are available, but so are hamburgers and enchiladas. Nightly entertainment ranges from folk to jazz.

El Palomar, *1344 Pacific Ave., 408/425-7575; lunch and dinner W-Sun; highchairs, booster seats; $; no cards.* Located in the old Palomar Hotel, this restaurant serves well-prepared, authentic Mexican food. Unusual menu items include crisp flautas, pozole (pork and hominy stew), menudo (tripe soup), and carne asada (barbecued beef). Children might especially enjoy the sopes (little tortillas shaped like boats and filled with tasty ground beef).

Old Theatre Cafe, *106 Walnut Ave., 408/426-0544; breakfast and lunch daily, dinner M-Sat; highchairs, booster seats; $; no cards.* This European-style coffee shop serves particularly good breakfasts. But it is best known for its German-Austrian bakery, which puts out such delights as Black Forest cake and Napoleons.

Tampico Kitchen, *822 Pacific Ave., 408/423-2241; breakfast, lunch, and dinner daily; highchairs and booster seats; $; MC, V.* Tasty Mexican food is served here in an American cafe-style atmosphere. Especially noteworthy are the nachos (tortilla chips smothered with cheddar cheese, chiles, and onions). Mariachis perform on Sunday evenings.

- # WHAT TO DO

Beach & Boardwalk, *400 Beach St./Riverside Ave., 408/426-7433; daily June-Sept, weekends Oct-May, call for hours; small fee for rides, all-day ride ticket $8.50.* Fortunately, this is one boardwalk which has not degenerated over the years. The mile-long arcade follows the beach. Thrill rides include a rickety wooden roller coaster, built in 1924 and rated by the *New York Times* as one of the ten best in the country, and a refreshing water flume ride. An old-fashioned merry-go-round, built in New Jersey in 1911 and one of only four remaining classic carousels in California, features 72 carved horses and 2 chariots as well as a 342-pipe organ. All this and miniature golf too!

Lighthouse Point, *on W. Cliff Dr.; museum open weekend afternoons, free.* Seal Rock, home to a herd of sea lions, is visible off shore from this light station. Surfers can be viewed from nearby Steamer Lane.

Mission Santa Cruz, *126 High St., 408/426-5686; daily 10-4; by donation.* The original mission, built in 1794, had a history of destruction. This half-size replica was built near the original mission site and houses a small museum.

Municipal Wharf, *near the Boardwalk.* Fishermen angle from the side of this half-mile long pier, and seafood restaurants, snack stands, and picnic tables are scattered along its length. Deep sea fishing trips originate at concessions located here.

Mystery Spot, *1953 Branciforte Dr. (3 miles north of town), 408/423-8897; daily 9:30am-5pm; adults $2.50, 5-11 $1.25.* Gravitational forces appear to be defied in this small (150 ft. diameter), quiet, cool spot in the redwoods. Finding it can be a bit of a mystery too.

Natural Bridges State Beach, *on W. Cliff Dr., 408/423-4609; $3/car.* While you picnic and sun on the sandy beach, you can marvel at the unusual sandstone arch and rock formations which have been pounded out by the surf. Swimming is not safe, but this is a good spot for exploring tidepools. From October to March large numbers of Monarch butterflies make their homes here; a nature trail leads to good viewing points.

Octagon Santa Cruz County Historical Museum, *118 Cooper St., 408/425-2540; M-Sat noon-5pm; free.* Exhibits of vintage clothing and photos change regularly. In 1882 this building was the County Hall of Records.

Pacific Garden Mall, *Pacific Ave. between Water & Cathcart Sts.* These five landscaped blocks comprise downtown Santa Cruz. The park-like setting features many conventional stores as well as boutiques, art galleries, and restaurants—many of which are located inside re-stored historic buildings.

Santa Cruz City Museum, *1305 E. Cliff Dr., 408/429-3773; Tu–Sat 10am–5pm; by donation.* Located across the street from a fine beach, this museum displays Indian relics and costumes as well as an unusual collection of sea shells.

Santa Cruz Yacht Harbor, *2200 E. Cliff Dr., 408/476-4992.* Bring a picnic lunch or pick up supplies at the deli located here. Then relax and enjoy watching the yachts sail in and out of the harbor while you sunbathe on the beach. Seals can often be observed frolicking close to shore.

The Last Supper, *526 Broadway, 408/426-5787; Tu–Sun 11am–4pm; by donation.* This life-size sculpted interpretation of Leonardo da Vinci's painting took 10 years to complete. It's located in the Santa Cruz Art League galleries.

University of California, Santa Cruz campus, *1156 High St., 408/429-0111.* Acquaint yourself with this scenic campus by taking a self-guided walking tour. Maps are available at the visitor information kiosk. A free shuttle bus loops the grounds during the school year but does not run in the summer. Hungry? Try the **Whole Earth Restaurant** (408/426-8285), which serves organic vegetarian food and is open to the public.

CAPITOLA

Capitola Chamber of Commerce
410 Capitola Ave.
Capitola 95010
408/475-6522

■ *ANNUAL EVENTS*

For information on the annual sand sculpture contest, arts and crafts fair, and floating parade of flower-covered boats down Soquel Creek—all of which occur during the September **Begonia Festival**—contact: Begonia Festival, P.O. Box 501, Capitola 95010.

Nearby Aptos is the home each August of the **Cabrillo Music Festival**, said to be one of the country's best small music festivals. A variety of works, including classic and contemporary, are presented along with world premieres. For information call 408/688-6466 or 425-6339.

■ *A LITTLE BACKGROUND*

This historic beach resort was founded in 1876. Now it is basically an artsy-craftsy beach town. The lovely beach offers

swimming in calm ocean waters or wading in the fresh water of Soquel Creek. Be cautious, however, as sometimes the creek water isn't so fresh.

Because it is such a popular spot, in the summer free shuttle buses are in service to take visitors from parking lots on Bay Avenue to the beach. Some shuttle bikes are also available for loan.

■ *ROUTE*
Located approximately 5 miles south of Santa Cruz on Hwy 1.

■ *WHERE TO STAY*

Capitola Inn, *822 Bay Ave., 95010, 408/462-3004; 2/$$-$$$, 4/$$$; some kitchens and fireplaces; pool; TVs; cribs; dining facilities; two-night minimum in summer; children under 14 stay free in parents' room.* This tasteful, modern lodging facility is within walking distance of the village and beach area. A free shuttle bus runs daily during the summer.

Capitola Venetian Hotel, *1500 Wharf Rd., 95010, 408/476-6471; 2/$-$$$, 4/$$-$$$; some kitchens, fireplaces, and ocean views; TVs; cribs; three-night minimum.* This mini-village of charming pastel stucco units is located right on the beach.

Harbor Lights Motel, *5000 Cliff Dr., 95010, 408/476-0505; 2/$-$$$, 4/$$-$$$; some kitchens, fireplaces, and ocean views; TVs; cribs.* This is an ordinary motel with an extraordinary location just across from the beach.

■ WHERE TO EAT

Charles Dickens Restaurant, *9051 Soquel Dr., Aptos, 408/688-7800; lunch M-F, dinner daily, Sun brunch; highchairs, booster seats, children's portions; $$; AE, MC, V.* Though you won't find gruel served in this cozy converted home, you will find homemade soups, salads, sandwiches, hamburgers, omelettes, and desserts—are you ready for avocado pie? At dinner the menu becomes continental with a large selection of seafood.

Greenhouse Restaurant at the Farm, *5555 Soquel Dr., Soquel, 408/476-5613; lunch and dinner daily, Sun brunch; booster seats; reservations suggested; $$; MC, V.* Dine in the huge garden greenhouse or in the Victorian front room of this *real* farmhouse located on a five-acre century-old working farm. Menu choices include quiches, hamburgers, fresh fish, steaks, and homemade soups—all served with freshly baked breads and including access to a salad bar. Also on the farm are a gift shop, garden nursery, bakery, and wine shop.

Mimi's Ice Cream Cart. In the summer be on the lookout for pretty Mimi pedaling her ice cream bike, and peddling cold ice cream to hot and hungry tourists. It's been awhile since I've seen Mimi. I do hope she's still around and hasn't become just another wispy legend.

Shadowbrook, *1750 Wharf Rd., 408/475-1511; dinner daily, weekend brunch; highchairs, booster seats, children's portions; reservations suggested; $$$; AE, MC, V.* Located on the banks of Soquel Creek, diners reach this smart restaurant by riding a bright red, self-operated cable car down the flower-laden hill from the street above—or they can walk down a winding path. The surf & turf menu features prime rib, salmon, and abalone. Dinners include a salad or clam chowder and fresh sourdough and brown breads. Entertainment and dancing is scheduled nightly in summer, weekends the rest of the year.

■ WHAT TO DO

Antonelli Begonia Gardens, *2545 Capitola Ave., Santa Cruz, 408/475-5222; daily 8am-5pm.* Acres of indoor plants, ferns, and beautiful begonia baskets may be viewed and purchased here. Peak of bloom is August and September, but a good show may be enjoyed June through November.

Bargetto Winery, *3535-A N. Main St., Soquel, 408/475-2258; daily 10am-5:30pm.* Take an informal tour of this small family winery

and do some tasting at the outdoor bar overlooking Soquel Creek.
Bargetto is known for fruit wines including olallieberry and apricot.

MONTEREY PENINSULA

■ *A LITTLE BACKGROUND*
Popular for years because of its proximity to San Francisco,
the Monterey Peninsula is well-established as a vacation destination. All types of overnight accommodations and restaurants are available. Once the off-season was the entire winter.
Now, due to the area's immense popularity, there is no off-
season. It is essential that you have reservations for lodging
as well as for most of the more popular restaurants.

■ *ROUTE*
Located approximately 115 miles south of San Francisco.
Take Hwy 101 to Hwy 17 to Hwy 1.

■ *STOPS ALONG THE WAY*
The Giant Artichoke, *Hwy 1, Castroville, 408/633-3204.* Located in
"the artichoke capital of the world," this novelty restaurant makes a
good rest stop. You may purchase picnic supplies or snack on artichoke specialties such as french-fried artichokes with a mayonnaise
dip, artichoke soup, artichoke nut cake, and steamed artichokes.
Other more standard short-order items are also available.

MONTEREY

Monterey Peninsula Visitors & Convention Bureau
P.O. Box 1770
(380 Alvarado St.)
Monterey 93940
408/649-3200

■ *ANNUAL EVENTS*
Contact the Visitors Bureau for information on these events:
Bing Crosby Golf Tournament, *January, in Pebble Beach, 408/624-0100.*
Adobe House Tour, *April, 408/372-2608.*

Laguna Seca Races, *Triple Crown in May, Historic Auto Races in August, Grand Prix in October, 408/373-1811.*

Scottish Highland Games, *July, 408/646-4010.*

Concours d'Elegance *(showing of classic vintage and antique cars), August, 408/649-8500.*

Jazz Festival, *September, (P.O. Box Jazz, Monterey 93940), 408/373-3366.*

■ WHERE TO STAY

Casa Munras Garden Hotel, *700 Munras Ave., 93940, 408/375-2411; 2/$$$; some fireplaces; pool; TVs; cribs; dining facilities; children under 13 stay free in their parents' room.* The grounds are spacious, attractive, and peaceful at this very large motel-like facility, and all rooms are furnished with brass beds.

Holiday Inn, *2600 Sand Dunes Dr., 93940, 800/238-8000, 408/394-3321; 2/$$$; pool; some ocean views; TVs; cribs; dining facilities; children under 12 stay free in their parents' room.* This hotel is located outside of town and is right on the beach. Spectacular views of Monterey Bay may be enjoyed from the higher-priced rooms.

Motel Row. Modern motel accommodations abound on Munras Ave.

■ WHERE TO EAT

Abalonetti, *53 Fisherman's Wharf, 408/373-1851; lunch and dinner W–M; highchairs, booster seats, children's portions; $; no cards.* In this tiny, unpretentious restaurant over half the menu is devoted to the house specialty—calamari (squid). The restaurant is named for a famous dish in which the squid is pounded tender, breaded, and sauteed in butter. Other seafood and Italian dishes are also available, and there is a nice view of Monterey Bay.

Clock Garden, *565 Abrego, 408/375-6100; lunch and dinner daily; booster seats; $$; AE, MC, V.* Diners have a choice of sitting inside this historic adobe, among the collection of antique clocks, or outside in the lovely courtyard garden. Sunday brunch features delicious hot muffins, orange marmalade served in a scooped-out orange shell, and frothy Ramos Fizzes. Reservations are not taken for brunch, so be there when they open or expect a wait. Lunch and brunch are casual and the best time to bring children.

Consuelo's, *361 Lighthouse Ave., 408/372-8111; lunch and dinner daily; highchairs, booster seats; reservations suggested; $$; AE, MC, V.* Situated in a lovely 1880 two-story Victorian mansion, complete with velvet-flocked wallpaper, this Mexican restaurant might more appropriately be located in one of Monterey's historic adobes. The various rooms of the house have been turned into semi-private dining areas. The menu offers typical Mexican fare along with a few more unusual items. My favorite is the flauta, made with shredded beef rolled in a chewy flour tortilla and then fried until crisp and topped with guacamole. Appetizers come with all dinners: *hot* carrots and peppers and a crisp quesadilla served on an elegant pedestal tray. For dessert don't miss the adobe pie with its oreo crust, coffee ice cream filling, and fudge and whipped cream topping. Olé!

Mike's Seafood, *25 Fisherman's Wharf, 408/372-6153; breakfast, lunch, and dinner daily; highchairs, booster seats, children's portions; no reservations; $; AE, CB, DC, MC, V.* Arrive early to take advantage of the lovely bay views afforded from the tables of this busy and popular seafood restaurant. Steaks, hamburgers, and chicken are also on the menu.

The Outrigger, *700 Cannery Row, 408/372-8543; lunch and dinner daily; highchairs, booster seats, children's portions; reservations suggested; $$; AE, CB, DC, MC, V.* Fruity Polynesian specialties, curries, steaks, and seafood are served in the dimly-lit, noisy dining room featuring spectacular views of Monterey Bay. A buffet lunch is available on weekdays. The comfortable bar juts out over the water and makes a good spot to enjoy a potent tropical drink concoction and perhaps some—careful with this one parents—*puu puus* (appetizers).

Sancho Panza, *590 Calle Principal, 408/375-0095; lunch and dinner daily; highchairs, booster seats; $; AE, MC, V.* Once inside you can see why this claims to be the funkiest Mexican restaurant in town. It reminds me of a Mexican roadhouse. I especially like the touch of recycling old Mexican newspapers as placemats. The patio is decorated with weathered hatch covers and timbers salvaged from Cannery Row's old sardine boats. The history of the building is described as "a Mexican country inn . . . located in a historic adobe built in 1841 . . . by a young Mexican for his bride." Fifteen children were raised here by that bride! The adobe was built when Monterey was still part of Mexico and is now protected by the State of California. My favorite menu items are the chispa (cheese and sauce on a flour tortilla), tostada (huge), chile verde burrito, guacamole, and Mexican hot chocolate flavored with cinnamon and crushed almonds. Freshly fried tortilla chips and salsa accompany each meal.

Sardine Factory, *701 Wave St., 408/373-3775; lunch and dinner M–Sat, dinner only Sun; highchairs, booster seats, children's portions; reservations essential; $$$; AE, CB, DC, MC, V.* Once this building housed a canteen patronized by cannery workers. Now it houses this elegant, dimly-lit award-winning restaurant. The kitchen offers fresh seafood and continental-style fare and is known for its white veal and well-aged beef. All dinners are accompanied by a plate of antipasto, hot cheese bread, soup, and a salad presented with *chilled* forks. Children are welcome, but I wouldn't want to be caught here with any whose behavior is unpredictable.

Spaghetti Warehouse, *Cannery Row, 408/375-1921; dinner daily, lunch on Sun and summer weekdays; highchairs; $; MC, V.* Diners enter this pizza parlor through a prohibition-era false phonebooth door. The menu features Italian items like ravioli, lasagna, fettucini, and various kinds of spaghetti as well as pizza.

Viennese Pastry and Coffee Shop, *469 Alvardo, 408/375-4789; breakfast and lunch daily; highchairs, booster seats; $; no cards.* Local residents come here for the superb pastries (including my personal favorite—the Viennese sacher torte) to down with a cup of coffee or spot of tea.

■ WHAT TO DO

Allen Knight Maritime Museum, *550 Calle Principal, 408/375-2553; Tu-F 10am–noon, 1–4pm, Sat & Sun 2–4pm, mid-June to mid-Sept; rest of year closed Tu-F 10-12; free.* See ship models, bells, compasses, and related items and learn about the area's naval history.

California Heritage Guides, *10 Custom House Plaza, 408/373-6454.* Guided walking tours through Monterey's historic area are arranged to fit your interests, schedule, and budget. Call for details and reservations.

California's First Theater, *Pacific/Scott, 408/375-4916; June–Aug W, Th, Sun 8pm, F & Sat 8:30pm; Sept–May F & Sat only; adults $4, 13–17*

$3, under 13 $2. Children over age five should enjoy visiting this ex-
saloon and boarding house for sailors. The first play was presented
in 1847, and the "Troupers of the Gold Coast" are still going strong.
Nowadays the melodramatic shows and olios change periodically, but
they are still presented in the tiny theater just like they were in the
old days—only now the old oak bar in the lobby serves only soda
pop. Best seating for kids is on the benches in the back. Call for
reservations and current production.

Cannery Row. Once an area of booming sardine canneries, Cannery Row
became a ghost town in 1945 when the sardines mysteriously disap-
peared from the area's ocean. Now this mile-long road houses restaurants, art galleries, shops, and a **Historical Wax Museum.** At press
time a major aquarium was being constructed and is scheduled to
open late in 1984. To get in the mood, you might want to read John
Steinbeck's *Cannery Row.* The Lee Chong's Heavenly Flower Grocery in Steinbeck's book is now the **Old General Store** (#835), the
La Ida Bar is now **Kalisa's Cosmopolitan Gourmet Restaurant** (#851),
and Doc's lab is now a private club (#800).

Edgewater Packing Company, *640 Wave St., 408/649-1899; open daily.*
This family entertainment center has a candy shop stocked with cotton candy, candy apples, and popcorn, a game room with antique
pinball machines and modern video games, a toy store which children
and limber adults can enter by crawling through a kitten's mouth,
and what may be the world's fastest merry-go-round. The restaurant
resembles an old-fashioned ice cream parlor and serves up breakfast,
lunch, and dinner items as well as Oscar Hossenfellder's "fabulous
formula" ice cream. The children's menu offers all their favorite
things; baby bottles are warmed and cheeks pinched at no charge. A
red 1915 Seagrave fire truck sits right in the restaurant begging children to climb on it.

El Estero Park, *Del Monte Ave./Camino El Estero/Fremont Blvd.* Enjoy
hiking and bike trails and a lake filled with hungry ducks. Paddle
boats and canoes may be rented, and children may fish from boats.
By the lake on Pearl St., **Dennis the Menace Playground** features
equipment designed by Hank Ketchum, creator of Dennis the Menace, who once lived in the area. Notable are the hedge maze and sus-
pension bridge. Picnic tables and a concession stand are available.

Fisherman's Wharf. Lined with restaurants and shops, the wharf also
offers some inexpensive entertainment. Sometimes an organ grinder
greets visitors at the wharf entrance, his friendly monkey anxious to
take coins from children's hands. Freeloading **sea lions** live around
the wharf pilings. If you toss them a fish (available at the bait shops),
they will put on a show. A **diving bell** offers a 30 foot plunge under

the water for a fish-eye view of Monterey Bay. Several businesses offer cruises of the bay and deep-sea fishing expeditions. For specific prices and schedules call **Sam's Fishing Fleet** (408/372-0577), **Monterey Fishing Trips** (408/373-3501), or **Frank's Fishing Trips** (408/372-2203).

Jacks Peak Stables, *550 Aquajito Rd., 408/375-4232; Tu–Sun 10am–4pm; $10/hr.* Over 50 miles of forest trails await you and your hired horse. Riding lessons can be arranged. Call ahead for reservations and details.

Kitty Hawk Kites, *1 Reservation Rd., Marina, 408/384-2622.* If you've ever longed to take up hang-gliding, this is the place to do it. Located on the dunes east of town, this school offers a three-hour beginning course with 5 flights for $47. Reservations are necessary.

Monterey State Historic Park, *115 Alvarado St., 408/373-2103; daily 9am–5pm; adults $1, 6–17 50¢.* Part of the California State Park System, this park consists of ten historical sites and preserved adobes. The fee admits you to all of the buildings and gardens and includes guided tours or the very special Stevenson and Larkin Houses and Casa Soberanes. Begin your tour and gather information at the Custom House located at 1 Custom House Plaza.

Presidio of Monterey Museum, *Pacific St. north of Decatur St., 408/242-8414; Thur-M 9am-12:30, 1:30-4pm; free.* The history of "Old Fort" Hill is told through dioramas, artifacts, and photographs. Next to the museum are ten historic sites including a 2,000-year-old Indian village site and ceremonial "rain rock," the ruins of Fort Mervine, and the site of Father Serra's 1770 landing.

PACIFIC GROVE

Pacific Grove Chamber of Commerce
P.O. Box 167
(Forest/Central Aves.)
Pacific Grove 93950
408/373-3304

■ *ANNUAL EVENTS*
Each year in late October hundreds of thousands of **Monarch butterflies** return to Pacific Grove to winter on the needles of favored local pine trees. There they dangle in huge clusters and are often overlooked as dull pieces of bark. They migrate all the way from western Canada and Alaska and stay until March, when they again fly north.

Somewhat of a mystery is how they find their way here each year since, with a lifespan of less than a year, no butterfly makes the trip twice. The stunning orange and black Monarchs somehow program this information into their progeny, which then return to these same trees the following fall and repeat the cycle.

Monarchs like to flutter about on sunny days between the hours of 10am and 4pm and this is the best time to view them. On cold and foggy days, which are quite common in this area, they cling to the trees and keep their wings closed—reacting to the weather somewhat like a golden poppy.

Leave your nets at home. To discourage people from bothering these fragile, lovely creatures, in Pacific Grove molesting a butterfly is a crime carrying a $500 fine.

To celebrate the annual return of the butterflies, the town of Pacific Grove, also known as *Butterfly Town USA*, hosts a special parade each year. School children dress up as butterflies and march along with the more traditional bands and majorette corps. Afterwards the local PTA sponsors a bazaar and carnival where celebrants enjoy old-fashioned fun and homemade foods. For the current year's date, contact the Chamber of Commerce.

Each April there is a **Victorian Home Tour.** Children under 12 are not permitted. Take your teenagers. For current information contact the Chamber of Commerce.

■ *WHERE TO STAY*

Andril Fireplace Cottages, *569 Asilomar Blvd., 93950, 408/375-0994; 2-4/$$; kitchens, fireplaces, TVs; cribs.* These woodsy cottages make for very comfortable lodging, especially for longer stays.

Asilomar Conference Center, *800 Asilomar Blvd. (P.O. Box 537), 93950, 408/372-8016; 2/$, 4/$-$$; some shared baths; some kitchens, fireplaces, and ocean views; pool; cribs; dining facilities.* Though this facility is used mainly as a conference grounds, it is part of the California State Park System and, when underbooked, makes rentals to the general public. Reservations may not be made more than one week in advance, but often there are last minute accommodations available. In Spanish the word "asilomar" means "refuge by the sea" and, indeed, the grounds are located in a quiet, scenic area just a short walk from the ocean. Guests may join in inexpensive, family-style conference meals at 7:30am, noon, and 6pm.

Beachcomber Inn, *1996 Sunset Dr., 93950, 800/453-4511, 408/373-4769; 2/$$, 4/$$-$$$+; some kitchens and ocean views; pool, sauna; TVs; cribs; dining facilities.* Factors rendering this otherwise ordinary motel special include its oceanfront location, the availability of some waterbeds, and free bikes for the use of guests.

Butterfly Grove Inn, *1073 Lighthouse Ave., 93950, 408/373-4921; 2-4/$-$$$; some kitchens and fireplaces; pool, hydrojet spa, TVs.* This facility offers a choice of motel rooms or suites in a vintage house. It is located on a quiet side street next to a two-acre field of easily accessible trees which the Monarchs particularly favor.

Butterfly Trees Lodge, *1150 Lighthouse Ave., 93950, 800/447-7400, 408/372-0503; 2/$$-$$$+, 4/$$$-$$$+; some kitchens, fireplaces, and ocean views; pool, sauna, jacuzzi; TVs; continental breakfast; cribs; two-night minimum on weekends.* This is an attractive and quiet motel located adjacent to a favorite butterfly nesting spot. Complimentary wine and cheese tastings are scheduled daily.

Centrella Hotel, *612 Central Ave., 93950, 408/372-3372; 2/$$-$$$, 4/$$$+; some shared baths; some fireplaces, ocean views, and TVs; continental breakfast; cribs; two-night minimum on weekends.* This restored turn-of-the-century Victorian has won awards for its interior decor which features antique furnishings and clawfoot tubs. Families with children under 12 are accommodated only in the more expensive cottage suites.

♥ **Seven Gables Inn,** *555 Ocean View Blvd., 93950, 408/372-4341; 2/$$$; ocean views; full breakfast; two-night minimum on weekends; no children under 13.* Located just across the street from the beach, this cheerful yellow Victorian mansion, built in 1886, lets both rooms and cottages.

Motel Row. Numerous motels are located at the west end of Lighthouse Ave. and on Asilomar Blvd.

■ *WHERE TO EAT*

♥ **Maison Bergerac,** *649 Lighthouse Ave., 408/373-6996; dinner W–Sun; reservations necessary; $$$; no cards.* A fixed-price classic French dinner may be enjoyed here in the Victorian ambiance of an 1892 Queen Anne mansion.

♥ **The Old Bath House,** *620 Ocean View Blvd., 408/375-5195; dinner daily, Sun brunch; booster seat; reservations suggested; $$$; AE, CB, DC, MC, V.* French and northern Italian cuisine are served here amid elegant Victorian decor. Every table has a good view of Monterey Bay. Entrees include items like rack of lamb, pheasant with raspberry sauce, and canneloni Romana. Divine dessert choices include mocha almond cheesecake and a cream puff filled with French vanilla ice cream and topped with hot fudge sauce.

The Tinnery, *631 Ocean View Blvd., 408/646-1040; breakfast, lunch, and dinner daily; highchairs, booster seats; $$; AE, CB, DC, MC, V.* Located at **Lover's Point**—the southern tip of Monterey Bay—this restaurant offers outstanding views of the bay. The eclectic menu includes appetizers like nachos and fried potato skins as well as entrees like huevos rancheros, linguini and clams, and prime rib.

■ *WHAT TO DO*

Butterfly Viewing. The densest clusters of Monarchs occur behind the Butterfly Grove Inn. Other good viewing spots are by the Butterfly Trees Lodge and on the west side of **George Washington Park** along Melrose St. south of Pine Ave. A statue honoring the butterfly is located at Lover's Point; a few butterflies can occasionally be seen fluttering there.

Les Josselyn Bicycles, *638 Lighthouse, 408/649-8520; daily 9am–5:30pm; $7.50/half day, $10/all day.* Choose from a large selection of bicycle rentals and then head on out to Cannery Row or Pacific Grove.

Lover's Point Marina, *626 Ocean View Blvd., 408/373-3304.* Glass bottom boats, first introduced here in 1892, operate during the summer. The trip allows visitors a chance to see the marine life which attracts scientists from all over the world. There is also a pleasant beach for sunbathing and wading as well as a grassy picnic area with barbecue pits.

Pacific Grove Museum of Natural History, *165 Forest Ave., 408/372-4212; Tu-Sun 10am–5pm; free.* Learn about the natural history of Monterey County through exhibits of butterflies, marine and bird life, native plants, shells, and Indian artifacts. Each year during the third weekend in April, this tiny museum sponsors a **wildflower show** with displays of as many as 500 varieties.

Point Piños Lighthouse, *on Asilomar Blvd., about two blocks north of the end of Lighthouse Ave., 408/373-3304; Sat & Sun 1–4pm; free.* The Coast Guard gives guided tours of this oldest of operating Pacific Coast lighthouses, built in 1855 out of granite quarried in the area. Doc's Great Tide Pool, from Steinbeck's *Cannery Row,* is located here. The terrain surrounding the lighthouse is a good spot to walk, picnic, and observe sea otters.

Poor Man's 17-Mile Drive. There is no charge for this scenic 4.2 mile drive which passes rugged seascapes and some impressive Victorian homes. Begin at Ocean View Blvd./3rd St. At Point Piños turn left on Sunset Dr. Tidepooling is good in several spots. From April to August the beautiful lavender ice plant (mesembryanthemum) cascades in full bloom over the rocky beach front.

CARMEL

Carmel Business Association
P.O. Box 4444
(Vandervort Court on San Carlos/Ocean)
Carmel 93921
408/624-2522

Tourist Information Center
P.O. Box 7430
(Ocean/Mission)
Carmel 93921
408/624-1711
This private agency is very helpful with information and will make lodging reservations.

■ *ANNUAL EVENTS*
Bach Festival, *July, (P.O. Box 575, Carmel 93921), 408/624-1521.*

■ *A LITTLE BACKGROUND*
A well-established weekend destination, Carmel is best known for its abundant shops, cozy lodging, and picturesque beach. It is also known for the things which it doesn't have: few sidewalks or street signs and no streetlights, house numbers, neon signs, jukeboxes, parking meters, or buildings over two stories

high. These absent items help Carmel to keep its small-town feeling.

Be careful. Eccentric laws in the town make it illegal to wear high-heeled shoes on the sidewalks, throw a ball in the park, play a musical instrument in a bar, or dig in the sand at the beach other than when making a sand castle.

Because Carmel is such a popular destination, it is important to make reservations for your accommodations far in advance, especially if you want to stay in one of its quaint inns. It seems that almost every weekend some special tournament, race, or house tour is scheduled in the area, making available lodging scarce.

■ WHERE TO STAY

Carmel River Inn, *26600 Oliver Rd., 93923, 408/624-1575; 2/$, 4/$–$$; some kitchens, fireplaces, and river views; pool; TVs; cribs; two-night minimum.* Located on the outskirts of town on the banks of the Carmel River, this lodging has ten acres of space for children to romp and explore. Guests have a choice of motel rooms or individual cottages.

Colonial Terrace Inn, *San Antonio/13th (P.O. Box 1375), 93921, 408/624-2741; 2/$–$$$, 4/$$$; some kitchens, fireplaces, and ocean views; TVs; cribs; continental breakfast.* In business since 1925, this crisp, attractive lodging is located in a quiet residential area just one block from the beach.

The Green Lantern, *7th/Casanova (P.O. Box 1114), 93921, 408/624-4392; 2–4/$$–$$$; some fireplaces and ocean views; TVs; continental breakfast; no infants.* An inn since 1926, this pleasant group of rustic multi-unit cottages is located on a quiet sidestreet just a few blocks from the village.

Highlands Inn, *located 4 miles south of town on Hwy 1 (P.O. Box 1700), 93921, 800/682-4811, 408/624-3801; 2–4/$$$+; some kitchens, fireplaces, ocean views, TVs; pool, hot tubs; cribs; includes full breakfast and dinner; dining facilities.* Located on the scenic outskirts of town, this legendary inn appears at first to be outrageously expensive. When you consider that two meals are included in the price and that the accommodations are truly luxurious, the price begins to seem a little more reasonable—at least for a splurge. The cliffside setting is spectacular, and guests have a choice of lanai rooms or cottages.

December is celebrated with a Scottish Christmas tree ceremony on December 7, the laying of the yule log on Christmas Eve, and a traditional dinner on Christmas day. On New Year's Eve there is a wassail bowl and hogmanay ball and dinner, and a special dinner on New Year's day.

The Homestead, *Lincoln/8th (P.O. Box 1285), 93921, 408/624-4119; 2/$-$$; some kitchens and fireplaces; TVs; two-night minimum on weekends.* This collection of motel units and cabins, located just a few blocks from the village, reminds me of a rural red farmhouse.

Lamp Lighters Inn, *Ocean/Camino Real (P.O. Box 604), 93921, 408/624-7372; 2/$$-$$$, 4/$$$; one kitchen, fireplace, and ocean view; TVs.* This gingerbread village has charming rooms and cottages and a convenient location between the village and the ocean. It very well may fulfill your fairytale fantasies.

Lincoln Green Inn, *Carmelo/15th (P.O. Box 2747), 408/624-1880; 2-4/$$$-$$$+; kitchens, fireplaces, TVs; cribs; two-night minimum on weekends.* Located on the outskirts of town just a few blocks from where the Carmel River flows into the ocean, this cluster of comfortable English housekeeping cottages features living rooms with cathedral-beamed ceilings and stone fireplaces.

The Lodge at Pebble Beach, *on 17 Mile Drive, Pebble Beach 93953, 408/624-3811; 2-4/$$$+; fireplaces, TVs; some ocean views; pool, wading pool, sauna; 14 tennis courts; cribs; dining facilities.* Complete luxury and the best of sporting facilities await guests. Golfers can enjoy playing some of the best courses in the country. Horse rentals and equestrian trails are nearby as are jogging and hiking trails, a parcourse, and several pools. Three restaurants and room service round out this totally civilized experience. Even if you don't stay in one of the bungalows or houses, you should stop in to enjoy the spectacular ocean view over a drink or meal.

San Antonio House, *San Antonio/7th (P.O. Box 3683), 93921; 408/624-4334; 2/$$$, 4/$$$-$$$+; some fireplaces and ocean views; cribs; full breakfast; two-night minimum on weekends.* This attractive guesthouse offers large rooms, a lovely garden, and a location in a quiet residential area just one block from the beach.

♥ **Sea View Inn,** *Camino Real/12th (P.O. Box 4138), 93921, 408/624-8778; 2/$-$$; some shared baths; continental breakfast; two-night minimum on weekends; no children under 12.* This converted three-story Victorian home offers pleasantly appointed rooms and sherry in the afternoon. It is located three blocks from the beach.

♥ **Stonehouse Inn,** *8th/Monte Verde (P.O. Box 2517), 93921, 408/624-4569; 2/$$-$$$; all shared baths; some ocean views; continental breakfast; two-night minimum on weekends; no children under 12.* Built in 1906, this rustic stone country house is close to the village. Rooms are named after authors and furnished with antiques.

♥ **Vagabond House Inn,** *4th/Dolores (P.O. Box 2747), 93921, 408/624-7738, 624-7403; 2/$$–$$$, 4/$$$–$$$+; some kitchens and fireplaces; TVs; full breakfast; two-night minimum on weekends; no children under 13.* Cozily furnished rooms open off a quiet, rustic flower-bedecked courtyard.

■ *OTHER*

♥ **John Gardiner's Tennis Ranch,** *P.O. Box 228, Carmel Valley 93924, 408/659-2207; April–Nov; $1,300–$1,400/person includes lodging, meals, and tennis instruction; some fireplaces and kitchens; 2 pools, jacuzzi.* Tennis clinics at this legendary spot, begun by John Gardiner in 1957, run Sunday–Friday and include 25 hours of instruction. Most are set up for mixed doubles; several are just for women. Lodging is in luxurious cottages on beautifully landscaped grounds, and meals are sumptuous.

■ *WHERE TO EAT*

Butcher Shop, *Ocean/Dolores, 408/624-2569; dinner daily; booster seats, children's portions; reservations advised; $$$; AE, CB, DC, MC, V.* This serious dining room specializes in prime rib, beef Wellington, and barbecued ribs but also serves Australian lobster tail and porterhouse steaks. Dinners include a relish plate, salad, home fries, a crock of baked beans, and hot cheese/bacon bread.

Clam Box, *Mission/5th, 408/624-8597; dinner Tu–Sun, closed most of Dec; highchairs, children's portions; no reservations; $$; no cards.* Customers happily wait in line at this tiny, cozy restaurant because they know they're going to enjoy themselves once they get a table. The menu is a combination of seafood and chicken items.

Cottage of Sweets, *Ocean/Lincoln, 408/624-5170; daily 10am–6pm.* Among the sweet surprises in this gingerbread candy cottage are imported chocolates, diet candy, gourmet jelly beans, and taffy.

Em Le's, *Dolores/5th, 408/624-2905; breakfast, lunch, and dinner daily; highchairs, booster seats; $; no cards.* Cozy and always crowded, Em Le's offers a large variety of breakfast items including blueberry pancakes and buttermilk waffles—my personal favorites. Pleasant views of the sidewalk, seen through lace curtains, add to its special Carmel charm.

Hector De Smet Bakery, *Ocean/Lincoln, 408/624-6265; daily 6:30am–8pm.* Caramel apples, cookie monster cupcakes, and alligators and turtles made of marzipan bread are just a few of the delicacies available at this popular bakery. The large selection of pastries and drinks may be enjoyed on the premises or as you walk the boutique-laden Carmel streets.

Hog's Breath Inn, *San Carlos/5th, 408/625-1044; lunch M–Sat, Sun brunch, dinner daily; booster seats, children's portions; no reservations; $$; MC, V.* Owned by actor Clint Eastwood, this rustic, secluded spot features a casual, cozy atmosphere. Many tables are located outdoors under a rambling old oak tree and are warmed by fireplaces and heaters when the temperature chills. The brunch menu offers eggs Benedict, omelettes, and eggs served with homemade blueberry muffins and homefried potatoes. Lunch features wonderful homemade soups, salads, sandwiches, and hamburgers. The bar drinks are excellent, especially the Irish coffee, and it is perfectly acceptable to stop in just for a drink.

♥ **La Boheme,** *Dolores/7th, 408/624-7500; dinner daily; booster seats; no reservations; $$; MC, V.* This colorfully decorated, cozy, and petite cafe serves a fixed menu of one meal choice. The menu changes each day. The European peasant-style dishes are served informal family-style.

Mediterranean Market, *Ocean/Mission, 408/624-2022; daily 9am–6pm.* At this well-stocked delicatessen patrons can choose such treats as freshly marinated artichoke hearts, exotic beers, and skinny French baguettes as well as such standards as sandwich meats, cheeses, soft drinks, and wines. Gourmet items such as caviar are also available— as well as picnic baskets to carry it all away in. Located practically next door is **Wisharts Bakery** (*M–Sat 9am–6pm*), which dispenses freshly baked desserts and breads. After selecting luncheon supplies, head out to the beach for a pleasant picnic.

Mrs. M's Fudge, *Mission/6th, 408/624-5331; daily until 9pm.* Seventeen kinds of homemade fudge and unusual "snow fruit" (apricots, peaches, pears, cherries, and walnut-stuffed prunes dipped in white chocolate) are just a few of the diet-deserting goodies available here.

♥ **Patisserie Boissiere,** *Mission/Ocean, 408/624-5008; breakfast, lunch, and dinner daily; reservations suggested; $$; no cards.* In this very elegant little French spot, snacks of homemade soups and quiches are available as well as more substantial items. Though it would be hard to do so, don't overlook the Parisian pastries: lemonpot cheesecake, chocolate eclairs, a wide variety of meringues, babas au rhum, and plenty more.

Rocky Point, *12 miles south of town on Hwy 1, 408/624-2933; lunch and dinner daily; highchairs, booster seats, children's portions; reservations advised; $$$; AE, MC, V.* Take a scenic drive down the coast toward Big Sur, and stop here for a charcoal-broiled steak or fresh seafood dinner. The spectacular view is included in the steep menu price.

Swedish Restaurant, *Dolores/7th, 408/624-3723; breakfast and lunch daily; booster seats; no reservations; $; no cards.* This cheerful spot is my favorite for breakfast. A large window allows diners to view the busy sidewalk traffic, and a fireplace warms the tiny dining room. Portions are generous, and most items are served with toasted homemade breads. The specialty, lingonberry pancakes, are memorably delicious.

Thunderbird, *26400 Carmel Rancho Blvd., 1 mile south of town in Barnyard shopping center, 408/624-1803; lunch and dinner daily; highchairs, booster seats, children's portions; no reservations; $; MC, V.* Dine among world-famous authors in this combination bookstore/restaurant. Sandwiches are available at lunch, full meals at dinner, coffee-and during the off hours.

Tuck Box Tea Room, *Dolores/Ocean, 408/624-6365; breakfast, lunch, afternoon tea W–Sun; no reservations; $; no cards.* This tiny spot, featuring fairytale architecture and verily reeking of quaintness, can be quite difficult to get into. If you ever notice it without a long line in front, go! The limited menu offers homemade scones with olallieberry preserves at breakfast and at lunch several entree choices such as shepherd's pie, cheese rarebit, or sandwiches. Afternoon tea features scones and cakes and, of course, plenty of English tea.

▪ WHAT TO DO

BEACHES

Carmel Beach, *at the foot of Ocean.* This world-famous beach, known for its white powdery sand and spectacular sunsets, is a choice spot for a refreshing walk, a picnic, or flying a kite. A **sand castle contest** is held here each year in October (contact the Carmel Business Association for details). Swimming is unsafe.

Carmel River State Beach, *at the end of Scenic Rd.* Very popular with families, this fresh-water lagoon is also a bird sanctuary. There are picnic facilities, and open fires are allowed.

San Jose Creek. Scuba divers come from all over to enjoy the undersea beauty of Carmel Bay. This is one of their favorite diving spots and is a good place to watch them while you picnic.

Brass Rubbing Centre, *Mission/8th, 408/624-2990; M–Sat 10:30am–5pm, Sun by appointment.* Once upon a time people would travel all the way to England to make wax-on-paper impressions of the brass plaques embedded in the floors of old churches. But the brasses have become so worn that this practice is now forbidden. This inexpensive hobby can still be enjoyed in domestic shops like this one, where you can make rubbings of brass reproductions.

Come Fly A Kite, *Ocean/Mission in Carmel Plaza, 408/624-3422; daily 10am–5pm.* If you forgot your kite, pick one up here and then head for the beach—the perfect spot to launch it.

Dansk II, *Ocean/San Carlos, 408/625-1600; daily 10am–6pm.* Get bargain prices on discontinued items and seconds from this expensive line of kitchen merchandise.

Mission San Carlos Borromeo del Rio Carmelo, *3080 Rio Rd., 1 mile south of town off Hwy 1, 408/624-3600; M–Sat 9:30am–4:30pm, Sun 10:30am–4:30pm, services on Sun; by donation.* Father Junipero Serra established this mission in 1770; he is buried here at the foot of the altar. A museum displays Indian artifacts, mission tools, and re-creations of the original mission kitchen and California's first library.

A beautifully landscaped courtyard garden accents the cemetery where over 3,000 mission Indians were buried. A **fiesta** is held each year on the last Sunday in September.

Pebble Beach Equestrian Center, *Portola Rd., Pebble Beach, 408/624-2756; group rides daily at 10am & 2pm, $15/person; reservations required.* It's strictly English saddles here; lessons are available. Rides follow the extensive bridle trails which wind through lovely Del Monte Forest.

Point Lobos State Reserve, *3 miles south of town off Hwy 1, 408/624-4909; daily until sundown; $2/car.* Described as "the greatest meeting of land and water in the world," Point Lobos allows the opportunity to see the rustic, undeveloped beauty of the Monterey Peninsula and offers self-guiding trails as well as guided ranger walks daily in summer. Sea otters may often be seen in the 1,250-acre reserve's protected waters. An interesting story has this area as the model for Spyglass Hill in Robert Louis Stevenson's *Treasure Island.* Dress warmly and bring along your binoculars and camera and maybe a picnic too.

17-Mile Drive, *located at Pebble Beach exit off Hwy 1 between Carmel and Monterey, 408/649-8500; daily; $4/car.* The scenery on this

world-famous drive is a combination of showplace homes, prestigious golf courses, and raw seascapes. Sights include the Restless Sea, where several ocean crosscurrents meet; Seal and Bird Rock, where herds of sea lions and flocks of shoreline birds congregate; the Pebble Beach

Golf Course, one of three used during the annual Bing Crosby Pro-Am Tournament; and the landmark Lone Cypress, clinging to its jagged, barren rock base. Picnic facilities and short trails are found in several spots. If you splurge on lunch or dinner at any of the three ocean-view restaurants (one is a reasonably-priced coffee shop) at the elegant Lodge At Pebble Beach, the gate fee will be deducted from your bill.

Take a Ride to Carmel Valley. Follow Carmel Valley Rd. to the Carmel Valley Village. Nearby on Equiline Rd. is **Rosie's Cracker Barrel**, an old-fashioned general store opened in 1927. Then backtrack and take Laureles Grade north and then Hwy 68 west to Monterey. On this scenic drive you will pass begonia gardens, regional parks, the **Laguna Seca Raceway,** and the tasting room of the **Monterey Peninsula Winery.**

Thinker Toys, *Ocean/Mission in Carmel Plaza, 408/624-0441; M–Sat 9:30am–9pm, Sun 10am–5:30pm.* This super toy store offers an exciting selection of puppets, dolls, workbooks, and puzzles. In another part of the Plaza, an annex houses a large selection of model trains. This is the place to bring your kids to choose a souvenir.

♥ **Tor House,** *26304 Ocean View Ave., 408/624-1813; tours F & Sat on the hour 10am–3pm, reservations required; adults $5, teenagers $1.50, no children under 12.* Poet Robinson Jeffers built this medieval-style house and tower retreat out of huge granite rocks hauled up by horse from the beach below. He did much of the work himself and was of the opinion that the manual labor cleared his mind and, as he put it, "my fingers had the art to make stone love stone." All of his major works and most of his poetry were written while he lived with his wife and twin sons on this craggy knoll overlooking Carmel Bay.

BIG SUR

■ *ROUTE*

Located approximately 145 miles south of San Francisco. Take Hwy 101 to Hwy 17 to Hwy 1.

■ *WHERE TO STAY*

Big Sur Lodge, *93920, 408/667-2171; 2/$–$$$, 4/$$–$$$; some kitchens and fireplaces; pool, sauna; dining facilities April–Dec.* Located in a redwood grove in **Pfeiffer-Big Sur State Park**, this lodging facility offers cabins and motel rooms as well as use of the park's facilities, which include ranger-led nature walks, campfires, and river swimming.

Esalen Institute, *93920, 408/667-2335; hot tubs.* Located on a breathtaking crest above the ocean, this legendary educational facility offers lodging and dining in conjunction with its workshops. Space is open to the general public when they are underbooked. Then a bed space runs $60/person/day and includes 3 meals. Special family rates are available. Self-exploration workshops include massage, Rolfing, vision improvement, etc. Call for further details and a copy of the workshop catalogue.

Ripplewood Resort, *93920, 408/667-2242; 2/$-$$, 4/$$; closed most of Dec; some kitchens and fireplaces; two-night minimum on weekends.* Rustic redwood cabins are located both above and below the highway. The ones below are more expensive but are also only a stone's throw from the river.

♥ **Ventana Inn,** *93920, 408/624-4812, 667-2331; 2/$$$-$$$+; some kitchens, fireplaces, and ocean views; pool, sauna; TVs; continental breakfast; dining facilities, closed in Jan; two-night minimum on weekends; young children discouraged.* The spectacular architecture of this inn has won awards, and the restaurant is known for its California-style cuisine which includes everything from a vegetarian platter to filet mignon. The secluded location 1,200 ft. above the ocean makes it a good choice for a restive, revitalizing, and hedonistic

retreat. Clothing is optional around the pool. Campsites are available at their adjacent facility.

■ WHERE TO EAT

Big Sur Inn, *408/667-2377; breakfast, lunch, and dinner daily; highchairs, booster seats; reservations suggested for dinner; $; no cards.* My favorite meal here is breakfast, especially when it's raining outside and I've managed to secure a table in front of the fireplace. The mellow, rustic, and informal setting is a complementary background to the fresh, simple foods produced by the kitchen. No alcohol is served; inquire about bringing your own. Rustic lodging is also available.

Glen Oaks Restaurant, *408/667-2623; dinner Tu–Sun, breakfast Sun; highchairs, booster seats; $; MC, V.* Classical music and tables with fresh flowers greet diners in this log cabin-like building. The breakfast menu offers such choices as whole trout with eggs and cornmeal cakes; dinner is a selection of continental items including seafood and pasta.

Nepenthe, *408/667-2345; lunch and dinner daily; highchairs, booster seats; $$; AE, MC, V.* Located at the top of a cliff 808 feet above the ocean and offering a breathtaking view of the coastline, this famous restaurant was designed by a student of Frank Lloyd Wright. Diners can sit inside, or outside on the more casual terrace. The menu features simple food including steaks, fresh seafood, baked chicken, homemade soups, and very good hamburgers. The atmosphere seems to have mellowed since the days the restaurant gained notoriety for turning away then Senator John F. Kennedy—because he wasn't wearing shoes. **Cafe Amphora,** located downstairs, serves brunch and lunch items on a patio that offers the same striking view.

■ WHAT TO DO

Big Sur is so non-commercial that there is almost nothing to list in this section. Note that most lodgings do not offer TV. Bring along a good book and relax, swim in the river, picnic on the beach, or take a hike through the woods.

Big Sur Trail Rides, *408/667-2666; April–Oct; reservations necessary.* Horses may be rented by the hour as well as for half-day nature rides or overnight pack trips into the Ventana Wilderness. Children must be at least 6.

SAN SIMEON

San Simeon Chamber of Commerce
P.O. Box 1
(204 E. Frontage Rd.)
San Simeon 93452
805/927-3500

■ *A LITTLE BACKGROUND*
Located in the small town of San Simeon on the wind-blown coast south of Big Sur, the spectacular **Hearst Castle** is perched atop La Cuesta Encantada (the enchanted hill) and is filled with art treasures and antiques from all over the world. Though considered by William Randolph Hearst himself to be unfinished, the castle contains 38 bedrooms, 31 bathrooms, 14 sitting rooms, a kitchen, a movie theater, 2 libraries, a billiard room, a dining hall, and an assembly hall! Exotic vines and plants inhabit the lovely gardens, and wild animals such as zebras, goats, and sheep still graze the hillsides—remnants of the private zoo which included lions, monkeys, and a polar bear.

Before 1958 visitors could get no closer than was permitted by the coin-operated telescope located on the road below. Operated now by the State of California as a Historical Monument, the castle is now open to the public. Four tours are available; all include a scenic bus ride up to the castle.

Reservations for the castle tours are essential and may be made at most Ticketron terminals. Be prepared to pay cash. For general information, the location of your nearest Ticketron terminal, or a mail order form call 800/952-5580. Tickets may also be purchased at the castle after 8am on the day of the tour. However, often none are available. And when they are available, they are usually sold out before noon. The charge for each tour is: adults $8, 6–12 $4.

Tour 1 is suggested for the first visit and includes gardens, pools, a guest house, and the main floor of the castle.

Tour 2 covers the upper floors of the castle, including Mr. Hearst's private suite, the libraries, a guest duplex, the kitchen, and the pools.

Tour 3 covers the 36-room guest wing, and includes gardens, pools, and a guest house.

Tour 4 stresses the gardens and is somewhat of a behind-the-scenes tour. It is given April–October only.

NOTE: Children under 6 are free only if they sit on their parent's lap on the bus ride. You will be walking about ½ mile and climbing approximately 300 steps on each tour; wear comfortable shoes. Tours take approximately two hours.

- **GETTING THERE**

  For a leisurely trip to Hearst Castle, try the train package offered by Key Tours (1510 Parkside Dr. #100, Walnut Creek, 415/945-8687). Via train is the way guests used to travel to the castle. Invitations always included tickets. Today you can still relax and enjoy the scenery—while Amtrak's Coast Starlight transports you to San Luis Obispo. There you are transferred to a bus for a lectured sightseeing tour of the coast, a stop in Cambria, and on to the San Simeon Lodge to spend the night. Next day you are bussed to the famed castle for a guided tour, then down scenic Highway 1 for a stop in the fishing village of Morro Bay, and then back to San Luis Obispo for the trip home. At press time the package price was not set; call for further details. The package does not include meals.

- **ROUTE**

  Located approximately 240 miles south of San Francisco. Take Hwy 101 to Hwy 17 to Hwy 1.

- **WHERE TO STAY**

  Cambria Pines Lodge, *2905 Burton Dr. (P.O. Box 1356), Cambria 93428, 805/927-4200, 927-3827; 2/$, 4/$$; indoor pool, sauna, whirlpool; TVs; dining facilities.* Located on a tree-lined hill above town, this spacious lodging facility consists mostly of cabins but a few lodge rooms are also available. Bikes may be rented.

  Cambria Shores Motel, *6276 Moonstone Beach Dr. (P.O. Box 63), San Simeon 93452, 805/927-8644; 2-4/$-$$; some ocean views; TVs; cribs; continental breakfast.* This modern motel is located on a wind-blown bluff across the street from the ocean and offers direct access to the beach.

  Cavalier Inn, *9415 Hearst Dr., San Simeon 93452, 800/528-1234, 805/ 927-4688; 2/$-$$$, 4/$$-$$$; some refrigerators, fireplaces, and ocean views; pool; TVs; cribs; dining facilities.* Located just 200 feet from the ocean, this large motel complex offers modern comfort.

  San Simeon Pines Resort Motel, *Hwy 1/Moonstone Beach Dr., Cambria (P.O. Box 115, San Simeon 93452), 805/927-4648; 2-4/$-$$$; some fireplaces; pool; TVs.* Located across the street from the ocean with direct access to the beach, this quiet facility offers a woodsy setting outfitted with a par 3 golf course, a playground, and a croquet lawn.

■ *WHERE TO EAT*

Brambles Dinner House, *4005 Burton Dr., Cambria, 805/927-4716; dinner daily; highchairs, booster seats, children's portions; reservations suggested; $$; AE, MC, V.* Located inside an English-style cottage with Victorian decor, this homey restaurant offers a menu dominated

by steaks, prime rib, and fresh seafood. A hamburger is also on the menu. English trifle is available in two sizes for dessert.

Grey Fox Inn, *4095 Burton Dr., Cambria, 805/927-3305; breakfast, lunch, and dinner daily, weekend brunch; highchairs; reservations suggested; $$; AE, CB, DC, MC, V.* This cozy, converted Spanish-style home offers delightful meals and terrace dining. Lunch features a soup and salad bar as well as a sandwich menu; continental-style dinner entrees change daily.

Sebastian's General Store, *San Simeon, 805/927-4217; store: daily 8:30am–6pm, cafe: breakfast and lunch daily.* Sebastian's was built in 1852, moved to its present location in 1878, and is now a State Historical Landmark. Inexpensive short order items are served in the outdoor cafe. In the winter watch for the Monarch butterflies which congregate in the adjacent eucalyptus and cypress trees.

■ WHAT TO DO

Bleschyu Miniature Golf Park, *on Hwy 1, 5 miles south of San Simeon, 805/927-4165; daily 10am–10pm.* A game arcade rounds out the activities.

The Soldier Factory, *789 Main St., Cambria, 805/927-3804; daily 10am–5pm.* The majority of items sold in this shop are designed, molded, and cast on the premises. Paper castles and forts, chess sets, and assorted sizes and styles of pewter soldiers from various wars are for sale. Prices range from $1.50 for a tiny unpainted pewter animal up to $700 for an elaborately painted *Alice in Wonderland* chess set. This store makes an ideal souvenir stop.

William Randolph Hearst State Beach, *San Simeon; daily 8am–sunset; $2/car.* This is a very nice swimming beach with a fishing pier.

MORRO BAY

Morro Bay Chamber of Commerce
P.O. Box 876
(385 Morro Bay Blvd.)
Morro Bay 93442
805/772-4467

■ ANNUAL EVENTS

Fire Muster, *September.* Teams of firemen compete in everything from bucket brigades to hose-cart races to hook-and-ladder climbing. There is even a parade of antique fire-fighting equipment and an old-fashioned Fireman's Ball. Contact the Chamber of Commerce for details.

■ *A LITTLE BACKGROUND*

A huge volcanic rock, visible from just about everywhere in town, is the reason Morro Bay is sometimes called "the Gibraltar of the Pacific." It stands 576 feet high and is now a State Monument. Peregrine falcons, an endangered species, nest at the top. Commercial fishing is the town's main industry, with albacore and abalone the local specialities.

All the town's lodgings fill up on weekends. Make reservations well in advance. Once here, look forward to strolling along Embarcadero to choose a seafood restaurant, most of which feature bay views.

■ *ROUTE*

Located approximately 230 miles south of San Francisco. Take Hwy 101 to Hwy 41 west.

■ *WHERE TO STAY IN TOWN*

Breakers Motel, *Morrow Bay Blvd./Market (P.O. Box 110), 93442, 805/772-7317; 2-4/$$; some fireplaces and bay views; pool; cribs; TVs.* This modern motel is located on pleasant, attractive grounds.

Cabrillo Motel, *890 Morro Ave., 93442, 805/772-8880; 2/$, 4/$-$$; some kitchens and bay views.* What this attractive, quiet motel lacks in facilities, it makes up for in its low price.

Golden Tee Resort Lodge, *19 Country Club Rd.*, 93442, 800/321-9566, 805/772-7313; *2/$$; some bay views; pool, toddler pool; TVs; cribs; dining facilities; children under 12 stay free in parents' room.* Located at the southern end of town in Morro Bay State Park, this large motel complex makes a quiet, restful spot to spend the night. A golf course and heron rookery are adjacent.

Log Cabin Motel, *851 Market, 93442, 805/772-7132; 2–4/$; some bay views; TVs; cribs; two-night minimum on weekends.* These motel units mimic the look of a log cabin. A few detached cabin units are available.

Point Motel, *3450 Toro Lane, 93442, 805/772-2053; 2/$; some kitchens and bay views; TVs.* Located at the northern end of town, this tiny motel has beach access.

■ *WHERE TO STAY NEARBY*

Madonna Inn, *100 Madonna Rd., San Luis Obispo 93401, 805/543-3000; 2/$$–$$$, 4/$$$–$$$+; some fireplaces; TVs; cribs; dining facilities.* Painted shocking pink (reputedly the owner's favorite color), this motel is hard to miss. Begun in 1960, it has been built one room at a time and now has over 100. Each room is unique (some might say weird) and decorated in the style of a different country or period of time—like the *Cave Man Room* with stone walls and the *Barrel of Fun* in which all the furniture is made out of barrels. A photo file at the check-in desk is available to help you decide. Beware—a few of the rooms are quite ordinary. Somehow it makes sense to find a motel like this located in the town where motels are said to have originated in 1925.

■ *WHERE TO EAT*

Dorn's Original Breakers Cafe, *801 Market St., 805/772-4415; breakfast, lunch, and dinner daily; highchairs, booster seats, children's portions; reservations suggested; $; no cards.* This casual restaurant offers a great bay view, hearty breakfasts, and a dinner menu of fresh fish and steaks.

Great American Fish Co., *1185 Embarcadero, 805/772-4407; lunch and dinner daily, breakfast in summer; highchairs, booster seats, children's portions; no reservations; $$; MC, V.* Items grilled over mesquite include fresh fish, shark, and bacon-wrapped local oysters.

Hungry Tiger, *781 Market Ave., 805/772-7321; lunch and dinner daily, Sun brunch; highchairs, booster seats, children's portions; reservations suggested; $$$; AE, CB, DC, MC, V.* This first-class restaurant features great bay views and is known for the fresh lobster it has flown in regularly. Fresh fish items are also available as well as steak and chicken.

The colorful children's menu offers fish, chicken, and hamburger dinners—each served with a Shirley Temple, soup or salad, dessert, and a glass of milk.

Rose's Landing, *725 Embarcadero, 805/772-4441; lunch Sat & Sun, dinner daily; children's portions; reservations essential; $$; AE, CB, DC, MC, V.* The best view here is from the downstairs bar. However, the upstairs restaurant has decent views from most of the tables and that is where the food is. Seafood and steaks dominate the menu. Complete dinners include clam chowder, salad, potato, vegetable, bread, beverage, and dessert.

The Whale's Tail, *945 Embarcadero, 805/772-7555; lunch and dinner daily; highchairs, booster seats, children's portions; no reservations; $; MC, V.* This tiny restaurant has no view but its menu offers soups, salads, hamburgers and assorted seafood and sandwiches. Fresh fish specials are available each night and cioppino (shellfish stew) is available on Thursdays.

Zeke's Wharf, *701 Embarcadero, 805/772-2269; lunch and dinner daily; highchairs, booster seats; no reservations; $; no cards.* Zeke's is very casual and offers really great views of the bay and rock. The menu features deep-fried seafood items as well as sandwiches, "dogs on a stick," and hamburgers.

■ *WHAT TO DO*

Centennial Stairway/Giant Chess Board, *Embarcadero/Front, 805/772-1214 x226.* At the stairway's base is one of the two largest chess boards in the U.S. (the other is in New York City's Central Park). The redwood pawns stand 18″ tall and pieces weigh from 18 to 30 pounds, making a game here physical as well as mental exercise. From noon to 5pm each Saturday the Morro Bay Chess Club sponsors chess on the giant 16 x 16 foot concrete board; the general public is welcome to challenge. The board is available to the public from 8am to 5pm daily, except for the hours mentioned above. Reservations must be made by filling out an application at the Recreation Office at 535 Harbor. Call for details.

Clam Digging. Go to it! World famous Pismo clams may be dug up on the beach just about anywhere.

Fishing. Fish from the pier, or go out on a chartered fishing boat.

Morro Bay Aquarium, *595 Embarcadero, 805/772-7647; daily 9am-dusk; adults 70¢, 6-12 35¢.* This teeny, tiny aquarium is a draw for the gift shop located in front. However, the price is right and over 300 live marine specimens may be observed as well as some preserved specimens. Very noisy seals beg to be fed.

Morro Bay State Park, *at the southern end of town, 805/772-2560.*
  Bird Sanctuary. Following a trail through the marsh and hills allows
    the possibility of catching glimpses of over 250 species of birds.
    This is said to be the third largest bird sanctuary in the world.
  Heron Rookery. No one is allowed inside the rookery, one of the last
    where the Great Blue Heron may be found, but the herons may be
    viewed from a special observation area with informative displays.
  Museum of Natural History, *805/772-2694; daily 10am–5pm; adults
    50¢, 6-17 25¢.* Located on a scenic perch over the bay, this mu-
    seum offers displays, lectures, slide shows, and movies about the
    wildlife and Indian history of the area. Guided tours are some-
    times available. In the winter, inquire about walks to see the
    Monarch butterflies which congregate in nearby eucalyptus groves.
Morro Rock Playground, *east of Morro Rock.* Children will enjoy this
    idyllic playground in the sand.
Tiger's Folly Harbor Cruises, *1205 Embarcadero, 805/772-2255; 2, 4, &
    6pm daily in summer, Sat & Sun in winter; adults $5, 4–12 $2.50.*
    A one-hour bay cruise may be taken aboard this sternwheeler.

■ *WHAT TO DO NEARBY*

Avila Beach, *20 miles south of town off Hwy 101.* This tiny, old-fashioned
    beach community is a great place to watch surfers and to swim in a
    generally mild surf. Notable among the many tiny diners is the **Sea-
    side Cafe,** where you can enjoy homemade fish and shrimp tacos,
    tangy chile verde burritos, and great guacamole. On the way to or
    from the beach, consider a stop at either the **Sycamore Mineral Springs**
    (805/595-7302), where you can rent an outdoor hot tub 24 hours a
    day, or **Avila Hot Springs** (805/595-2359), where you can rent inner
    tubes to use in the warm pool.

Cayucos, *six miles north of town on Hwy 1.* The pleasant little beach
    town of Cayucos has a fine beach with a gentle surf. There is a pier
    to fish from, and equipment rentals are readily available. Consider
    lunch or dinner at **The Way Station,** a nineteenth century traveler's
    rest stop once again functioning as such.

Gum Alley, *next to 733 Higuera, San Luis Obispo.* This vulgar, tacky
    eyesore is a cheap thrill for gum aficionados. For over a decade gum
    chewers have been depositing their product on these brick walls.
    Some have even taken the time to make designs. It quite resembles
    the underside of a school desk.

Mission San Luis Obispo de Tolosa, *Monterey/Chorro Sts., San Luis
    Obispo, 805/543-6850; daily 9am–4pm; admission 50¢, family $1.*
    Built in 1772, this is referred to as "the Prince of Missions" and

features a museum and gardens. Nearby is the **Judge Walter Murray Adobe** (M, W, F noon–4pm), the **County Historical Museum** (W–Sun 10am–4pm; free), and the **Art Center** (daily noon–5pm).

PG&E Energy Information Center, *San Luis Bay Drive exit off Hwy 101, 7 miles south of San Luis Obispo, 805/595-2327; daily 9am-5pm; free.* The various exhibits, displays, and "surround-sound" film may be viewed in about an hour. Picnic facilities are available. A free 1½ hour bus tour to the Diablo Canyon Nuclear Power Plant overlook leaves daily at 10am and 2pm. Call for more information and reservations.

SOLVANG

Solvang Chamber of Commerce
P.O. Box 465
(1623 Mission Dr.)
Solvang 93463
805/688-3317

■ *ANNUAL EVENTS*

Theaterfest, *P.O. Box 1700, Santa Maria 93456, 805/922-8313.* Summer open-air theater runs July–Sept. No children under 3 permitted.

Danish Days, *September.* Contact Chamber of Commerce for details.

■ *A LITTLE BACKGROUND*

Located north of Los Angeles in Santa Barbara County, Solvang (meaning literally "sunny field" in Danish) is about a 6 hour drive from the Bay Area via Hwy 101. This replica Danish town seems right out of a Hans Christian Andersen tale; its business section features authentic Danish architecture complete with thatched roofs and hand-carved storks nesting by the chimneys.

Solvang is a popular shopping destination because it holds hundreds of specialty shops offering a wide variety of giftwares, many imported from Europe. It is especially popular around Christmas, when seasonal decorations add to the festive air.

Many restaurants and outdoor cafes offer Danish menus. Half the fun is walking around and selecting an appealing spot. Also, many excellent bakeries turn out breads, cookies, and dessert pastries.

■ *ROUTE*

Located approximately 90 miles south of Morro Bay, 300 miles south of San Francisco. Take Hwy 101 to Hwy 246 east.

■ *WHERE TO STAY*

All these lodging facilities are located within easy walking distance of the village center.

Chimney Sweep Inn, *1554 Copenhagen Dr., 93463, 805/688-2111; 2-4/$$-$$$+; some kitchens and fireplaces; jacuzzi; TVs; cribs; continental breakfast.* The quiet grounds here are beautifully landscaped and include a very large outdoor chess board. A few cottages are available in addition to the motel units.

King Frederik Motel, *1617 Copenhagen Dr., 93463, 800/528-1234, 805/688-5515; 2/$, 4/$$; pool, hot spa; TVs; cribs; continental breakfast.* This modern motel has a very attractive pool area.

Royal Copenhagen, *1579 Mission Dr., 93463, 805/688-5561; 2/$, 4/$$; pool; TVs; cribs; continental breakfast at nearby bakery.* This unusual motel resembles an Old World Danish village; many rooms are reproductions of actual Danish buildings.

Svendsgaard's Danish Lodge, *1711 Mission Dr., 93463, 805/688-3277; 2/$-$$, 4/$$-$$$; some kitchens and fireplaces; pool, jacuzzi; TVs; cribs; continental breakfast.* This pleasant motel has a secluded pool area.

■ *WHERE TO STAY NEARBY*

♥ **The 1880 Union Hotel,** *362 Bell St. (P.O. Box 616), 14 miles north of town, Los Alamos 93440, 805/928-3838, 344-2744; 2/$$$; F-Sun only; some private baths; one fireplace; pool, jacuzzi; full breakfast; dining facilities; two-night minimum; no children under 16.* This wooden hotel is gradually being restored to the way it was in 1880, when it served as lodging for Wells-Fargo stagecoach passengers. Rooms are tastefully decorated with antiques, and guests have use of the 1880 Brunswick pool table, manicured outdoor garden, and jacuzzi—picturesquely situated in a Victorian gazebo. In the morning guests are given a tour of the town in a circa 1918, 15-passenger touring car. Moderately-priced homecooked meals are served family-style in the beautifully appointed dining room, furniture for which came from a Mississippi plantation. Amenities are available for children in the dining room; reservations are suggested.

■ *WHERE TO EAT IN TOWN*

Belgian Cafe, *475 First St., 805/688-6316; breakfast and lunch daily; highchairs, booster seats; reservations suggested; $; AE, MC, V.*

Dining here is al fresco on a patio decorated with profusely blooming flowers. The menu offers a huge selection of gigantic Belgian waffles as well as crepes, Danish sausage, salads, sandwiches, and homemade soups. Local fruit wines are also available.

Ellen's Danish Pancake House, *1531 Mission Dr., 805/688-5312; breakfast, lunch, and dinner daily; booster seats; no reservations; $; MC, V.* Danish pancake balls (*aebleskiver*) are the specialty at this informal cafe. In addition a variety of pancakes and omelettes are served, and all menu items are available all day.

Little Mermaid, *1546 Mission Dr., 805/688-6141; breakfast, lunch, and dinner daily; highchairs, booster seats, children's portions; reservations suggested for dinner; $; MC, V.* This cute little cottage has a charmingly decorated interior and specializes in Danish foods. Breakfast specialties include Danish pancake balls (*aebleskiver*) as well as tasty Danish-style hash and mild Danish veal sausage.

■ WHERE TO EAT NEARBY

Andersen's Pea Soup Restaurant, *Avenue of Flags, Buellton, 3 miles west of town, 805/688-5581; breakfast, lunch, and dinner daily; highchairs, booster seats, children's portions; reservations suggested; $$; AE, CB, DC, MC, V.* A reproduction of a Swiss chalet, this famous restaurant offers thick pea soup as well as homemade breads, thick creamy milkshakes, and other substantial foods. Children are given their own menus and a pea-green crayon to color them with. This keeps most kids busy for at least ten seconds. Colorful, free postcards are available at each table. The gift shop sells that famous soup by the can or case, fresh from the pea soup factory in Stockton. Outside the kids can ride coin-operated mechanical horses and cars.

Mattei's Tavern, *5 miles north of town on Hwy 154, Los Olivos, 805/688-4820; dinner daily; highchairs, booster seats, children's portions; no reservations; $$; AE, CB, DC, MC, V.* Built in 1886, this tavern was formerly a stagecoach stop. Now it is a bar and restaurant as well as a State Historical Landmark. Steak and seafood dominate the menu, and there is a salad bar.

■ WHAT TO DO IN TOWN

Ballard School, *2425 School St., Solvang, 805/688-4812; M–F 7:30am–3pm, closed June–Sept; free.* Built in 1883, this one-room little red schoolhouse now makes a good spot to picnic.

Honen (*hen*), *board on Alisal Rd. by Rasmussen's, 805/688-4282; daily from noon on, in winter no rides M & Tu; adults $1.50, children $1.* Tour the town on a replica 1800s Danish streetcar pulled by two blond Belgian draft horses.

Mission Santa Ines, *1760 Mission Dr., 805/688-4815; M–Sat 9:30am–4:30pm, Sun noon–5pm; adults 50¢, under 16 free.* This 19th in the chain of 21 California missions, referred to as the "hidden gem," is situated in a scenic location on the outskirts of town. Founded in 1804, it is fully restored and features hand-painted murals and lovely gardens. Recorded tours are available.

■ *WHAT TO DO NEARBY*

La Purisima Mission State Historic Park, *west on Hwy 246 near Lompoc; 805/733-3713; daily 9am–5pm; adults 50¢, 6–17 25¢.* Located on 1,000 acres, this mission is completely restored and provides an accurate picture of what mission life was like here over 150 years ago. It is the best preserved of the 21 missions.

Lompoc, *west on Hwy 246 to Junction of Hwy 1.* Over one-third of the world's flower seed is grown in this fertile valley. Spring and summer provide a stunning show of color, and a **Flower Festival** (805/736-3110) is held here each June.

Nojoqui Falls Park, *on Alisal Rd. 6½ miles south of town; free.* This 60-acre park contains a 168 ft. waterfall, picnic facilities, hiking trails, and playground facilities.

COAST NORTH

Redwood Empire Association
One Market Plaza
Spear Street Tower, suite 1001
San Francisco 94105
415/543-8334

Information and brochures on the counties north of San
Francisco may be obtained M–F 9am–5pm. A *Visitor's
Guide* pamphlet is available free if picked up in person or
for $1 by mail.

■ *A WORD OF CAUTION*

The rocky cliffs and beaches along the coast are scenic and
beautiful. In our appreciation of the beauty, we sometimes
forget that they are also dangerous. Standing at the edge of a
cliff with the surf pounding at our feet is tempting, but it is
also hazardous. People have been washed out to sea just that
way. Don't be one of them. Be careful. Stay on trails. Obey
posted signs. And take special care not to let children run
loose.

HIGHWAY 1 LODGING

■ *ROUTE*

From San Francisco, take Hwy 101 to Hwy 1 north.

■ *WHERE TO STAY / WHAT TO DO*

MUIR BEACH

The Pelican Inn, *10 Pacific Way, 94965, 415/383-6000; 2/$$$; full break-
fast; dining facilities.* Built in 1979 to resemble an English country
inn, the Pelican offers snug rooms furnished with English antiques,
canopied beds, and oriental carpets. Elegant pub fare and afternoon
tea are available in the dining room.

POINT REYES

Inns of Point Reyes, *P.O. Box 145, Inverness 94937, 415/663-1420.* Contact for information on the area's bed and breakfast inns.

Point Reyes Hostel, *P.O. Box 247, Point Reyes Station 94956, 415/669-7414.* Formerly a ranch house, this hostel offers a kitchen and outdoor barbecue as well as two cozy common rooms with wood-burning stoves. Currently it is open only to groups and families—no individuals. See also p. 219.

Point Reyes National Seashore, *west of Olema, 415/663-1093; daily; free.* Known for its beaches and hiking trails, this rustic windblown area also offers a replica of a Miwok Indian village, a Morgan horse farm, hike-in campsites, and a picturesque old lighthouse. Horses may be rented nearby to use on over 70 miles of equestrian trails, and whale-watching is prime during the winter.

BODEGA BAY

Bodega Bay Lodge, *P.O. Box 357, 94923, 800/528-1234, 707/875-3525; 2/$$-$$$; some kitchens, fireplaces, and ocean views; enclosed whirlpool spa; TVs; cribs; children under 18 stay free in parents' room.* This is a woodsy, modern Best Western motel.

Chanslor Ranch, *Hwy 1 (P.O. Box 327), 94923, 707/875-3386; 2/$$, 4/$$$; cribs; full breakfast; dining facilities; two-night minimum.* Pack 'em up and move 'em out to this 700-acre working cattle and sheep ranch. Lodging consists of comfortable rooms in the ranch house and a bunkhouse that sleeps 12. Hearty breakfasts and family-style dinners are served in the ranch house dining room. Wind-down activities include horseback riding (fee), hiking, fishing, nearby golfing, and local sightseeing—or you can help milk a cow!

George Haig Realty, *P.O. Box 38, 94923, 707/875-2711.* Lodging ranging from cozy cottages to luxurious homes can be rented through this resource.

JENNER

Murphy's Jenner by the Sea, *Hwy 1 (P.O. Box 69), Jenner 95450, 707/865-2377; 2/$-$$$+, 4/$$$-$$$+; some kitchens, woodstoves, and ocean views; 2 hot tubs; full breakfast; dining facilities; two-night minimum on weekends.* Located 70 miles north of San Francisco where the Russian River runs into the ocean, this lodging facility offers cabins, lodge rooms, and private homes. The restaurant operates May–Oct (schedule varies) and offers family amenities. Seafood, steak, and rack of lamb are house specialties but vegetarian meals are also available. The bar has a stone fireplace and library with books and games, and classical music and jazz are sometimes presented live on weekends. Live plays are often scheduled next door on weekends.

Fort Ross State Historic Park, *19005 Hwy 1, 11 miles north of town, 707/847-3286; daily 10am–5pm; $2/car.* Built in 1812 as a trading outpost by Russian and Alaskan hunters, this historic fort has been authentically restored by the state. The compound consists of a stockade, two blockhouses, a Russian chapel, the Rotchev and Kuskov Houses, a Russian well, and the Officials' Barracks. Picnic facilities are available.

Salt Point Lodge, *23255 Hwy 1, Jenner 95450, 707/847-3234; 2/$–$$$, 4/$$; some fireplaces and ocean views; hot tub and sauna; TVs; cribs; dining facilities.* This secluded lodging facility has motel-like units.

♥ **Timber Cove Inn,** *14 miles north of town, 95450, 707/847-3231; 2–4/$$–$$$+; some fireplaces and ocean views; dining facilities; two-night minimum on weekends March–Dec; children discouraged.* Perched on a rocky seaside cliff, this inn offers many rooms with magnificent ocean views and some with sunken tubs and jacuzzis. Self-contained, the bar and dining room are done in a dramatic Japanese-modern style of architecture and also feature ocean views. You know you're here when you see the tall Bufano sculpture jutting above the lodge.

POINT ARENA

Oz, *P.O. Box 147, 95468, 707/882-2449; private cabins and meals available when no workshops are scheduled; all shared baths; fireplaces; sauna, hot tub, isolation tank; meals included.* Oz is located in a redwood forest "just this side of the rainbow." It is an ecotopian community with limited electrical facilities. Lodging is in private cabins with kerosene lanterns and outhouses. Guests provide their own bedding. The lack of structure allows as much or as little interaction with others as is desired. A week-long family camp is scheduled each July, and workshops on such subjects as Tai Chi, polarity therapy, and filmmaking are scheduled throughout the year.

THE SEA RANCH

Homes. *Rams Head Realty, P.O. Box 123, 95497, 707/785-2427; $$–$$$+; two-night minimum.* Staying in an award-winning vacation home and enjoying the beauty of the wind-swept coastal scenery are two compelling reasons to visit The Sea Ranch. A bar and restaurant are located in the nearby lodge, and guests have use of the swimming pools, tennis courts, saunas, hiking and jogging trails, and a children's playground. Horse rentals and a golf course are available at extra charge.

Lodge. *60 Sea Walk Dr. (P.O. Box 44), 95497, 707/785-2371; 2/$$–$$$+, 4/$$$–$$$+; some fireplaces and ocean views; 2 pools; cribs; dining facilities.*

GUALALA

Mar Vista Cottages, *35101 Hwy 1, 95445, 707/884-3522; 2/$, 4/$$; some kitchens, fireplaces, and ocean views; hot tub; cribs.* These cottages are just a short walk from a sandy beach with a gentle surf. Two ponds and assorted geese and ducks are located on the nine acres of land.

♥ **Old Milano Hotel,** *38300 Hwy 1, 95445; 707/884-3256; 2/$$-$$$+; Dec–Mar open weekends only; some shared baths; some kitchens and ocean views; hot tub; continental breakfast; two-night minimum on weekends; no children.* Built originally in 1905 as a railroad rest stop and pub, this cliffside Victorian hotel is now recorded in the National Register of Historic Places. A cottage and a converted caboose are available in addition to the hotel rooms—all of which are named after Italian operas.

Serenisea, *36100 Hwy 1, 95445, 707/884-3836; 2-4/$-$$$; kitchens, fireplaces, ocean views; some TVs; two-night minimum on weekends.* These ocean-front cottages are located on a scenic bluff. Serenisea also manages a group of local homes, all of which have dramatic ocean views, decks, kitchens, fireplaces, and TVs or stereos.

St. Orres, *Hwy 1 (P.O. Box 523), 95445, 707/884-3303; 2/$$-$$$+, 4/$$$-$$$+; some shared baths; some kitchens, fireplaces, and ocean views; full breakfast; dining facilities; two-night minimum on weekends.* Built of weathered old wood in a Russian style of architecture, this striking inn offers rooms as well as three detached cabins. Families are welcome but restricted to the more expensive cabins.

ELK

♥ **Harbor House,** *5600 Hwy 1 (P.O. Box 369), 95432, 707/877-3203; 2/$$$-$$$+; in December open weekends only; some fireplaces and ocean views; full breakfast and dinner included; no children.* Built entirely of redwood in 1917, this lovely inn offers five rooms and four cottages. A path leads to a private beach where guests may sun, explore tidepools, or gather driftwood.

MENDOCINO

Fort Bragg-Mendocino Coast Chamber of Commerce
P.O. Box 1141
(332 N. Main St.)
Fort Bragg 95437
707/964-3153

■ *A LITTLE BACKGROUND*

For a rejuvenating, quiet escape from the hectic pace of city life, pack up your car and head for Mendocino. Now a Historical Monument, this tiny artists' colony is built in a pastel Cape Cod-style of architecture and exudes the feeling that it belongs to a time past. To really slow down your system, consider parking your car and not using it for the duration of your visit. You can get anywhere in town with a short walk.

Keep in mind that Mendocino has a limited water supply and be careful not to waste. Also, there is a Volunteer Fire Department whose alarm has been known to go off in the middle of the night. Resembling the scream of an air raid siren, it can be quite startling—even if you know what it is.

The night life here is of the early-to-bed-early-to-rise variety. My family's agenda usually consists of dinner out, a stroll through town, a nightcap at the Mendocino Hotel or Sea Gull Inn, and then off to bed.

Be sure to make your lodging reservations at least a few weeks in advance; in-town lodging is limited and popular.

■ *ROUTE*
Located approximately 150 miles north of San Francisco. Take Hwy 101 to Hwy 1, or Hwy 101 to Hwy 128 west to Hwy 1.

■ *STOPS ALONG THE WAY*
On the drive to Mendocino, a picnic makes a good lunch stop. Several wineries off Hwy 101 have picnic facilities. **Geyser Peak Winery** (707/433-6585), located a mile north of Geyserville at the Canyon Rd. exit, has picnic tables, barbecue facilities, and a self-guided nature trail. The facilities are, however, somewhat difficult to locate. Ask for directions in the tasting room. **Italian Swiss Colony** (707/894-2541), at the Asti exit, has a deli stocked with picnic supplies and a shaded area with tables.

More picnic spots are found along Hwy 128. The best are **Indian Creek City Park** located just east of Boonville, **Anderson Valley Historical Museum** (open Th, F, and Sat 11–4, Sun 1–4) just west of Boonville, and the **Masonite Corporation Demonstration Forest** just past Navarro.

If you prefer to stop at a restaurant, **Souverain Winery** (707/433-3141, off Hwy 101 at the Independence Lane exit in Geyserville) offers an elegant luncheon and a huge Sunday brunch. Menu choices include delicious fresh soups and salads, varied entrees, and fancy desserts. Diners are seated outdoors with a view of the vineyards. Highchairs and booster seats are available and children are welcome. Reservations are suggested.

The **New Boonville Hotel** (707/895-3478), on Hwy 128 in Boonville, serves lunch and dinner daily. It is celebrated for using only local ingredients, many of which are grown or raised on the restaurant's own land. Menu items vary from chicken pot pie and pizza to grilled rabbit and duck to a BLT and hamburger. The atmosphere is casual, prices reasonable, and booster seats are available. Reservations are suggested.

While in Boonville note that the townspeople speak an

unusual dialect known as *Boontling.* For example, public telephones are labeled *Buckey Walter.*

Highland Ranch *(P.O. Box 150, Philo 95466, 707/895-3294)* offers the rural pleasures of fishing and swimming in two ponds as well as a tennis court and hot tub. Most days horseback riding is available at additional charge. Lodging is in modern redwood cabins with fireplaces, and three full meals are included. There is a two-night minimum, and the ranch is closed Nov–March.

■ *WHERE TO STAY IN TOWN*

♥ **Joshua Grindle Inn,** *44800 Little Lake Rd. (P.O. Box 647), 95460, 707/937-4143; 2/$$; some fireplaces and ocean views; continental breakfast; children discouraged.* Built in 1879, this small inn has a New England country atmosphere and antiques in every room. Bikes are available for guests to use, and airport pickup via a '48 Chevy woodie can be arranged.

MacCallum House Inn, *45020 Albion St. (P.O. Box 206), 95460, 707/937-0289; 2-4/$-$$$+; some private baths; some fireplaces and ocean views; cribs; continental breakfast; dining facilities; two-night minimum May–Oct.* Built in 1882 by William H. Kelley for his newlywed daughter, Daisy MacCallum, this converted Victorian home features charming rooms decorated with antiques. Accommodations are also available in the Greenhouse, Carriage House, Watertower, Gazebo, and Barn.

♥ **The Mendocino Hotel,** *45080 Main St. (P.O. Box 587), 95460, 707/937-0511; 2/$$-$$$+; some private baths; some ocean views; continental breakfast; dining facilities; no children under 14.* Built in 1878, this hotel has been renovated in Victorian style. Its rooms combine modern convenience with nineteenth century elegance. The hotel also offers lodging in a house and apartment located across the bay; both feature a fireplace and kitchen.

Mendocino Village Inn, *44680 Main St. (P.O. Box 626), 95460, 707/937-0246; 2/$-$$; some shared baths; some fireplaces, ocean views, and TVs; two-night minimum on weekends.* Built in 1882, this Victorian home is known as "the house of the doctors" because it was originally built by a doctor and then bought in turn by three other doctors. All the cozy rooms are different and decorated in old-fashioned style.

Sea Gull Inn, *10481 Lansing St. (P.O. Box 317), 95460, 707/937-5204; 2/$, 4/$-$$; dining facilities.* Over 100 years old, this rustic, non-cutesy inn has a casual atmosphere.

Sea Rock, *11101 N. Lansing St. (P.O. Box 286), 95460, 707/937-5517;*

2/$-$$$+, 4/$$$-$$$+; some kitchens and fireplaces; ocean views, TVs; two-night minimum on weekends. These cottage units are located on a rural road ¼ mile from town. Guests have access to a private cove and beach.

♥ **Whitegate Inn,** *499 Howard St. (P.O. Box 150), 95460, 707/937-4892; 2/$$-$$$; some shared baths; some fireplaces and ocean views; continental breakfast, full breakfast on weekends; two-night minimum on weekends; no children under 16.* Built in 1880, this Victorian home has been refurbished and decorated with antiques and now offers tasteful lodging.

■ *WHERE TO STAY NEARBY*

Big River Lodge, *P.O. Box 487, Mendocino 95460, 707/937-5025, 937-5615; 2-4/$$$-$$$+; some kitchens and ocean views; fireplaces, TVs; continental breakfast; cribs; two-night minimum on weekends.* Located on the outskirts of town, these modern luxury motel rooms are decorated with antiques, fresh flowers, and the work of local artists. Guests may borrow bicycles.

♥ **Glendeven,** *8221 N. Hwy 1, Little River 95456, 707/937-0083; 2/$$-$$$; some shared baths; some fireplaces and bay views; full breakfast; two-night minimum on weekends; no children under 7.* Built in 1867, this Maine-style farmhouse overlooks the headland meadows and bay at Little River. Rooms are furnished eclectically with antiques and contemporary art, and the atmosphere is casual.

Heritage House, *5200 N. Hwy 1, Little River 95456, 707/937-5885; 2/$$$-$$$+, 4/$$$+; closed Dec and Jan; some fireplaces and ocean views; full breakfast and dinner included; dining facilities.* Located on a craggy stretch of coast, this inn offers a luxurious escape from city living. Guests are housed in cottages furnished with antiques. Meals are served in a cliffside dining room; male guests are encouraged to dress in jacket and tie. If it all looks familiar, you may have seen it before in the film *Same Time Next Year* which was filmed here.

Little River Inn, *Hwy 1, Little River 95456, 707/937-5942; 2/$$-$$$, 4/$$$-$$$+; ocean views; some fireplaces; cribs; two-night minimum on weekends.* Built in 1853, this house became an inn in 1929 and now offers cozy attic rooms, cottages, and standard motel units as well as a 9-hole golf course for the use of guests.

Mendocino Coast Holiday Reservations, *P.O. Box 1143, Mendocino 95460, 707/937-5033; $-$$$+; two-night minimum.* This vacation home rental service will arrange lodging in studios, cabins, cottages, inns, and estate homes located on the Mendocino coast.

■ *WHERE TO EAT IN TOWN*

Cafe Beaujolais, *961 Ukiah, 707/937-5614; breakfast and lunch daily, dinner May–Oct; highchairs; $$; AE, MC, V.* Breakfast in this converted Victorian home is the usual items prepared with unusual care along with such delights as homemade coffeecake, croissants, cashew granola, fruit salad with creme fraiche, and Mexican hot chocolate. Lunch begins at 11:30; the menu changes daily and includes a variety of sandwiches, quiches, casseroles, soups, and salads. All this plus a large variety of specialty coffees and fresh flowers decorating each plate!

Mendocino Hotel, *45080 Main St., 707/937-0511; breakfast, lunch, and dinner daily; highchairs, children's portions; $$; AE, MC, V.* Consider a stop in the bar to enjoy a fancy drink among its stained glass and oriental carpet splendor. The dining room is somewhat formal and furnished in old-fashioned oak. Fresh seafood and steak entrees and deepdish pie desserts are on the dinner menu along with hamburgers and grilled cheese sandwiches.

Mendocino Ice Cream Co., *Main St., 707/937-5884; Sun–Thur 9am–7pm, F & Sat to 11pm, in winter daily to 6pm.* People wait in long lines here to get their ¼ lb. ice cream cones. And, indeed, the award-winning ice cream is very good. My favorite is Black Forest, rich chocolate ice cream with chocolate and cherry chips. The foot-long hot dogs are pretty good too. Wooden booths are available for enjoying a soda, hamburger, sandwich or some such informal delight.

Sea Gull Inn, *10481 Lansing St., 707/937-5204; breakfast, lunch and dinner daily; highchairs, children's portions; $$; no cards.* The specialty here is fresh food prepared simply. The great breakfasts include eggs, pancakes, and hot cereal. The premier choice on the dinner menu is fresh fish from the local catch, grilled or broiled to order. A buttery chicken Kiev, assorted veal dishes, and a nightly vegetarian special are also available. Dinners come with homemade soup or green salad, fresh vegetable, baked potato with mounds of sour cream, and a crusty loaf of French bread. The upstairs **Cellar Bar** is a good choice for an Irish Coffee. Children are welcome until 9pm, when the live music begins.

■ *WHAT TO DO IN TOWN*

For a listing of current local events, check the postings in the entryway to the Sea Gull restaurant.

- Take the little path behind the church on Main Street down to the beach to **do some beachcombing.**
- **Make a kelp horn.** Cut the bulb off the end of a long, thin piece of fresh bull kelp. Rinse out the tube in the ocean so that it is hollow.

Wrap it over your shoulder and blow through the small end. The longer the tube, the greater the resonance.

- **See a movie** at the **Mendocino Art Center**, 540 Little Lake St. Showings are usually scheduled for weekend evenings. There is also an irregular schedule of Sunday afternoon concerts and plays. Call 707/937-5818 for details.
- Bring along your **bikes**. This is the perfect spot to ride.
- **Go whale-watching** at **Mendocino Headlands State Park**. December through March, whales migrate close to shore and can sometimes easily be seen *breaching* (jumping out of the water). Binoculars are handy to have along.

Catch a Canoe, *located off Hwy 1 at Comptche-Ukiah Rd., 707/937-0273; daily 9am–6pm; $8–$10/hr; reservations recommended.* Drifting down calm Big River affords the opportunity to picnic in the wilderness, swim in a secluded swimming hole, and observe a variety of wildlife. Canoe rentals include paddles and life jackets.

Kelley House Museum, *45007 Albion St., 707/937-5791; daily 1–4pm (Dec & Jan, F–Sun 1–4pm and by appt.); $1 donation.* A gigantic cypress tree grows in the front yard of this home built by William H. Kelley in 1861. The restored first floor displays a collection of photos from the 1800s and changing exhibits of local artifacts and private collections. Inquire about the schedule of walking tours.

■ *WHAT TO DO NEARBY*

Pygmy Forest, *located south of town on Airport Rd.* The leached soil in this forest produces miniature trees. The 1/3 mile trail takes about 15 minutes to walk. A brochure, describing the various types of trees, is available at the trailhead.

Ricochet Ridge Ranch, *27011 Albion Ridge Rd., Albion, 95410, 707/937-4894; daily 9am-9pm; $10/hr.* Equestrian excursions vary from two-hour guided rides to four-day overnight trips. Meal trips, camping expeditions, and tours with overnight inn lodging can be arranged. All this and ponies too!

FORT BRAGG

■ *WHERE TO STAY*

Beachcomber Motel, *21800 N. Hwy 1, ½ mile north of town, 95437, 707/964-2402; 2/$, 4/$-$$; some kitchens and ocean views; TVs; cribs.* This ordinary motel is in an extraordinary location just 200 ft. from the beach.

Colonial Inn, *533 E. Fir St. (P.O. Box 565), 95437, 707/964-9979; 2/$-$$, 4/$$; closed in Oct; some fireplaces, some ocean views; TVs.* Located in a quiet residential area, this huge old woodframe house has tastefully decorated rooms.

The Grey Whale Inn, *615 N. Main St., 95437, 800/382-7244, 707/964-0640; 2/$$, 4/$$$; some shared baths; some kitchens, fireplaces and ocean views; continental breakfast.* This unusual hotel was a hospital from 1915 to 1971. An inn since 1976, it now offers spacious, pleasantly decorated rooms, a few with private decks. Well-behaved children are welcome.

Ocean View Lodging, *21950 N. Hwy 1, ½ mile north of town, 95437, 707/964-4595; 2/$-$$, 4/$-$$$; some kitchens; ocean views and TVs; cribs; continental breakfast.* Located by a secluded sandy beach, this lodging facility has some rooms with decks.

Pine Beach Inn, *4 miles south of town on Hwy 1 (P.O. Box 1173), 95437, 707/964-5603; 2-4/$-$$; tennis courts (no fee); TVs; cribs; dining facilities Apr-Oct.* These modern motel units are located on twelve acres of private land. Facilities include a private beach and cove.

▪ *WHERE TO STAY NEARBY*

These lodgings are located approximately 35 miles east via Hwy 20.

Emandal, *16500 Hearst Rd., Willits 95490, 707/459-5439; open all of August and some weekends; rates vary according to age; cribs; includes three meals per day.* This 1,000-acre working cattle and pig farm is located on the Eel River about 16 miles northeast of Willits. Makings for the homecooked meals are grown on the farm. Emandal has been a guest ranch since 1908. Guests are housed in rustic one-room cabins dating from 1916 and may hike and swim in the river. Stays of less than a week can sometimes be arranged, usually on weekdays.

Orr Hot Springs, *13201 Orr Springs Rd., Ukiah 95482, 707/462-6277; 2/$$, 4/$$$; communal kitchen; pool, hot tubs.* In the 1800s, when this mineral springs resort was built, patrons reached it via stagecoach. Now this secluded spot is easier to reach. Facilities include some hot tubs (bathing suits optional) and a natural rock swimming pool filled with cool mineral spring water. Lodging is in primitive cabins or on the floor in a loft area in the lodge, and guests must bring their own food. Campsites and day use rates are also available.

▪ *WHERE TO EAT*

Cap'n Flint's, *32250 N. Harbor Dr., Noyo, 707/964-9447; lunch and dinner daily; highchairs, children's portions; no reservations; $; no cards.* Popular with locals, the menu here offers various types of fish and chips, Louis salads, and the house specialty—shrimp wontons made with a tasty cream cheese filling. Also available are hamburgers, hot dogs, assorted sandwiches, and mixed wine drinks. Though the decor is well-worn mix-matched furniture, the view of the picturesque harbor is excellent.

Egghead Omelettes, *326 N. Main St., 707/964-5005; breakfast and lunch daily; booster seats; no reservations; $; no cards.* This cheerful, popular, and tiny diner serves a large variety of huge omelettes. Regular breakfast items are also available, and at lunch sandwiches join the menu. Enclosed booths allow for dining privacy.

The Flying Bear, *356 N. Main St., 707/964-5671; daily 10am–5pm.* In this candy shop they hand-dip their homemade chocolate-covered creams, they make their own marshmallow for the rocky road, they roast their own almonds for the English toffee, and they make thick peanut brittle fresh each day. All without the use of preservatives, of course.

Piedmont Hotel, *102 S. Main St., 707/964-2410; lunch Tu-F, dinner Tu–Sun; highchairs, booster seats, children's portions; $$; MC, V.* The menu in this noisy, popular spot includes Italian specialties, fried

At Northspur, half-way to Willits on the Skunk Train Line.

chicken, fresh seafood, and homemade desserts. Served family style, the dinners include soup, salad, entree, and beverage.

■ **WHAT TO DO**

Georgia-Pacific Guest House Museum, *Main St., 707/964-5651; W–Sun 8:30am–4:30pm; free.* Get a sense of this area's history by viewing the old logging photos and artifacts on display in this beautifully restored mansion made entirely of redwood. The display outside in the manicured gardens includes a steam donkey.

Georgia-Pacific Nursery, *90 W. Redwood Ave., 707/964-5651; M–F 9am–4pm April–Oct; free.* Visitors get a view of 4 million seedling trees and may take a walk along a nature trail or make use of the picnic tables. The nursery closes November 1, when the seedlings are taken out and planted.

Mendocino Coast Botanical Gardens, *18220 N. Hwy 1, 2 miles south of town, 707/964-4352; daily 9am–5pm; adults $3, 12–17 $1.50.* Enjoy a self-guided tour through 47 acres of flowering plants. The garden is known for its rhododendrons, fuchsias, and native California plants. Picnic facilities, a restaurant, and a nursery are available, and concerts are often scheduled in the summer.

Skunk Train, *foot of Laurel St., 707/964-6371; round trip: adults $12, 5–11 $6, under 5 free if they don't occupy a seat; train leaves at 9:45am and returns at 5pm; reservations suggested.* For those of you with little skunks who love trains—voilà—the skunk train. The train gets its name from the fact that the original logging trains emitted unpleasant odors from their gas engines. They smelled not unlike skunks. Now a steam engine usually pulls the train in the summer (the Super Skunk) and a diesel engine is used the rest of the year (the Skunk). The train travels through two deep mountain tunnels and 40 miles of dense redwood forest, over 31 bridges and trestles, and makes stops along the way to deliver mail. It runs between Fort Bragg and Willits, where there is a stopover for lunch. Several other schedule choices are available. Like many town attractions, this one is owned by Georgia-Pacific Co.

Weller House Museum, *524 Stewart St., 707/964-3061; summer Tu–Sat 10am–5pm, winter weekends by appt; donation.* Listed on the National Register of Historic Places, this is a private 1886 Victorian home open for public touring. The owners guide visitors through 9 of the 18 rooms in their unaltered home, built almost entirely of local redwood. Of special interest is the attic ballroom. Family possessions include a hand-cranked record player, an extensive collection of beaded purses and antique toys, and antiques from various periods.

EUREKA

Eureka Chamber of Commerce
2112 Broadway
Eureka 95501
707/442-3738

In summer, guided tours of the town leave the Chamber office on Tuesdays and Thursdays at 9am. The $12.50 charge (children under 12 $8) includes lunch. Call for reservations.

Eureka/Humboldt County Convention and
Visitors Bureau
123 F St.
Eureka 95501
707/443-5097

■ *A LITTLE BACKGROUND*
Ambitious logging activity has, over time, changed the scenery

here quite a bit. The best of the remaining virgin redwoods are in this area's State Parks, all of which were established in the 1920s.

The winter off-season is an uncrowded (and cold) time to visit the quiet north coast redwood country around Humboldt Bay. Pack your warmest clothing, kiss the sunshine goodbye, and prepare to enjoy the stunning beauty of this quiet, foggy area.

Eureka and nearby Arcata are both known for their well-preserved Victorian homes. Arcata, a smaller town and home of Humboldt State University, also has a number of interesting restaurants in its downtown square.

■ *ROUTE*

Located approximately 275 miles north of San Francisco. Take Hwy 101 all the way.

■ *WHERE TO STAY IN TOWN*

Eureka Inn, *7th/F Sts., 95501, 707/442-6441; 2–4/$$–$$$+; some kitchens and fireplaces; pool, jacuzzi, sauna; TVs; cribs; dining facilities.* Built in English Tudor style in 1922 and now a National Historic Landmark, this is *the* place to stay and is within walking distance of many attractions.

Motel Row. Plenty of last-minute accommodations can usually be found along 4th St. and Broadway, both of which are lined with motels.

■ *WHERE TO STAY NEARBY*

Arcata Crewhouse Hostel, *1390 I St., Arcata, 707/822-9995; summer only.* This restored Victorian home is a popular stopover with bicyclists. See also p. 219.

Avenue of the Giants. See p. 84.

Benbow Inn, *445 Lake Benbow Dr., Garberville 95440, 70 miles north of town, 707/923-2124; 2/$$–$$$+, 4/$$$+; closed Jan–Mar; some fireplaces, mountain views, and TVs; dining facilities; no infants.* This magnificent English Tudor inn has blooming English gardens, rooms furnished with antiques, a communal fireplace and library, and an elegant dining room and taproom bar. Facilities include a putting green, 9-hole golf course, lawn games, and a private beach on a lake. Movies are scheduled each evening.

Bishop Pine Lodge, *1481 Patricks Point Dr., Trinidad 95570, 23 miles north of town, 707/677-3314; 2/$, 4/$$; some kitchens; TVs; cribs.* These rustic, secluded cabins are located in the redwoods. Forest and ocean trails are nearby, and a playground is on the premises.

♥ **The Gingerbread Mansion,** *400 Berding St. (P.O. Box 937), Ferndale 95536, 15 miles south of town, 707/786-4000; 2/$$; all shared baths; continental breakfast; no children under 10.* Originally built in 1894 as a doctor's home, this carefully restored Victorian mansion, complete with gables and turrets, has been painted cheery colors. Bicycles and picnic baskets are available for loan, and afternoon tea is served in the parlor.

Hartsook Inn, *Hwy 101, Piercy 95467, 70 miles south of town, 707/247-3305; 2/$, 4/$$; closed Nov–April; some kitchens; cribs; dining facilities.* These scattered cottages and motel units are located in a majestic 30-acre redwood setting adjoining **Richardson Grove State Park.** Guests may swim in the Eel River and have use of a children's playground, lawn games, a putting green, and a lounge with fireplace. See also p. 84.

Historic Requa Inn, *451 Requa Rd., Klamath 95548, 65 miles north of town, 707/482-5231; 2/$–$$, 4/$$–$$$; closed mid-Oct through Mar; some private baths; continental breakfast; dining facilities.* In the style of an English country inn, this historic hotel features steak and kidney pie and rack of lamb on its dining room dinner menu. It is located at the mouth of the Klamath River just 30 miles south of the Oregon border.

■ *WHERE TO EAT*

Lazio's Seafood Restaurant, *at the foot of C St. (near Old Town),*

707/442-2337; breakfast, lunch, and dinner daily; highchairs, booster seats, children's portions; no reservations; $$; AE, CB, D, MC, V.
Fresh seafood, caught by the restaurant's own commercial fishing operation, is the specialty here. Picture windows allow diners to watch the fishermen bringing in the catch. It's usually crowded, so expect a short wait.

Samoa Cookhouse, 445 W. *Washington (from Hwy 101 take Samoa Bridge to end, turn left on Samoa Rd., take first left turn), 707/442-1659; breakfast, lunch, and dinner daily; highchairs, booster seats, children's portions; no reservations; $$; AE, CB, D, MC, V.* The fare changes daily in this "last of the western cookhouses," which was formerly owned by the Georgia-Pacific Corporation to feed its loggers. There are no menu choices. Just sit down and the food starts arriving. Hearty, delicious, and huge family-style meals are served at long tables in three large, noisy dining halls. A typical lunch might consist of marinated 3-bean salad, soup, homemade bread with butter, assorted jams and honey, coleslaw, scalloped potatoes, deep-fried cod with tartar sauce, mixed vegetables, coffee or tea, and butterscotch pudding topped with whipped cream. A fantastic value! Most items are cooked with fresh ingredients. The only item not included in the fixed-price is milk. After dining you can wander through a mini-museum and purchase freshly-baked loaves of bread and toy logging trucks for souvenirs of your visit. Several unmarked turnoffs from Samoa Rd. lead to driftwood-strewn beaches.

■ WHAT TO DO

Carson Mansion, 2nd/M Sts. Built in 1885, this is said to be the most photographed house in the United States and the "queen" of Victorian architecture. The house is now a private club and may be viewed only from the exterior.

Clarke Memorial Museum, 240 E St./3rd, 707/443-1947; Tu–Sat 10am–4pm, closed in April; by donation. In this airy high-ceilinged building built in 1912, you'll see an extensive collection of pioneer relics, local Indian baskets and artifacts, and historical photographs of the area as well as Victorian clothing, furniture, and antique weapons.

Coast Oyster Co., foot of A St., 707/442-2947; free. Take a self-guided tour of this oyster processing plant located behind Lazio's restaurant. Hours are irregular; call for current schedule.

Fort Humboldt State Historic Park, 3431 Fort Ave., 707/443-7952; daily 8am–5pm; free. This was U. S. Grant's headquarters in 1854. Exhibits include locomotives, a restored logger's cabin, and displays of pioneer logging methods. The view of Humboldt Bay makes it a nice spot for a picnic.

Dolbeer steam donkey at Fort Humboldt.

Humboldt Bay Harbor Cruise, *foot of C St., 707/445-1910; at 1, 2:30, and 4pm, daily in summer, schedule varies rest of year; adults $4, 12-17 $3, 6-11 $2.* The one hour cruise aboard the *M/V Madaket*— which once ferried workers to the lumber mills across the bay in Samoa—allows a view of the bustling activity and native wildlife of the bay.

Old Town, *1st/2nd/3rd Sts. from C to G Sts.* This waterfront area consists of restored commercial and residential buildings. Many restaurants are located here as well as interesting shops. Antique hunting is especially good.

Sequoia Park and Zoo, *Glatt/W Sts., 707/443-7331; May–Oct Tu–Sun 10am–7pm, Nov–Apr until 5pm; petting zoo open in summer only; free.* The backdrop for this combination zoo-playground-picnic area is a 52-acre grove of virgin redwoods. Visitors may also enjoy hiking trails, gardens, and a duck pond.

■ *WHAT TO DO NEARBY*

The Avenue of the Giants, Humboldt Redwoods State Park, *Weott, 707/946-2311; free.* Millions of years ago, when dinosaurs roamed the earth, gigantic redwood forests were plentiful. After the Ice Age, the redwood survived only in a narrow 500-mile strip along the northern coast of California. Before the logging days on the north coast, it is estimated the area contained 1½ million acres of redwoods.

Now only 100,000 acres remain—preserved by the State Parks system. Approximately half of these huge old trees are found in Humboldt Redwoods State Park, home of the Avenue of the Giants.

The Avenue of the Giants, which is actually the old Hwy 101, begins a few miles north of Garberville near Phillipsville and continues on for approximately 40 miles to just south of the town of Pepperwood, where it rejoins the busy new Hwy 101. This breathtaking route parallels the freeway and the Eel River and winds through grove after grove of huge redwoods. Unusual sights along this unique stretch of road are numerous. Near Myers Flat, the **Shrine Drive-Thru Tree** has a circumference of approximately 64 ft. and provides the opportunity to take an unusual picture. The **Children's Forest,** located across the south fork of the Eel River, is a 1,120-acre memorial to children. **Williams Grove** features picturesque picnic and swimming sites on the Eel River. Near Weott the 9,000-acre **Rockefeller Forest,** referred to by some as "the world's finest forest," features hiking trails leading to the Flatiron Tree, Giant Tree, and 356 ft. Tall Tree as well as equestrian trails and horse rentals.

Lodging facilities are scattered along the route. A few of the best are:

Benbow Inn. See p. 80.

Hartsook Resort. See p. 80.

Humboldt State Park, *800/952-5580.* Excellent camping.

Miranda Gardens Resort, *P.O. Box 186, Miranda 95553, 707/943-3011; 2-4/$-$$; pool; TVs; cottages and motel units.*

Richardson Grove State Park, *800/952-5580, 707/247-3318; $; mid-Oct to Apr.* Stark, unfurnished cabins have indoor plumbing, showers, and kitchens but you must bring almost everything else, including a bed. Campsites are also available.

Whispering Pines Motel, *P.O. Box 246, Miranda 95553, 707/943-3160; 2/$, 4/$-$$; some kitchens; pool; TVs; cribs.*

•**Squirrel Bus Tour,** *Garberville, 707/986-7526.* Narrated tours of the Avenue are available. Rates and schedules vary.

Confusion Hill, *Hwy 101, Piercy, 707/925-6456. Hill: open all year; adults $2, 6-12 $1. Train: April–Sept.; adults $2, 3-12 $1.* You have a choice here of visiting a spot where gravity appears to be defied and water runs uphill or of taking a train ride through a tree tunnel to the crest of a hill in the redwoods.

Covered Bridges, *take Hwy 101 south to Elk River Rd., follow Elk River Rd. to either Bertas Rd. or Zane Rd.* These two all-wood covered bridges were constructed in 1936.

Demonstration Forests. To educate the public about modern forestry practices, many lumber firms have set up self-guided tours through parts of their forests. Picnic facilities are usually available.

Louisiana Pacific Corporation, *on Hwy 1 one mile north of Rockport.*

Louisiana Pacific, *Samoa Division, on old Hwy 101 one mile north of Trinidad.*

Masonite Corporation, *on Hwy 128 west of Navarro.*

Pacific Lumber Company, *on Hwy 101 four miles south of Scotia.*

Rellim Redwood Company, *on Hwy 101 three miles south of Crescent City.*

Simpson Timber Company, *on Hwy 299, one mile east of Blue Lake (10 miles east of Arcata).*

Drive-Thru Tree Park, *Hwy 1, Leggett, 707/925-6363; daily dawn to dusk; $2/car.* Most average-size cars can squeeze through the hole in this 315 ft. high, 21 ft. diameter redwood tree. Bring your camera. Nature trails and lakeside picnic areas are available.

Ferndale, *15 miles south of town.* This entire town is composed of well-preserved and restored Victorian buildings. Located in farm country, the town is a State Historical Landmark. It is also an artists' colony and is filled with antique shops, galleries, restaurants, and bed-and-breakfast lodging. See also p. 80, The Gingerbread Mansion.

Humboldt State University, *Arcata, 707/826-3928.* Find out what's happening on campus (concerts, films, plays, etc.).

Klamath Jet Boats, *60 miles north of town, Klamath, 707/482-4191; daily June–Oct; adults $20, 4-11 $8; reservations required.* Trips leave at 9am and return at 3pm. A stop is made at a lodge for lunch, or guests may bring along a picnic.

Pacific Lumber Company, *on Hwy 101 27 miles south of town, Scotia, 707/764-2222; M–Th 7:30-11am & 1-3:30pm; free.* Take a self-guided tour through the world's largest redwood lumber mill. Get your pass for the hour tour in the old First National Bank building, now a logging museum. Scotia is one of the last company-owned lumber towns in the west and is built entirely of redwood.

Redwood National Park, *40 miles north of town, Orick, 707/464-6101.* This magnificent National Park encompasses 106,000 acres and three State Parks. Ranger-led interpretive programs are scheduled daily May through October. During the summer horses may be rented to ride on some of the scenic trails accessible only on horseback; overnight pack trips may also be arranged. Inquire about inner tube float trips on the Smith River. **Prairie Creek Redwoods State Park,** *on Hwy 101, Orick, 707/488-2861; daily 9am-5pm; free.* The eight-mile gravel road to Gold Bluffs Beach and Fern Canyon passes through a beautiful forest into an area of fern-covered cliffs. This park tends to

be foggy and cold and is a refuge for one of the few remaining herds of native Roosevelt elk. **Shuttle Bus to Tall Trees Grove,** *707/488-3461; daily June–Sept, call for schedule; adults $2, under 12 50¢.* In summer a bus takes visitors to within a mile of the Tall Trees Grove, which contains the world's tallest tree (367.8 ft.) as well as the third and sixth tallest trees. The rest of the year it is an 8½ mile walk each way.

WINE COUNTRY

■ *A LITTLE BACKGROUND*
California's first wineries were appendages of the 21 Franciscan missions which were built a day's ride (by horseback) from each other in a chain reaching from San Diego to Sonoma. The wine was produced by the missions for sacramental use. Eventually the church gave up producing wine and the art passed into the realm of private enterprise.

Presently Sonoma County is home to over 90 wineries and Napa County is home to over 110. Both areas are literally erupting with new small family wineries. Winemaking is becoming a hobby with many city folk who have bought themselves little vineyard retreats.

The best route for wine tasting in this area is along Hwy 29 between Oakville and Calistoga. When visiting this stretch of highway, which is heavily concentrated with wineries, the problem is to remain selective in tasting and to not get too heavily concentrated oneself. Experts suggest not planning to taste at more than four wineries in one day.

Young children can be difficult on a winery tour. Out of courtesy for the other tour participants (a noisy child interferes with the guide's presentation), parents might consider selecting a member of their party to stay with the children while the rest go on the tour. Or visit a winery with a self-guided tour. Most wineries allow tasting without going on a tour, and it is a nice idea to bring along some plastic wine glasses and a bottle of grape juice so the children can "taste" too.

Many wineries have picnic areas. An ideal agenda is to tour a winery, taste, and then buy a bottle of the wine you enjoy most to drink with a picnic lunch.

Because the Wine Country is so close to the Bay Area, this trip can easily be made into a one-day adventure.

SONOMA

Sonoma Valley Chamber of Commerce
453 E. 1st St.
Sonoma 95476
707/996-1033

■ *ROUTE*

Located approximately 45 miles north of San Francisco. Take Hwy 101 to Hwy 37 to Hwy 121 to Hwy 12.

■ *WHERE TO STAY*

El Pueblo Motel, *896 W. Napa St., 95476, 707/996-3651; 2/$, 4/$-$$; pool; TVs; cribs.* Located on the outskirts of town, eight blocks from the plaza, this is a spacious pleasant motel.

Sonoma Hotel, *110 W. Spain St., 95476, 707/996-2996; 2/$-$$, 4/$$$-$$$+; some private baths; continental breakfast; dining facilities.* Dating from the 1870s when it was the town theater, this hotel is located on the town square and has rooms furnished in carefully selected turn-of-the-century antiques. Private bathrooms have clawfoot tubs and room 3 boasts a carved rosewood bed said to have once been owned by General Vallejo. The restaurant specializes in hearty country fare and serves lunch and dinner in the dining room daily except Wednesday; an old-fashioned bar adjoins.

Sonoma Mission Inn, *18140 Hwy 12, Boyes Hot Springs 95416, 800/ 862-4945, 707/996-1041; 2-4/$$$+; some kitchens; pool, spa facilities; TVs; cribs; continental breakfast; dining facilities.* Built in the 1920s, this sedate luxury resort features a pink adobe architecture and rooms cooled with old-fashioned ceiling fans. Though children are welcome, this is an adult-oriented resort.

■ WHERE TO EAT

Au Relais, *691 Broadway, 707/996-1031; lunch and dinner W-M; high-chairs; reservations suggested; $$; AE, DC, MC, V.* How many French restaurants do you know of where you can take the kids? Au Relais, meaning literally "a place to rest," is reminiscent of a French country inn and has a friendly atmosphere. Diners can be seated inside this converted Victorian house or, on a warm afternoon, outside on the flower-bedecked patio. Dinner entrees include standard French items like cassoulet (a casserole of meats and white beans) and several daily specials. Desserts include chocolate truffle cake, fresh fruit sorbets, peach melba, creme caramel, and various coffees. The lunch menu is similar but less expensive and also offers crepes, sandwiches, and omelettes.

Big 3 Fountain, *Hwy 12, Boyes Hot Springs, 707/996-8132; breakfast and lunch daily; highchairs, booster seats; $; MC, V.* This airy, noisy dining room offers seating on stools at the fountain counter, at ice cream parlor tables, or in comfy booths. Toasters are right on the tables and lemon slices pretty-up the water glasses. The menu offers typical coffeeshop fare, exceptional cottage fries, and fancy ice cream creations.

Cafe Pilou, *464 E. 1st St., 707/996-2757; breakfast, lunch and dinner Tu-Sun; booster seats; reservations suggested; $$; AE, V.* This cozy cafe has a charming country-French decor. Local wines are available by the glass, and wonderful Sonoma Bakery sourdough bread is served with meals. The menu includes made-from-scratch soups, salads, omelettes, French toast, a huge hamburger (served with thin French fries), and several daily specials.

■ PICNIC FARE

Fantasie Au Chocolat, *40 W. Spain St., 707/938-2020; Th-Sat 10am-9:30pm, Sun-W 10am-5:30pm.* A chocoholic's dream come true, this specialty shop handmakes truffles and candies as well as tortes laced with Grand Marnier.

Sonoma Cheese Factory, *2 Spain St., 707/938-5225; daily 9am-6pm.* This crowded shop stocks hundreds of cheeses (including their famous varieties of Sonoma Jack made from old family recipes), cold cuts, salads, marvelous marinated artichoke hearts, and cheesecake flown in from New Jersey. Sandwiches are made-to-order. If you wish to eat here, a few tables are available inside as well as out on the patio. The workings of the cheese factory may be viewed in the back.

Sonoma French Bakery, *468 E. 1st St., 707/996-2691; W-Sat 8am-6pm, Sun 7:30am-noon, closed last two weeks of August.* This renowned bakery makes sourdough French bread which is so delicious that people are willing to wait in line to purchase it. Personally, I favor the sweet French bread. The Basque baker hails from the French Pyrenees and makes the bread without yeast. Flutes, rolls, croissants, gateau Basque bread, French and Danish pastries, and chocolantines are just a few of the other delights available.

Sonoma Sausage Company, *453 W. 1st St., 707/938-8200; M–Sat 9:30am–5:30pm, Sun noon–6pm.* Over 65 kinds of sausage—including hot beer sausage, Nurnberger bratwurst, smoked Hawaiian Portugese, and Kalbs leberwurst—are available here. They're all made with Old World techniques from 100% meat (no fillers), and some are smoked and ready to eat.

■ WHAT TO DO

Depot Museum, *270 W. 1st St., 707/938-9765; W–Sun 1–4:30pm; adults 50¢, 9-18 25¢.* Operated by volunteers from the Sonoma Historical Society, this tiny museum is housed in the restored North West Pacific Railroad Station and features changing historical and railroad exhibits. An adjacent park has a playground and picnic area. A bicycle path, which follows the old railroad track, originates here.

Sonoma State Historic Park, *located along Spain St., 707/938-1578; daily 10am–5pm; adults 50¢, 6-17 25¢; admission includes barracks, mission, and Vallejo home.* This extensive park preserves structures dating from the early 1800s when General Vallejo, founder of Sonoma, was Mexico's administrator of northern California. The two-story, whitewashed adobe barracks once housed his soldiers; it now contains historical exhibits. Vallejo drilled his soldiers across the street in what is now the town square. Next door and across the street from the barracks, the well-preserved remnant of Mission San Francisco Solano, founded in 1823 and the most northerly and last in the chain of California missions, exhibits a collection of mission watercolors by Chris Jorgensen. An impressive old prickly pear cactus forest graces the mission courtyard. General Vallejo's home, a Victorian Gothic with original furnishings, is located about one mile east. Shaded picnic tables and another giant prickly pear garden are found there.

Sonoma Town Square Park. This old-fashioned park is great for picnics. Children may frolic at the playground and feed the ducks in the tiny pond.

Toscano Hotel, *E. Spain St., 707/938-0510; tours on Sat & Sun 1–4pm, Tu 11am–1pm; by donation.* Built in 1858, this is a beautifully restored hotel.

Train Town, *20264 Broadway, 707/938-3912; daily in summer 10:30am–5pm, weekends rest of year; adults $2.10, 2-16 $1.50.* On this 15-

minute ride on the Sonoma Gaslight and Western Railroad, the steam locomotive winds through ten acres. Passengers pass through forests and a tunnel, cross a 70 ft. double truss bridge and a 50 ft. steel girder bridge, and make a five-minute stop at a miniature mining town— where the train takes on more water and the engineer distributes food for the kids to feed the ducks and swans.

Vasquez House, *129 E. Spain St. in El Paseo de Sonoma, 707/938-0510; tours W–Sun 1–5pm; by donation.* Built in 1856, this refurbished woodframe house features a tearoom serving homemade pastries and tea.

■ WHAT TO DO NEARBY

Aero-Sport, *at the airport off Hwy 121 two miles north of Sears Point Raceway, Schellville, 707/938-2444; weekends 9am–5pm; weekdays by appointment; scenic ride/$35, one loop and one roll/$40, full aerobatic ride $50; reservations suggested.* Chuck Hunter takes riders on 15-minute flights in his Stearman biplane, once used to train World War II combat pilots. Have your picnic *after* this excursion. Old and antique planes may also be viewed at the airport.

Jack London State Historic Park, *off Hwy 12 in Glen Ellen, 707/938-5216; daily 8am–dusk, museum 10am–5pm; $2/car.* Located in the Valley of the Moon, this park contains the ruins of Jack London's dream castle Wolf House (reached by a pleasant one-mile trail), his

Ruins of Wolf House, Jack London State Historic Park.

grave, and a museum—The House of Happy Walls—built in his mem-
ory by his widow. The park, given to the state by London's nephew,
provides ample room for picnicking and romping. To get yourself in
the mood for this trek you may want to read a London classic such
as *The Call of the Wild* or *Martin Eden.*

Morton's Warm Springs, *1651 Warm Springs Rd., Kenwood, 10 miles
north of town, 707/833-5511; May–Sept only, Tu–F 10am–6pm,
Sat & Sun to 8pm; adults $2–$3, 2–11 $1.50–$1.75.* Two large pools
and one toddler wading pool allow everyone in the family to enjoy a
refreshing summer swim. Lifeguards are on duty. There are picnic
tables and barbecue pits, a snackbar, and a large grassy area for sunbathing. Dressing rooms and lockers are available. A special teenage
rec room is equipped with a juke box, ping pong tables, and pinball
machines. A few rules: all drinks must be in cans, no glass allowed,
no cutoffs in the pools.

■ WINERIES

Buena Vista Winery, *18000 Old Winery Rd., 707/938-1266; tasting daily
10am–5pm.* Founded in 1857, this is California's oldest winery.
Though it went through a period of decline when it was vacant and
then used as a women's prison, it has been restored to its original
charm. It has the finest picnic area of any winery I've been to.
Tables, shaded by stately old eucalyptus trees growing on the banks
of a tiny brook, encircle the vine-covered entrance to the winery's
limestone cellars. Visitors may take a self-guided tour through its
limestone cellars and taste wines in the old Press House. A **Midsum-
mer Mozart Festival** is scheduled each August; call for details.

Chateau St. Jean, *8555 Hwy 12, Kenwood, 10 miles north of town,
707/833-4134; tasting daily 10am–4:30pm.* This relatively new
winery, which specializes in white varietals, was built in 1975. It
offers self-guided tours, tasting in its 1920s chateau, and a grassy,
shaded picnic area with fountains and several fish ponds.

Hacienda Wine Cellars, *1000 Vineyard Lane, 707/938-3220; tasting daily
10am–5pm.* Though there are no tours here, there is tasting. If you
decide to picnic on one of the tables, wine glasses may be borrowed
from the tasting room. If you want to feed the ducks and geese that
often wander up from the nearby pond, bring along appropriate
provisions.

Sebastiani Vineyards, *389 E. 4th St., 707/938-5532; tours and tasting
daily 10am–5pm.* This winery has been continuously owned by the
same family since 1904—longer than any other in the country. Take
time to view the world's largest collection of carved oak wine casks.

An adjacent museum houses Indian artifacts, including an extensive collection of arrowheads. Children are thoughtfully served grape juice when their parents are tasting.

YOUNTVILLE

Yountville Chamber of Commerce
P.O. Box 2064
Yountville 94599
707/944-2929

■ *ROUTE*

Located approximately 60 miles north of San Francisco. Take Hwy 101 to Hwy 37 to Hwy 121 to Hwy 29.

■ *WHERE TO STAY*

Burgundy House, *6711 Washington St. (P.O. Box 2766), 94599, 707/ 944-2855; 2/$-$$$+; some shared baths; kitchens and fireplaces in cottages; continental breakfast; children welcome in cottages only.* The stone walls of this former brandy distillery are 22″ thick. The rooms in the main inn are nicely decorated with antiques, all of which are for sale. A collection of antique games are available for play. The cottages have two bedrooms and offer a comfortable amount of space for families. More rooms are available in the ultra-modern **Bordeaux House** located down the street at 6600.

♥ **Magnolia Hotel,** *6529 Yount St. (P.O. Drawer M), 94599, 707/944-2056; 2/$$$-$$$+; some fireplaces; pool, jacuzzi; full breakfast; dining facilities; no children under 16.* Located in the center of town, the rooms in this three-story stone building are decorated with antiques. The well-reviewed French restaurant serves a five-course dinner on Friday and Saturday.

Napa Valley Lodge, *Hwy 29 (P.O. Box L), 94599, 800/528-1234, 707/ 944-2468, 2/$$$-$$$+; some kitchens and fireplaces; pool, whirlpool, hot tub; TVs; cribs; children under 12 stay free in parents' room.* This attractive modern motel is located on the outskirts of town, across the street from a public park and playground. Bicycles are available for rent.

Silverado Country Club, *1600 Atlas Peak Rd., Napa 94558, 800/622-0838, 707/257-0200; 2-4/$$$-$$$+; some kitchens and fireplaces; 5 pools; 15 tennis courts; TVs; cribs; dining facilities.* Accommodations are in modern condominiums and facilities include two 18-hole golf courses.

■ *WHERE TO EAT*

The Diner, *6476 Washington St., 707/944-2626; breakfast and lunch Tu–Sun, dinner Thur–Sun; highchairs, booster seats; no reservations; $; no cards.* This unpretentious spot offers seating at either the counter or in comfortable booths, and meals are made of quality ingredients. Breakfast features the house specialty of crispy cornmeal pancakes with smoky links as well as potato pancakes and old-fashioned oatmeal with nuts and raisins. Lunch features sandwiches and hamburgers and ice cream fountain specialties. Dinners are basically hamburgers and Mexican items; the flautas are especially good.

♥ **Domaine Chandon,** *California Dr., 707/944-2892; lunch and dinner daily in summer, closed M & Tu rest of year; reservations suggested; $$$; AE, MC, V.* The spacious dining room at this winery is lovely, but in good weather the terrace is the premier spot to be seated. Marvelous, unusual courses (smoked quail or perhaps trout in champagne sauce stuffed with seafood mousse) comprise the a la carte lunch and dinner menu. The winery's sparkling wines are available by the glass.

♥ **French Laundry,** *6640 Washington St., 707/944-2380; dinner W–Sun; reservations essential; $$$; no cards.* With only one seating, the dining pace here is leisurely, with enough time between courses to take a stroll in the garden. Located inside an attractive old building, the kitchen specializes in freshly prepared, innovative cuisine and serves a fixed-price five-course dinner.

Mama Nina's, *6772 Washington St., 707/944-2112; lunch and dinner Thur–Tu, Sun brunch; children's portions; reservations suggested; $$; AE, MC, V.* Homemade pastas such as gnocchi, tagliarini pesto, and fettucine Alfredo are the house specialty, but dishes like scampi and veal piccata are also available. My favorite is the Tortellini Nina—small circles of pasta filled with a mix of ground veal, parmesan cheese, and spices and topped with a delicate sauce of cream, butter, minced chicken breast, and parmesan cheese. Pizza and calamari are available only out on the more casual patio—a good (and cool) choice for families. Two super desserts are the sandpie (an oatmeal cookie crust filled with vanilla ice cream and topped with hot fudge sauce and chopped peanuts) and the mudpie (a chocolate cookie crust filled with coffee ice cream and topped with hot fudge sauce).

Mustards, *7399 Hwy 29, 707/944-2424; lunch and dinner daily; reservations suggested; $$; V.* This relatively new bar and grill features a cool, screened porch and tables set with white nappery and shining wineglasses. The atmosphere is casual and chic and the menu imaginative. Lunch includes salads and sandwiches; dinner brings on items like barbecued baby backribs, mesquite-grilled rabbit with mustard

seeds, and New York steak with salsa. The onion rings are superior,
and you can order old-fashioned tapioca for dessert.

Vintage 1870. See *What To Do.*

- **WHAT TO DO**

Adventures Aloft, *6525 Washington St., 707/255-8688; $110/person;
reservations necessary.* Tour the Napa Valley via hot air balloon.
Trips average one hour in the air; altitude and distance depend on
which way the wind blows. Rides include an after-flight champagne
celebration and a flight certificate. **Napa Valley Balloons,** 707/253-
2224, offers a similar experience.

Vintage 1870, *Washington St., 707/944-2451; daily 10am–5:30pm.*
This lovely old brick building, a former winery, now houses a number of interesting specialty shops and restaurants. Inexpensive, tasty
lunches may be enjoyed at the **Chutney Kitchen** and the **Vintage
Cafe.** The **Court of Two Sisters** bakery offers fancy pastries and tiny
quiches as well as coffee. The **Kitchen Store Deli** has picnic supplies
and **The Wurst Place** features fresh sausage without nitrates. From
the children's play area, hot air balloons can often be viewed taking
off. In the summer the **Valley Theatre Co.** (707/944-8925) puts on
performances in the theatre. The adjacent **Vintage Rail Shops** are
located inside old train cars.

Wild Horse Valley Ranch, *20 miles s.e. of town off Hwy 121 at the
end of Coombsville Rd., Napa, 707/224-0727; daily 9am–3:30pm;
reservations necessary; $8/hr.* Breakfast ($20), lunch, and dinner
($25) rides are available as well as lessons. Overnight rides are occa-
sionally scheduled. No children under 7.

ST. HELENA

St. Helena Chamber of Commerce
P.O. Box 124
(1508 Main St.)
St. Helena 94574
707/963-4456

- **WHERE TO STAY**

♥ **Chalet Bernensis Inn,** *225 Hwy 29, 94574, 707/963-4423; 2/$$–$$$;
some private baths; some fireplaces; continental breakfast; two-night
minimum on weekends; no children under 15.* Located next door to
Sutter Home Winery, this Victorian mansion offers rooms decorated

with antiques in either the upstairs of the main house or in the replica of a tank tower located adjacent.

El Bonita Motel, *195 Main St., 94574, 707/963-3216; 2–4/$-$$; some kitchens; pool; TVs; cribs.* This motel has a shaded, grassy pool area and is an alternative to classy, cutesy, and expensive Wine Country lodging.

Harvest Inn, *One Main St., 94574, 707/963-WINE; 2–4/$$$-$$$+; some fireplaces; pool, jacuzzi; TVs; cribs; continental breakfast.* Set on a 21-acre working vineyard, this relatively new English Tudor-style inn has beautifully landscaped grounds complete with a carp pool and ducks. Rooms are furnished with antiques.

♥ **Wine Country Inn**, *1152 Lodi Lane, 94574, 707/963-7077; 2/$$$-$$$+; some fireplaces; continental breakfast; no children.* Built in the style of a New England inn, this attractive, quiet lodging is located back from the main highway on top of a country hill.

■ *WHERE TO EAT*

♥ **Auberge Du Soleil**, *180 Rutherford Hill Rd., Rutherford, 707/963-1211; lunch and dinner Thur–Tu; reservations suggested; $$$; AE, MC, V.* Located off The Silverado Trail near the Rutherford Hill Winery, this elegant French restaurant has plush inside seating as well as more rustic seating outside on the balcony overlooking the valley. Dinners are fixed-price, lunch a la carte with a two-course minimum. The beautifully executed dishes change regularly. A memorable luncheon I enjoyed here included quail eggs in aspic, beef strips in black truffle sauce, and hazelnut souffle.

♥ **Miramonte**, *1327 Railroad Ave., 707/963-3970; dinner W–Sun, closed part of Dec. & Jan; reservations suggested; $$$; no cards.* The five-course, fixed-price nouvelle dinners at this well-reviewed restaurant change each week and tend to be very unusual and interesting. The chef produces sophisticated dishes with a Japanese flair. Outdoor seating is available.

Napa Valley Olive Oil Manufactory, *835 McCorkle Ave., 707/963-4173; daily 8am–6pm.* In addition to an unusual cold press olive oil, you can purchase cheeses, sausage, olives, a variety of pastas and sauces, and cracked walnuts. A picnic area is available outside.

Oakville Grocery, *7856 Hwy 29, Oakville, 707/944-8802; daily 10am–6pm.* Everything needed to put together a fantastic gourmet picnic is available here. Select from a large variety of mustards, vinegars, jams, fresh fruits, imported beers, mineral waters, natural juices, cheeses, and other deli items.

■ WHAT TO DO

Bale Grist Mill State Historic Park, *on Hwy 29, 3 miles north of town, 707/942-4575; daily 10am-5pm; adults 50¢, children 25¢.* Reached via a shaded, paved streamside path, this grist mill once ground grain for farmers from the 1840s through the turn-of-the-century. The damp site and slow-turning millstones were reputedly responsible for the exceptional cornmeal produced here. Now interpretive displays are located inside the gable-roofed mill house, and the state hopes someday to restore the 45 ft. waterwheel to full operation.

Lake Berryessa, *take Hwy 128 east, 707/966-2111.* This manmade lake is over 25 miles long, 3 miles wide, and has 165 miles of shoreline. Boats and waterskis may be rented, campsites and resort facilities are available, and the swimming and fishing are excellent.

Silverado Museum, *1490 Library Lane, 707/963-3757; Tu-Sun noon-4pm; free.* Located in The Hatchery, a stone building dating from 1884, this library houses Robert Louis Stevenson memorabilia. I suggest a family read-in of *A Child's Garden of Verses* or *Treasure Island* before or after this visit.

■ WINERIES

Beaulieu Vineyard, *1960 Hwy 29, Rutherford, 707/963-2411; tours and tasting daily 10am-4pm.* Founded in 1900 by Frenchman Georges deLatour, Beaulieu is now owned by the Heublein Corporation. An informative film is shown periodically. Two small adjacent restaurants (not affiliated with the winery) serve lunch.

Beringer Vineyards, *2000 Hwy 29, 707/963-7115; tours and tasting daily 9:30am-3:45pm.* The Visitor's Center is located in the Rhine House—a beautiful oak-paneled, stained-glass-laden reproduction of a nineteenth century German house. Unfortunately, picnicking is not permitted on the beautifully landscaped grounds.

Christian Brothers, *2555 Hwy 29, 707/963-2719; tours and tasting daily 10am-4:30pm.* This landmark winery is built of locally quarried volcanic stone and displays a collection of over 800 corkscrews. In addition to its commercial wines, the winery still produces sacramental wines. Winery revenues are used to help operate The Christian Brothers Schools.

Rutherford Hill, *at the end of Rutherford Hill Rd., Rutherford, 707/963-9694; tasting daily 11am-4:30pm, tour at 11am.* A wonderful hillside picnic area overlooks the valley and boasts plenty of tables sheltered by old oak trees.

V. Sattui/St. Helena Cheese Factory, *Hwy 29, Oakville, 707/963-7774; daily 9am-5pm.* Taste wine while you select edibles to enjoy in the spacious picnic area outside.

Sterling Vineyards, Calistoga.

CALISTOGA

Calistoga Chamber of Commerce
P.O. Box 321
(1458 Lincoln Ave.)
Calistoga 94515
707/942-6333

- *A LITTLE BACKGROUND*
Often called "the Hot Springs of the West," Calistoga is enjoying a renaissance as a popular weekend and summer retreat. The name originated from a combination of California and Saratoga (a New York spa). For the town's history, I suggest reading *The Silverado Squatters* by Robert Louis Stevenson.
  The town sits on top of a hot underground river. Its many unpretentious spas are geared to helping visitors relax, unwind, and get healthy in their pools filled from hot springs. Most offer services such as mud baths, steam baths, and massages and most make their mineral pools available for a small fee for day use.
  Don't miss taking a mud bath. The mud is made from volcanic ash, collected from nearby Mount St. Helena, which is mixed with naturally heated mineral water. After a period of nude immersion, the bather takes a mineral bath, a steam bath, and then, swaddled in dry blankets, rests and cools. Ahhh!

■ ROUTE

Located approximately 10 miles north of St. Helena. Follow route to St. Helena, then continue north on Hwy 29.

■ WHERE TO STAY

Calistoga Spa, *1006 Washington St., 94515, 707/942-6269; 2/$, 4/$$; some kitchens; 3 pools; TVs; cribs; four-night minimum in summer.* In addition to lodging in motel rooms and cottages, this conveniently located spa offers three pools: a 105° covered jacuzzi, a 100° open-air mineral pool, and a very interesting 85° Roman olympic outdoor pool. Mud baths, mineral baths, steam baths, and massage are available.

Dr. Wilkinson's Hot Springs, *1507 Lincoln Ave., 94515, 707/942-4102; 2/$-$$, 4/$$; some kitchens; 2 pools; TVs; cribs; two-night minimum on weekends.* Operated by the Wilkinson family, this pleasant spa features both an indoor hot mineral water pool with a view of the nearby foothills and a cooler outdoor swimming pool. Mud baths, mineral baths, steam baths, and massage are available. Lodging is in motel units. Cottages are available at a nearby location, but children are not permitted there.

Mountain Home Ranch, *3400 Mountain Home Ranch Rd., 94515, 6 miles from town, 707/942-6616; 2/$, 4/$-$$; closed Dec–Feb; some shared baths; some kitchens; 2 pools, hot springs; TVs; cribs; dining facilities.* The atmosphere in this rural spot is informal and accommodations are a choice of modern or rustic cabins or lodge rooms. Activities include swimming, hiking, movies, campfires, dancing, and supervised activities for children. Most activities are available only during the summer, when the rates are higher and include both breakfast and lunch.

Mount View Hotel, *1457 Lincoln, 94515, 707/942-6877; 2/$$-$$$+; pool, hot tub; cribs; continental breakfast; dining facilities; two-night minimum on weekends.* This attractive hotel, built in 1917 and decorated in a '30s Art Deco style, is a National Historic Monument. The dining room has a French menu with specialties like roast duck and milk-fed veal. Live entertainment is often scheduled in the lounge. Packages are available.

Pacheteau's Original Calistoga Hot Springs, *1712 Lincoln, 94515, 707/942-5589; 2/$; closed Dec; some kitchens; pool; TVs; two-day minimum.* This is said to have been the first spa in town. It is also said that in 1880 Robert Louis Stevenson wrote part of *Silverado Squatters* while he vacationed here. The spa facilities include a 90° geyser mineral water swimming pool which is open to the public for a day-use fee and is especially popular with children. Accommodations are 1930s housekeeping cottages in which the bathrooms have piped-in hot sulphur water. Mud baths are available.

Triple S Ranch, *4600 Mountain Home Ranch Rd., 94515, 4 miles from town, 707/942-6730; 2/$; closed Jan-Mar; pool; dining facilities.* Small red and white cabins nestle under shady trees in this quiet country setting. On the spacious grounds is a pool in a scenic setting and an informal ranch house dining room.

■ *WHERE TO EAT*

Calistoga Inn, *1250 Lincoln Ave., 707/942-4101; dinner Tu-Sat; high-chairs; reservations suggested; $$$; MC, V.* The specialty is simply-treated seafood, and the menu changes daily. Past offerings have included ceviche of barracuda, poached halibut with saffron sauce, grilled marlin with ginger sauce, and fish stew. Duck, veal, steak, and a pasta are also usually on the menu as well as irresistable desserts like raspberries with chocolate crème fraîche and Santa Rosa plum sorbet. Also, inexpensive lodging is available upstairs.

Silverado Restaurant, *1374 Lincoln, 707/942-6725; breakfast, lunch, and dinner daily; highchairs, booster seats, children's portions; $$; no cards.* Comfortable booths with views of the sidewalk parade combine with fresh and tasty food to make the Silverado a pleasant spot to dine. Lunch is informal with a menu of hamburgers, sandwiches, omelettes, and homemade soups and desserts as well as a large choice of non-alcoholic drinks and alcoholic fruit daiquiris. Dinner is fancier and features mesquite-grilled items.

The Village Green, *1413 Lincoln, 707/942-0330; breakfast, lunch, and dinner daily; highchairs, booster seats; $; no cards.* This place has been around almost forever and has an informal, unpretentious atmosphere with comfortable booths and counter seating. Short order items dominate the menu including hamburgers, homemade French fries with the skins still on, spaghetti, design-your-own-omelettes, and ice cream fountain items.

■ *WHAT TO DO*

Bike Rentals, Hauschildt's Ice Cream Parlor, *1255 Lincoln, 707/942-9923; daily from 11am; $2-$2.50/hour.* Regular bikes and two-seat tandems may be rented here. Also gigantic, messy ice cream cones may be purchased at the crowded counter inside this converted gas station.

Bothe-Napa Valley State Park, *3601 Hwy 29, 707/942-4575; daily 8am-dusk; $2/car.* You can picnic, hike, swim in the pool (summer only), and camp in this lovely park.

Bothe-Napa Valley State Park.

Calistoga Soaring Center, *1546 Lincoln, 707/942-5592; daily 9am–dusk; $35/1 person, $46/2; reservations suggested on weekends.* The 20-minute glider ride/sightseeing trip covers up to ten miles and reaches altitudes of up to 2,500 ft. and speeds of up to 70 mph.

Old Faithful Geyser, *1299 Tubbs Lane, 707/942-6463; daily 9am–dusk; adults $2, 6–11 $1.* One of only three geysers in the world that erupt regularly and merit the name *Old Faithful* (the other two are in Yellowstone National Park in Wyoming and on North Island in New Zealand), this geyser erupts approximately every 40 minutes and shoots 350° water 60–150 ft. in the air in a show that lasts 3–4 minutes. Chickens roam freely on the idyllic site, located in the crater of an extinct volcano, and plenty of picnic tables are available.

Petrified Forest, *4 miles west of town on Petrified Forest Rd., 707/942-6667; daily 9am–5pm; adults $3, under 10 free.* A self-guided ¼ mile path leads through this unusual 502-acre forest containing redwood trees over 6 million years old and as large as 126 ft. long. There is also a small museum and picnic tables.

Sharpsteen Museum and Sam Brannan Cottage, *1311 Washington St., 707/942-5911; daily in summer noon–4pm, rest of year F–M; free.* This exceptionally well-designed museum shows an elaborate and extensive diorama of Calistoga as it appeared in 1865, when Sam Brannan opened the first town spa and began its career as a resort area. The beautifully furnished cottage displays the style in which wealthy San Franciscans lived when they vacationed here in the late 1800s.

■ *WINERIES*

Chateau Montelena Winery, *1429 Tubbs Lane, 707/942-5105; tasting daily 10am–4pm, guided tour at 11am & 1:30pm by appointment.* This hard-to-find, small stone winery offers a very unusual picnic area. Small Jade Lake holds two islets, reached via footbridge, which in turn hold miniature picnic pagodas. The lake is stocked with ducks and geese and even a berthed Chinese junk. Reservations are necessary to use the picnic facilities.

Sterling Vineyards, *1111 Dunaweal Lane, 707/942-5151; daily Apr–Oct, W–Sun Nov–Mar, 10:30am–4:30pm; self-guided tour; gondola ride, adults $3.50, under 16 free.* Accessible to the public only by special gondola cars, this winery was built to resemble a Greek monastery. It features stunning and unusual white stucco, cubist archtecture. Visitors enjoy wine tasting at tables on the outdoor terrace. The gondola ride takes four minutes. Each adult is given a $2 credit toward the purchase of Sterling wines, which in California are available for sale only at the vineyards. Picnic facilities are available at the base of the hill. See photo on p. 98.

CLEAR LAKE

Lake County Chamber of Commerce
P.O. Box 517
(875 Lakeport Blvd.)
Lakeport 95453
707/263-6131

- *A LITTLE BACKGROUND*

From the 1870s into the early 1900s, this area was world-famous for its health spas and huge luxury resort hotels.
Then, for various reasons, it fell into a state of disrepair and slowly lost its acclaim. Now it is basically a reasonably-priced family resort area. In fact, many of the resorts are very run-down and accordingly inexpensive.

The lake measures 25 miles by 8 miles. The 70-mile drive around the lake takes 2½ to 3 hours. Spring-fed, Clear Lake is the largest fresh-water lake totally within California (Lake Tahoe is partially in Nevada).

The most scenic drive to get here is via Hwy 29 through the heart of the Wine Country. The rolling hills are strewn with blazing wild flowers during the spring and with brilliantly colored foliage during the fall. Make the drive during daylight; the two-lane road is tedious and dangerous to drive at night, and you also miss the lovely scenery.

Clear Lake is situated on volcanic terrain, which gives it an unusual physical appearance and a profusion of hot springs. Many years ago the Pomo Indians lived here. They had a legend which said that if there is no snow on Mount Konocti in April, the volcano will erupt. If you heed legends, be sure to check the April snowfall before you make your vacation reservations. Lake County's first traffic light was installed in 1982, and there are still no parking meters.

■ ROUTE

Located approximately 50 miles north of St. Helena. Follow route to St. Helena and continue on Hwy 29. An alternate route follows Hwy 101 north to Hwy 175 east.

■ WHERE TO STAY

Jules Resort, *14195 Lakeshore Dr. (P.O. Box 880), Clear Lake Highlands 95422, 707/994-6491; 2–4/$; kitchens; pool, sauna; TVs; cribs; one-week minimum July–Sept.* Stay in a pleasant old cabin and sunbathe by the lakefront pool. Facilities include a game room, private beach, fishing pier, and launching ramp; miniature golf is available across the street.

Konocti Harbor Inn, *8727 Soda Bay Rd., Kelseyville 95451, 800/862-4930, 707/279-4281; 2–4/$$–$$$+; closed Nov–Feb; some kitchens and lake views; 2 pools, 2 wading pools; 8 tennis courts (fee); TVs; cribs; dining facilities.* Nestled in the shadow of Mount Konocti on the rim of the lake, this beautifully landscaped resort enjoys a superb setting. It is reminiscent of luxury resorts in Hawaii but is a lot easier to reach and much less expensive. The list of facilities is extensive: tennis lessons, a playground, a teenage recreation room, a running/ bike trail, feature films, a bar with live music in the evenings, a paddlewheel boat cruise (fee), a miniature golf course (fee), and a marina which rents equipment for fishing, waterskiing, and paddle boating. The resort even has its own gas station. In the summer college students are hired to run day camps to entertain children age 5–12; babysitting can usually be arranged for younger children. Tennis, golf, and fishing packages are available. The dining room has stunning lake views, offers an Italian continental menu, and is comfortably set up for children. A coffee shop serves more informal meals.

Skylark Motel, *1120 N. Main St., Lakeport 95453, 707/263-6151; 2/$, 4/$–$$; some kitchens and lake views; pool; TVs.* These modern motel units and cottages are located lakefront. The spacious, well-maintained grounds feature a large lawn area, swings, and a wading area in the lake.

Will-o-Point Resort, *1 First St., Lakeport 95453, 707/263-5407; 2–4/$$; some kitchens and lake views; TVs; cribs; dining facilities.* The attractive cabins here are bargains when rented by groups of 4 to 8 people. Campsites and RV hookups are also available. Facilities include a fishing pier, boat ramp, bait and tackle shop, boat rentals, recreation room, and sandy beach. This 13-acre waterfront resort is located adjacent to a public park equipped with a tennis court, waterfront playground, children's wading pool, and roped-off lake swimming area.

■ *WHAT TO DO*

Fishing, hunting, swimming, boating, rock hunting, golfing, and waterskiing are the big activities here.

Nice lakefront public parks and beaches are located in Lakeport and Clearlake Highlands.

RUSSIAN RIVER

Russian River Chamber of Commerce
P.O. Box 255
(14034 Armstrong Woods Rd.)
Guerneville 95446
707/869-9009

■ *ANNUAL EVENTS*
Contact the Chamber of Commerce for details on these annual events:

Banana slug races and recipe contest bake-off, *March.*

Rodeo, *June.*

Country Music Festival, *June.*

Jazz Festival, *September.*

■ *A LITTLE BACKGROUND*
Once upon a time in the '20s and '30s this was a summer resort area favored by wealthy San Franciscans who traveled here by ferry and train. Then it faded in popularity and became a pleasant and uncrowded retreat. Today it is regaining its former popularity and is recovering from a state of decay. The area has also become very popular with gays, and many resorts catering only to gays have opened.

Each year in the last two weeks of July, many of the world's

109

most powerful political, military, and corporate leaders meet here at 2,700-acre Bohemian Grove.

Guerneville, the area's hub, is surrounded by many smaller towns. There are numerous public beaches, but many more beaches are privately owned and not open to the public. Also, there are many unofficial nude beaches. Inquire when in town so that you may easily find them or avoid them, depending on your attitude.

■ *ROUTE*

Located approximately 75 miles north of San Francisco. Take Hwy 101 past Santa Rosa to Hwy 116 (River Road West exit) to Guerneville.

■ *WHERE TO STAY*

Brookside Lodge, *Hwy 116/Brookside Lane (P.O. Box 382), Guerneville 95446, 707/869-2470; 2/$-$$, 4/$$-$$$; some kitchens and fireplaces; pool; TVs; cribs.* Accommodations are in a choice of motel rooms or cottages and facilities include a playground, recreation room, and spacious, attractive grounds.

Centennial Associates, *17120 Hwy 116 (P.O. Box 361), Guerneville 95446, 707/869-2805.* This realty company rents a number of private homes and studio units—many right on the river. There is a two-night minimum.

Johnson's Resort, *P.O. Box 386, Guerneville 95446, 707/869-2022; 2-4/$; closed Oct–May; some kitchens and river views; TVs.* Some of these rustic old hotel rooms and cabins are located right on the river. Reservations are taken only for stays of at least a week, but rooms are often available on a first-come, first-served basis. The beach is one of the best-equipped in the area with a slide into the water, picnic tables, and rentals of boats and beach paraphernalia.

Northwood Lodge, *19400 Hwy 116 (P.O. Box 188), Monte Rio 95462, 707/865-2126; 2/$-$$$, 4/$$-$$$; some kitchens and fireplaces; 2 pools, hot tub; TVs; cribs; dining facilities.* This comfortable, modern facility offers motel rooms as well as cabins in the woods. A golf course is adjacent.

♥ **Ridenhour Ranch House Inn,** *12850 River Rd., Guerneville 95446, 707/887-1033; 2/$$-$$$, 4/$$$; closed Dec & Jan; some shared baths; hot tub; continental breakfast; two-night minimum on weekends; no children under 10.* This historic redwood ranch house, circa 1906, is decorated with English and American antiques, quilts, and fresh flowers. Guests may enjoy the cozy living room and fireplace, secluded beaches are just a short walk away, and the lawn beckons for a game of croquet.

Riverlane Resort, *16320 First St. (P.O. Box 313), Guerneville 95446, 707/869-2323; 2/$, 4/$$; some kitchens, fireplaces, and river views; pool, hot tub; TVs; cribs.* Located by the river, this pleasant resort offers a private beach, recreational equipment, and movies in the evenings.

Southside Resort, *13811 Hwy 116, Guerneville 95446, 707/869-2690; 2-4/$-$$; some kitchens, fireplaces, and river views.* Tucked under a bridge, these charming yellow cottages provide dots of color on the green, woodsy grounds. In July and August they are available only on a weekly basis. The private beach has a shallow wading area safe for children, and a recreation area is available for guests. Evening campfires, movies, and campsites are also available.

- **WHERE TO EAT**

Cazanoma Lodge, *1000 Kidd Creek Rd., Cazadero, 13 miles from Guerneville, 707/632-5255; March to mid-May and mid-Sept. through Nov, dinner F-Sun, Sun brunch; mid-May to mid-Sept, dinner also on W & Th; closed Dec-Feb; highchairs, booster seats, children's portions; reservations suggested; $$; MC, V.* German specialties include a sausage platter with sauerkraut and barbecue spareribs, but the really unusual item offered in this 1926 lodge is catch-your-own-trout. That's right. The customer here has the option of catching his own trout from the pond, to make sure it is really fresh. For the unimpressed, the kitchen will do the job with a net. Live music is sometimes scheduled on weekends. Cabins and lodgerooms ($) are also available in this tranquil forest setting.

The Occidental Three, *take Main St. through Monte Rio into Occidental.* All three of these restaurants serve multi-course, family-style Italian dinners. All have highchairs, booster seats, and a reasonable plate charge for small children. All are moderately priced and offer less expensive ravioli and spaghetti dinners which include less side dishes. Reservations are suggested at prime dining times during the summer. **Fiori's** (707/823-8188), **Negri's** (707/823-5301), **Union Hotel** (707/874-3662).

Skippy's Hacienda Inn, *11190 McPeak Rd., Forestville, 707/887-2366; dinner July-Sept Thur-Sun, Oct-June F-Sun; highchairs, booster seats, children's portions; reservations suggested; $$; MC, V.* This comfortable restaurant has a steak and seafood menu and is famous for its jukebox filled with old tunes. When making reservations ask for directions; it's hard to find.

▪ WHAT TO DO

Canoe Trips. W. C. Bob Trowbridge, *20 Healdsburg Ave., Healdsburg, 707/433-7247; April–Oct, daily 8am–6pm; $28/canoe/day, reservations necessary.* Trips are unguided. The canoe fee includes life jackets, paddles, and canoe transport. An additional $1/person charge provides for a ride back to the starting point. Children must be at least six. An after-canoeing barbecue is served from 4 to 7pm each weekend. It includes steak or chicken, vegetable, baked beans, salad, garlic bread, and beverage. The charge is $5–$6, and reservations are necessary. Trowbridge has 8 other rental sites on the river. Those, as well as other concessions, also rent canoes by the hour.

Cazadero, *west on Hwy 116.* Located on Austin Creek, this is a charming and tiny logging town.

Duncan Mills, *west on Hwy 116.* This town was once a lumber village but now is home to a number of shops, the **Blue Heron Inn** vegetarian restaurant (707/865-2269), a riverside campground with private beach (707/865-2573), and horse rentals (707/865-9982).

Korbel Champagne Cellars, *13250 River Rd./Hwy 101, Guerneville, 707/887-2294; tasting and tours daily 10am–3pm.* Korbel is over a century old and produces champagne and brandy as well as wine.

Pee Wee Golf and **J's Amusements,** *13803 Hwy 116, 707/869-2887; daily in summer.* Various kiddie rides and entertainments await the family in search of cheap thrills.

Swimming. Anywhere you choose to lay your blanket on the banks of the Russian River is bound to be nice. A prime spot is under the Monte Rio bridge, where parking and beach access is free. Another choice spot is **Johnson's Beach** (see *Where to Stay*). The beaches are lined with pebbles, so bring along waterproof sandals or tennis shoes to wear in the water.

SACRAMENTO

Sacramento Convention & Visitors Bureau
1311 I St.
Sacramento 95814
916/449-5291

■ *ANNUAL EVENTS*

Dixieland Jazz Festival, *Memorial Day Weekend, 1011 2nd St., Sacramento 95814, 916/448-1251.*

California State Fair, *August, P.O. Box 15649, Sacramento 95813, 916/924-2000.*

■ *A LITTLE BACKGROUND*

Sacramento has been the state capital since 1854. Most of the major historic attractions are concentrated in the downtown area.

Mark Twain wrote colorfully of this city, "It is fiery summer always, and you can gather roses, and eat strawberries and ice-cream, and wear white linen clothes, and pant and perspire at eight or nine o'clock in the morning."

■ *GETTING THERE*

By Cruise Ship. Exploration Cruise Lines offers a 4-day, 3-night cruise through the Delta to Sacramento. Passengers sleep aboard a shallow-draft ship in stateroom accommodations, and informal family-style

meals are included. Stops are scheduled in Sausalito, Stockton, Sacramento, and Locke. The fare ranges from $239–$359. Make reservations through your travel agent.

By Ferry. *Delta Travel Agency, 1540 West Capitol Ave. (P.O. Box 813), West Sacramento 95691, 916/372-3690; $81/person, special rates for children.* Cruise from San Francisco through the Delta region to Sacramento. The package includes roundtrip boat tickets, bus transfers, and hotel accommodations in Sacramento. One-day and one-way trips are also available.

By Train. Amtrak trains leave for Sacramento daily from San Jose, San Francisco (via bus connection to Oakland), and Oakland. Special family fares are available. Call 800/872-7245 for fare and schedule information and to make reservations.

Scenic Route by Car. *Take Hwy 80 to Hwy 24 to Walnut Creek, Hwy 680 to Concord, Hwy 4 to Antioch, Hwy 160 to the outskirts of town, then Hwy 5 into Sacramento.* This route takes about six hours.

■ *ROUTE*

Located approximately 80 miles north of San Francisco. Take Hwy 80 all the way.

■ *STOPS ALONG THE WAY*

The Nut Tree, *Hwy 80/Hwy 505, Vacaville, 707/448-1818; breakfast, lunch, and dinner daily; highchairs, booster seats, children's portions; reservations suggested; $$; AE, MC, V.* There is plenty to do at the Nut Tree besides eat. For a small fare a colorful miniature train transports passengers around the spacious grounds. Numerous shops are stocked with quality merchandise. The toy shop is a great place to pick up travel games and books for children. Outside there are free rocking horse rides, puppet shows, and climbing structures for kids and wooden benches for the old folks. An outside snack bar serves a memorable fresh orange slush along with an assortment of other short order items. The striking restaurant features a colorful decor and a huge glass-enclosed area housing a variety of plants and exotic, brightly colored birds. The food is as well-prepared as the setting is pleasant. Parents of babies will be interested to know that Gerber's baby food is on the menu!

■ *WHERE TO STAY*

Modern motels abound. Call your favorite chain for reservations or contact the Chamber of Commerce for a list.

■ *WHERE TO EAT*

Buffalo Bob's Ice Cream Saloon, *Front/K Sts., Old Sacramento, 916/441-4788; breakfast, lunch, and dinner daily; highchairs, booster seats; $; no cards.* A variety of sandwiches (including grilled cheese and peanut butter & jelly) and hot dogs are available here, as is old-time sarsaparilla to wash it all down. Ice cream concoctions dominate the menu and include exotic sundaes such as Fool's Gold (butter brickle ice cream topped with butterscotch and marshmallow, whipped cream, almonds, and a cherry) and the Sierra Nevada (peaks of vanilla ice cream capped with hot fudge, whipped cream, almonds, and a cherry).

China Camp, *1015 Front St., Old Sacramento, 916/441-7966; lunch M-F, dinner daily; booster seats; reservations suggested; $$; MC, V.* During the period after gold was discovered in Coloma in 1849, Chinese immigrants found it difficult to come by the ingredients and utensils traditionally used in their cooking. They learned to improvise by marinating their food with ethnic sauces. China Camp serves a re-creation of how that food most probably tasted. The rustic decor features brick walls, spacious wooden booths, and architecture designed to give diners the feeling they're inside an old mining camp. Unusual items include beef-in-clay-pot, immigrant's beef, beggar's hen, and drunk steak, but hamburgers and squidburgers are available too—all served on pretty floral dishes. Homemade desserts include banana cream pie, apple pie, and mud pie with mint ice cream.

Fanny Ann's Saloon, *1023 2nd St., Old Sacramento, 916/441-0505; lunch and dinner daily; no reservations; $; no cards.* The raucous ambiance and funky decor provide the makings for instant fun. Children and adults alike enjoy the casual atmosphere and American-style fare of half-pound hamburgers, assorted styles of 9″ hot dogs, giant French fries, and huge bowls of homemade soup. A variety of sandwiches and salads are also available. Place your order with the cook at the window in back and then relax with a game of pinball or a downright cheap drink at the old bar. When I inquired whether there were booster seats, the cheerful hostess replied, "I'll hold the kids on my lap."

Los Padres, *J St., Old Sacramento, 916/443-6376; lunch and dinner daily, breakfast Sat & Sun; highchairs, booster seats, children's portions; no reservations; $$; AE, MC, V.* The lovely old brick walls of this nicely appointed restaurant are decorated with paintings of the California missions. The Early California/Mexican cuisine includes nachos (tortilla chips topped with refried beans and melted cheddar cheese), quesadillas (small corn tortillas topped with melted Jack cheese and guacamole), and a green enchilada (corn tortilla filled with king crab and guacamole and topped with green sauce and sour cream). Fresh tortillas and European pastries and breads are made in the restaurant's downstairs bakery, where food for take-out is also available.

River Galley, *Levee Rd., Broderick, 916/372-0300; lunch and dinner Tu-Sun; booster seats; reservations suggested; $$; AE, MC, V.* Sacramento's only floating restaurant specializes in seafood but also serves steaks, prime rib, and a hamburger. Call for directions; it is difficult to find.

■ *WHAT TO DO*

American River Parkway. This is basically 23 miles of water fun. To request a map, send a stamped self-addressed envelope to: *County of Sacramento, Department of Parks and Recreation, 3711 Branch Center Rd., Sacramento 95827, 916/366-2061.*

Bike Trail. The paved **Jedediah Smith National Recreation Trail** runs for 23 miles along the American River. Get a free map from: *Sacramento County Parks Dept., room 106, 3701 Branch Center Rd., 95827, 916/366-2072.*

Fishing. The best month for salmon and steelhead is October. Favorite spots are the Nimbus Basin below the dam and Sailor Bar. A state license is required.

Inner Tubing. A good area is from Sailor Bar to the Watt Avenue Bridge.

Nature Walks. The **Effie Yeaw Nature Center** *(in Ancil Hoffman Park, 916/489-4918; M, Tu, Th, F 1:30-5:30pm, Sat & Sun 11am-5pm)* has two self-guided nature trails. Guided tours are available Saturday and Sunday 11am–5pm.

Raft Trips. Trips begin in the area north of the Sunrise Blvd. exit off Hwy 50. A number of companies rent rafts and provide shuttle bus return.

Swimming. For a refreshing swim in the river or to sun on its sandy banks take the Watt exit off Hwy 50.

California Almond Growers Exchange, *18th/C Sts., 916/446-8409; M-F 10am, 1, & 2pm, closed in July; free.* Take a one-hour tour of the world's largest almond factory, see a 25-minute film about the history of almonds, and do a little tasting.

Capitol, *10th St./Capitol Mall, 916/324-0333; free.* Specialized tours stressing the architectural restoration, the history, and the legislative process (January–September only, when the legislature is in session) operate daily on the hour from 9am–4pm. During busy times additional tours are scheduled each half-hour. Tours of the surrounding grounds, home to hundreds of varieties of trees and flowers, are scheduled weekdays at 12:10 and weekends at 1pm as weather permits; this tour does not operate in the winter. Tickets may be picked up in the basement a half-hour before the tour. A small museum and a 10-minute orientation film entertain visitors while they wait. A short order cafeteria serves meals and snacks. In 1981 the Capitol was remodeled to the tune of $68,000,000 in what is said to be the largest restoration project in the history of the country. The main reason for the project was to make the building earthquake safe. Restored now to its turn-of-the-century decor, it is quite a showcase.

Some restored offices on the first floor are open for display but are
no longer used.

Crocker Art Museum, *216 O/3rd Sts., 916/446-4677; Tu 2-10pm, W-
Sun 10am-5pm; adults $1, 13-18 50¢.* The oldest art museum in
the West, this Victorian building circa 1874 houses a gallery of special exhibitions in addition to its permanent collection of European
and American paintings. Cultural events such as lectures, films, and
Sunday afternoon concerts are often scheduled. Call for current
schedule and tour information. Picnic tables are located in a lovely
park across the street.

Governor's Mansion, *16th/H Sts., 916/445-4209; tours daily 10am-
4:30pm; adults $1, 6-17 50¢ (ticket admits visitor to Sutter's Fort
on the same day).* Built in 1878, this Victorian Gothic house was
bought by the state in 1903 for $32,500. During the next 64 years
it was home to 13 governors and their families. Now it is an interesting museum.

Music Circus, *15th/G Sts., adjacent to the Sacramento Civic Theater,
916/441-3163; evening performances nightly during July & Aug;
$10.* Claiming to be "the only tent theater west of the Mississippi"
and seating 2,500, the Music Circus presents summer stock musicals
which are suitable for the entire family. Call for current schedule.

Old Sacramento. Located on the Sacramento River, Old Sacramento
was the kickoff point for the gold fields. It was the western terminus
for both the Pony Express and the country's first long distance telegraph, and the country's first transcontinental railroad started here.

Said to be the largest historic preservation project in the West,
Old Sacramento is a 28-acre living museum of the Old West. Vintage
buildings, wooden sidewalks, and brick streets recall the period from
1850 to 1880. Restaurants and shops as well as historic exhibits make
it an entertaining and educational spot to visit.

Guided tours of the town begin at the Central Pacific Railroad
Depot daily at 10:30am and 1:30pm. For more information call
916/445-7373.

California State Railroad Museum, *111 I St., 916/445-7373; daily
10am-5pm, in summer to 9pm; adults $3, 6-17 $1 (ticket admits
visitor to Central Pacific Passenger Station on same day).* This
gigantic three-story building houses 21 beautifully restored railroad cars and engines. A film, slide show, and assorted interpretive displays tell the history of American railroading.

Central Pacific Railroad Depot, *930 Front St., 916/445-7373; daily
10am-5pm; adults 50¢, 6-18 25¢.* Inside this reconstructed train
depot, visitors step back in time to an era when riding the train was
the chic way to go. Visitors are given a tour wand which picks up
recorded descriptions of the various displays.

Old Eagle Theatre, *925 Front St., 916/446-6761; tours Tu–Sun 10am–5pm, free; performances F & Sat eves, $3.50, reservations suggested.* A reconstruction of California's first theater building built in 1849, the Eagle now presents Gold Rush era plays and musicals. Call for current schedule.

Sacramento Science Center and Junior Museum, *3615 Auburn Blvd., 916/485-4471; M–Sat 9:30am–5pm, Sun from noon; adults $2, 3–15*

$1. This museum is of special interest to children and features a live animal hall, walk-through aviary, self-guided nature trail, and hands-on exhibits. A picnic area is available.

Sutter's Fort State Historic Park, *2701 L St., 916/445-4209; daily 10am-5pm; adults $1, 6-17 50¢ (ticket admits visitor to Governor's Mansion on same day).* This fort is a reconstruction of the settlement founded in 1839 by Captain John A. Sutter. Exhibits include carpenter, cooper, and blacksmith shops as well as prison and living quarters. Hand-held audio wands are loaned to visitors for self-guided tours. The cannon is fired daily at 11am & 2pm.

State Indian Museum, *2618 K St., 916/445-4209; daily 10am-5pm; free.* Located adjacent to Sutter's Fort, this museum was established in 1940 and has continuously changing exhibits on Indian culture. A permanent basket collection, featuring colorful Pomo feather baskets, and samples of bark clothing are particularly interesting. Films and puppet shows are often presented on weekends. Call for details.

William G. Stone Navigation Lock, *Visitor's Overlook, at end of South River Rd. (take West Sacramento exit off Hwy 80), 916/371-7540; overlook open daily dawn to dusk; free.* Operated by the U.S. Army Corps of Engineers, this is the only ship navigation lock in California.

It passes smaller craft such as barges and tug boats. It has an unpredictable operation schedule dependent on ship traffic, however you
can usually count on usage by recreational boats on fair weather
weekends.

William Land Park, *Freeport Blvd. between 13th Ave. and Sutterville Rd.*
This 236-acre park has a supervised playground, wading pool (daily
in summer 1–5pm), fishing for children under 16, a 9-hole golf course,
kiddie rides, and pony rides. Also:

Fairytale Town, *Tu–Sun 10am–5pm, closed Dec & Jan; adults $1,
3–12 50¢.* Nursery rhymes and fairy tales come alive in this amusement park.

Zoo, *daily 9am–4:30pm; adults $2, 6–12 50¢.*

YOSEMITE NATIONAL PARK

National Park Service
Yosemite National Park 95389
209/372-1000

■ *ANNUAL EVENTS*

Spending Christmas at the Ahwahnee Hotel and attending the memorable **Bracebridge Dinner** is a pleasure not many get to enjoy. This expensive experience ($85/person) requires that participants apply for reservations a full year in advance. Applications are so numerous that guests must be chosen by lottery. Since 1927 the fare at the elegant 3½ hour dinner, held on the evenings of December 24 and 25, has been traditional Old English Christmas foods such as Peacock Pie, Boar's Head, and Wassail. Pageantry, readings, and carols entertain diners between courses.

■ *A LITTLE BACKGROUND*

> "Yosemite Park is a place of rest. A refuge . . . in which one gains the advantage of both solitude and society . . . none can escape its charms. Its natural beauty cleanses and warms like fire, and you will be willing to stay forever. . ."
>
> *—John Muir*

And if you did stay forever, you would be privileged to enjoy the spectacular beauty of the park's dramatic seasonal changes. Most visitors see this grand National Park in the summer, when it is at its worst with clogged roads, crowded accommodations, and even smog. All this makes it hard to focus on what you came for—the scenic, natural beauty of the High Sierra. If you want to catch a glimpse of the Yosemite described by Muir, consider a visit in the off-season: in fall when the colorful foliage change is spectacular, in winter when snow blankets the valley floor, in spring when the falls are at their fullest.

Yosemite was designated a National Park in 1890. Among the scenic wonders here are El Capitan, the largest piece of exposed granite in the world, and Yosemite Falls, the highest in the Northern Hemisphere.

Remember that falls and rivers can be dangerous as well as beautiful; keep a good grip on your children when hiking.

A $3 admission fee is collected at all park entrances, and visitors are given an activities newsletter and map.

■ *ROUTE*
Located approximately 240 miles east of San Francisco. Take Hwy 80 to Hwy 580 to Hwy 205 to Hwy 120. To minimize the need for chains in winter consider taking low elevation Hwy 140 in from Merced.

■ *STOPS ALONG THE WAY*
Numerous cafes and produce stands are located along Hwy 120. Fast-food heaven is in Oakdale, and there are several cafes in the rustic mountain town of Groveland. In the summer the **Groveland Motel** (209/962-7865) offers inexpensive lodging in carpeted tepees.

Hershey Chocolate Company, *1400 S. Yosemite Ave., Oakdale, 209/ 847-0381; tours M–F 8:15am-3pm; free.* Half-hour tours allow visitors to see such delights as chocolate being mixed in huge vats and kiss-wrapping machines. After the tour all visitors receive a sweet treat.

Knights Ferry Covered Bridge, *turnoff is about 12 miles east of Oakdale off Hwy 108.* Built in 1864, this bridge is still in use. A park with picnic tables, hiking trails, and a cold swimming hole is on the freeway side of the Stanislaus River. On the other side is a rustic town with a store and another park.

Oakwood Lake Resort, *874 E. Woodward Rd., Manteca, 209/239-9566; May–Oct, hours vary; admission for age 5 and older $3, all rides $3/half hour, all-day pass $13.* The main attraction here is the eight fiberglass waterslides. Most feature over 60 ft. of enclosed tunnel and several 360° turns. A free, open slide is available for small children and the timid. More daring is required for the Rapids Ride, which is maneuvered on an inner tube, and the Rampage Ride, in which riders sit on a plastic toboggan and drop 63 ft. down a steep slide and then skim across the water. Resort facilities include a swimming lagoon, hot tubs, an outdoor roller skating rink, playgrounds, barbecue and picnic areas, and overnight camping.

Riverbank and Stanislaus County Cheese Companies *(from Modesto take Hwy 108 to Riverbank).* **Riverbank,** *6603 Second St., 209/869-2803; 9am–5pm.* **Stanco,** *3141 Sierra Ave., 209/869-2558; 9am–6pm.* If you are interested in taking a tour, call ahead for the schedule. Specialty cheeses made by these two companies include teleme and assorted varieties of cheddars and Jacks. Picnic supplies are available for purchase. A riverside picnic may be enjoyed in town at **Jacob Myers Park,** located at First St. across the Burneyville Ferry Bridge.

■ *WHERE TO STAY*

Yosemite is always crowded, but is especially so in the summer. Reservations are essential. Call 209/373-4171 for information or to make reservations at any park facilities. Rates range from $ to $$$+. Children under three stay free in their parents' room; cribs are available. A bargain Midweek Ski Package is available in the winter.

Ahwahnee Hotel; *$$$+; pool, playground, tennis courts.* This is a very sedate luxury hotel. Some cottages are also available.

Campgrounds; *open April–Oct, a few are open year-round.* Make reservations through Ticketron. See p. 224.

Curry Village; *$–$$.* Accommodations and facilities are similar to Yosemite Lodge (see below), but inexpensive tent-cabins are also available.

High Sierra Trail Camps; *$$.* These five camps provide tent accommodations complete with linens and two meals.

Tuolumne Meadows Lodge; *$.* This facility is located at the eastern entrance and is all tent-cabins.

Wawona Hotel; *$–$$; closed in winter; pool, tennis court, 9-hole golf course.* This 1876 Victorian hotel is located at the south entrance (Hwy 41) near the Mariposa Grove of Big Trees, 30 miles from the valley.

White Wolf Lodge; *$.* Located at Tioga Pass, 31 miles from the valley.

Yosemite Lodge; *$–$$; pool, bike rentals.* Accommodations vary from frugal (old cabins without plumbing) to luxurious (modern hotel rooms).

Other. Midpines Hostel, *P.O. Box 173, Midpines 95345, 209/742-6318.* Not part of the park, this inexpensive lodging is located on Hwy 140 about 35 miles west of Yosemite. See also p. 219.

■ *WHERE TO EAT*

All facilities are open daily and equipped with highchairs and booster seats.

Ahwahnee Hotel, *209/372-4611 x408; breakfast, lunch, and dinner daily; children's portions; reservations essential.* The best time to dine in the rustic splendor of this elegant dining room is during daylight hours. Only then can you take full advantage of the spectacular views of the valley offered by the 50 ft. floor-to-ceiling windows. Dinner is expensive and men are expected to wear coat and tie and women to dress accordingly. Guests of the hotel receive the select dining times, so be prepared for either an early or late seating. Children fit in best at breakfast or lunch. January–March ski buffets are presented each Thursday evening.

Curry Village and Yosemite Lodge Cafeterias; *breakfast, lunch, and dinner daily.* Meals here are quick and inexpensive.

Four Seasons Restaurant, *Yosemite Lodge; breakfast, lunch, and dinner daily; children's portions.* The dinner menu offers good old American fare—steak, fried chicken, fish, and hamburgers.

Mountain Room Bar, *Yosemite Lodge.* This is the place to get rid of the kinks developed on the long drive in.

Mountain Room Broiler, *Yosemite Lodge; dinner only.* The walls in this stunning room are papered with striking black and white photo murals; floor-to-ceiling windows look out on Yosemite Falls. The menu features trout, lobster, and well-aged, charcoal-broiled steak as well as corn-on-the-cob, artichokes, and hot cheese bread.

Picnic. Request a box lunch from your hotel kitchen the evening before you need it, or pick up supplies at Degnan's Deli in the Village.

■ WHAT TO DO

Ansel Adams Gallery, *in the Village.* Exclusive special edition photographs from this well-known photographer are available here.

Bicycle Rentals, *Yosemite Lodge (209/372-1208, daily 9am–5pm) and Curry Village (209/372-1200, daily 8am–8pm) April–Oct; $1.50/hour, child carriers available.* A bicycling map and information about ranger-led bike tours may be obtained when you rent your bike. A **Yosemite Bike Rally** is scheduled each spring (209/372-1491).

Bus Tours, *209/372-1240; valley floor $8, grand tour $18.50.*

Glacier Point, *an hour drive from the valley.* From this spot you can enjoy a 270° view of the high country, or you can look down 3,242 ft. for a bird's-eye view of the valley. Several trails lead down to the valley. Consider arriving in the morning (get the one-way ticket on the Glacier Point Bus Tour) so that you can spend the afternoon hikking back down.

Hiking. Enjoy a ranger-guided walk or take any of the many self-guided trails. Check in the park brochure for maps.

Indian Cultural Museum, *next to the Village Visitor Center; W–Sun 9am–noon, 1–4pm.* Visitors learn about the Awanichi Indians through artifacts, cultural demonstrations, and recorded chants. Behind the museum is a reconstructed Indian village. A self-guided trail points out plants used by the Indians for food, clothing, and shelter.

Inner Tube Float Trip. Scenic and calm is the area on the Merced River between Pines Campground and Centinnel Bridge. Raft rentals are available.

Junior Ranger Program. This program is available in the summer for children in 3rd grade and above. There is a nominal charge and reservations are necessary. Consult the activities newsletter for details.

Mariposa Grove of Big Trees, *35 miles from the valley on Hwy 41; tours 8am–7pm May–Oct; free.* Several hundred giant sequoias are located in this 250-acre grove. Free open-air trams take visitors on guided tours. In winter, this is a choice spot for cross-country skiing.

Movies. Scenic movies and slide shows are scheduled some nights. Check the activities newsletter for times and locations.

Pioneer History Center, *25 miles from the valley on Hwy 41, 209/375-6321; daily 9am–5pm.* This village of restored pioneer buildings is reached by walking across an old covered bridge. In the summer history comes to life with occasional demonstrations of soap making, yarn spinning, rail splitting, and other pioneer crafts—sometimes there is even an old-fashioned square dance and stagecoach rides.

Rock Climbing Lessons, *Village Sport Shop and Tuolumne Meadows, 209/372-1244 and 372-1335 (summer only).* Learn rock climbing at Yosemite Mountaineering School, one of the finest in the world. Basic classes are held daily year-round and cost $25/person. Beginners are taught safety essentials for dealing with the area's granite rock and can expect to climb as high as 80 ft. in the first lesson. Snow and ice climbing are, ironically, offered only in the summer. Children must be at least 14 to participate.

Valley Stables *(inquire about other park locations), guided two-hour horse trips leave at 8am, 10am, and 1pm; $12.50/person; half-day* *mule trips/$18, all day/$29.* Said to have the largest rental stock in the United States, these stables will also arrange for custom pack and/or fishing trips. Burros and ponies may be rented by parents for their young children to ride; parents must lead ($5/hour). As an alternative to hiring a babysitter, consider the 9:30am–3:30pm **burro picnic** for children ages 7–12 ($15).

Winter Activities. See pp. 202 and 205.

Yosemite Mountain Sugar Pine Railroad, *an hour drive from the valley on Hwy 41, Fish Camp, 209/683-7273; train: Sat & Sun mid-June through Sept, adults $5.50, 3-12 $3.25; railcars: daily mid-April through mid-Oct, weekends rest of year, adults $3.75, 3-12 $2.25.* The cars on this narrow-gauge steam railway are carved out of logs. Passengers may stopover at the midway point of the scenic four-mile ride to picnic or hike. Moonlight rides, which include a steak-fry and campfire program, are scheduled Saturday nights at 7pm mid-June through August; adults $16, 3-12 $10. Quaint Jenny railcars operate on same route as the train. This railroad is not affiliated with Yosemite National Park.

SEQUOIA AND KINGS CANYON NATIONAL PARKS

Superintendent
Sequoia/Kings Canyon National Parks
Three Rivers 93271
209/565-3341

- *A LITTLE BACKGROUND*

Though located just south of Yosemite National Park, these two scenic National Parks are often overlooked. It's a shame because they, too, offer spectacular scenery and are much less crowded.

Their main attraction is the enormous sequoia trees, with their vibrant cinnamon-colored bark, located in Sequoia Park's Giant Forest. The largest is the General Sherman Tree which towers 275 ft. high, measures 36½ ft. in diameter, and is 3–4,000 years old—higher than Niagara Falls, as wide as a city street, and already middle-aged when Christ was born! It is said to be the largest living thing on this planet. Mt. Whitney is also located in Sequoia Park and at 14,495 ft. is the highest point in the United States outside of Alaska. It is a 2–3 day hike to its peak.

Admission to the parks is $4/car.

- *ROUTE*

Located approximately 250 miles southeast of San Francisco.

Take Hwy 80 to Hwy 580 to Hwy 99 south to Hwy 180 east.
In winter take Hwy 198 through Visalia to Giant Forest,
where most snow activities are centered.

■ *WHERE TO STAY*

Park Lodging. *Guest Services, Sequoia National Park 93262, Sequoia
209/565-3373, Kings Canyon 209/335-2314; $; some private baths;
some kitchens and fireplaces; cribs; dining facilities.* At Sequoia lodging includes spartan and deluxe cabins as well as motel rooms. Kings
Canyon has similar facilities, but they are generally less luxurious
and there are less of them.

Arrangements can be made to backpack into a camp facility with
furnished tents. Campsites are available on a first-come, first-served
basis. In the summer Lodgepole Campground may be reserved
through Ticketron (see p. 224). Another option is to hike 11 miles
into the high Sierra tent-cabin camp at Bearpaw. Dinner and breakfast are included, and reservations are necessary. The best way to
make reservations is to call for a park brochure which explains the
various options in detail. If interested, inquire about the ski packages.

If you are unable to get lodging at the park facilities, two privately
owned lodges are nearby:

Kings Canyon Lodge, *P.O. Box 853, Kings Canyon 93633, 209/335-
2405.*

Wilsonia Lodge, *P.O. Box 808, Kings Canyon National Park 93633,
209/335-2311.* See also p. 204.

See also **Montecito-Sequoia Lodge,** pp. 204 and 210.

■ *NEARBY GUEST RANCHES*

Snowline Lodge, *44138 E. Kings Canyon Rd., Kings Canyon 93621,
209/336-2300; 2/$$, 4/$-$$; some kitchens and fireplaces; pool;
dining facilities.* Located 8 miles from Kings Canyon, this resort has
both motel units and cabins. The ranch covers 450 acres and is adjacent to Sequoia National Forest. Activities include horseback riding,
hayrides, square dances, campfires, and outdoor sports like volley
ball, horseshoes, and archery. Week-long, everything-included packages available.

Valley View Citrus Ranch, *14801 Ave. 428, Orosi 93647, 209/528-2275;
2/$; some shared baths; 1 tennis court; crib; full breakfast.* Located
40 miles from Kings Canyon, this is a friendly bed and breakfast. All
but one room is in the Ranch House.

Wonder Valley Ranch Resort, *Box 71 Star Route, Sanger 93657, 209/
787-2551, 415/986-3063; 2-4/$$-$$$; some fireplaces; pool, jacuzzi;
tennis courts; dining facilities; children permitted in July & Aug. only.*

Located 25 miles from Kings Canyon, this resort has both motel units and cabins and 52 acres of grounds. Activities include horseback riding, hayrides, buggy rides, and boating on a private lake.

■ WHAT TO DO

Bicycle Rentals, *in Cedar Grove.*

CAVES:

> **Boyden Cavern,** *in Kings Canyon; daily June–Sept 10am–5pm, May & Oct 11am–4pm; adults $3, 6–12 $1.50.* This cave is located in spectacular 8,000 ft. deep Kings River Canyon, the deepest canyon in the United States. Guided tours take about 45 minutes.
>
> **Crystal Cave,** *in Sequoia; F–Tu in summer 10am–3pm; $1, under 12 free.* This 50° cave is reached via a ½-mile trail. The guided tour takes about an hour.

Fishing. Most popular spots are along Kings River and the forks of the Kaweah River.

Horse Rentals, *in Cedar Grove, Giant Forest at Wolverton, General Grant Grove, Owens Valley, and Mineral King.*

Lodgepole and Grant Grove Visitor Centers, *daily in summer 8am–5pm, rest of year from 9am; free.* See exhibits on the area's wildlife as well as displays on the Indians and sequoias. Inquire here about the schedule of nature walks and evening campfire programs.

Swimming and Sunbathing, *at "Bikini Beach."*

Trails. Over 900 miles of hiking trails are in these parks.

Unusual Trees. Most of these are encountered on the drive along the 46-mile General's Highway, which connects the two parks. This highway is usually closed by snow December through May.

> **Auto Log.** Drive your car onto it for a photograph.
>
> **Room Tree.** Climb a ladder and enter down through a burn hole into the "room" and then exit through another burn hole.
>
> **Senate Group and House Group of Sequoias.** These are the most symmetrically formed and nearly perfect of the sequoias.
>
> **Tunnel Log.** Drive your car inside this tunnel carved through a tree which fell across the road long ago.

Winter Activities. See Grant Grove Ski Touring Center p. 202, Montecito-Sequoia Nordic Ski Center p. 204, Sequoia Ski Touring Center p. 204, and Wolverton Ski Bowl p. 205.

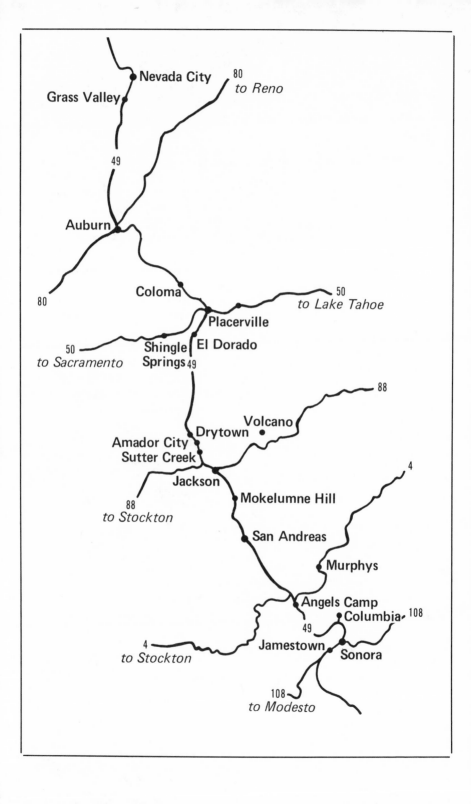

GOLD RUSH COUNTRY

■ *A LITTLE BACKGROUND*
Technically the Mother Lode stretches from Melones north
to Auburn, where the primary gold vein was located. It takes
at least three of four days to really see the entire area. If you
are going for only a weekend, don't attempt to drive the entire route from south to north. Visit just one portion, and
then go back another time to see the rest. Do slow down and
take the time to explore side roads off Hwy 49 and visit towns
whose names intrigue you.

Because the area is steeped in history, I recommend doing a
little reading for some background information. Two books
about the area which are good for reading out loud are *The
Celebrated Jumping Frog of Calaveras County* by Samuel L.
Clemens (Mark Twain) and *The Luck of Roaring Camp* by
Bret Harte.

And here's some advice on staking a claim:

> **"A gold mine is a hole in the ground with a liar at the
> entrance."**
>
> *—Mark Twain*

■ *ROUTE*
Located approximately 135 miles east of San Francisco.
Take Hwy 80 to Hwy 580 to Hwy 205 to Hwy 120 to Hwy 49.

JAMESTOWN

■ *WHERE TO STAY*

Jamestown Hotel, *Main St. (P.O. Box 539), 95327, 209/984-3902;*
2/$$-$$$, 4/$$$; hot tub; continental breakfast; dining facilities.
Built in the 1850s and recently remodeled, the Jamestown Hotel is
furnished with Victorian antiques and cozy patchwork quilts. Many
rooms are suites with a sitting room. Lunch and dinner are served
daily in the nicely appointed dining room downstairs. The eclectic
menu offers prime rib, seafood, chicken, veal, and Mexican items.
Total consideration is given to children: highchairs, booster seats,
children's portions and even hamburgers and grilled cheese sand-
wiches are available. Adjacent to the dining room is an attractive
saloon which specializes in fancy drinks.

■ *WHERE TO EAT*
Smoke Cafe, *18228 Main St., 209/984-3184; dinner Tu–Sun, closed Dec;*

highchairs, booster seats, children's portions; no reservations; $$; no cards. This friendly spot serves tasty Mexican cuisine. Specialties include pollo de mole poblano and chile verde. A hamburger is also available.

■ *WHAT TO DO*

Gold Prospecting Tours, *18172 Main St., 209/984-4162; daily at 9:30am and then every 2 hours; 1 hour family rate $35.* Learn the basic principles of gold prospecting. All equipment is supplied and you keep any gold you find. All-day trips and trips by river raft or helicopter can also be arranged.

Railtown 1897 State Historic Park, *209/984-3953; open spring & summer, Sat & Sun at 11am, 1:30 & 3pm; adults $7.95, 5-12 $3.95; roundhouse tours: daily 9am-5pm; adults $1.95, 5-12 95¢.* A historic steam train, the Mother Lode Cannonball, takes passengers on a one-hour, 12-mile round trip to the historic site of Chinese Camp. Tours of the Roundhouse are also available.

SONORA

Tuolumne County Chamber of Commerce
P.O. Box 277
Sonora 95370
209/532-4212

■ *A LITTLE BACKGROUND*

This bustling town is a popular stopover spot for skiers and other travelers on their way to vacation cabins and recreation. Because it is a crossroads, it has been built up more than most Gold Rush towns and is far from quiet. But if you get off the main streets, you'll find a taste of the old Sonora—Victorian homes, quiet streets, and a bit of a country feeling. A brochure outlining a self-guided tour of the town's Victorian homes and churches is available for a small charge from the Chamber of Commerce.

■ *WHERE TO STAY*

Gunn House, *286 S. Washington St., 2/$-$$; pool; TVs; cribs; continental breakfast.* Built in 1850, this two-story adobe house was once the residence of Dr. Lewis C. Gunn. Rooms are restored and furnished with antiques. The cozy office is staffed with helpful personnel, and a cocktail lounge is located by the pool.

- ■ *WHERE TO EAT*

    Europa Coffee Shop, *275 S. Washington St., 209/532-9957; breakfast, lunch, and dinner daily; highchairs, booster seats; no reservations; $; no cards.* Popular with local residents, the Europa is open round-the-clock, offers a huge choice of dinner entrees, and is well-known for homemade pies. Almost everything is made from scratch and cooked just to perfection. The bargain dinners include homemade soup, salad, choice of potato, a canned or frozen vegetable (I said *almost* everything), garlic bread, coffee, and dessert.

- ■ *WHAT TO DO*

    Autumn Colors Drive. Take Hwy 108 about 15 miles east for a dazzling tour of fall leaf colors.

    Sonora County Museum, *158 W. Bradford Ave., 209/532-4212; M-F 9am-5pm, also summer weekends 10am-3pm; free.* Located inside a jail built in 1866, this museum displays various relics from the Gold Rush era.

    UFO Exhibit and Library, *115 S. Washington, 209/532-3116, 533-2821; daily in summer 10am-5pm, M-Sat in winter; adults $1.50, 13-19 $1, 7-12 75¢, special family rate.* This is said to be the world's largest collection of UFO data. Exhibits include replicas of aliens, eyewitness tapes, and what is claimed to be videotapes of UFO flights and crashes.

COLUMBIA STATE HISTORIC PARK

P.O. Box 151
Columbia 95310
209/532-4301

- ■ *ANNUAL EVENTS*

    Fire Muster, *May.* Contact park for details. For description of a muster, see p. 53.

- ■ *A LITTLE BACKGROUND*

    In her prime, with over 6,000 people calling her home, Columbia was one of the largest mining towns in the southern Mother Lode. Her nickname, "Gem of the Southern Mines," was reference to the $87 million plus in gold mined there (a figure calculated when gold was $35 an ounce).

    Since 1945 this reconstructed Gold Rush town has been a State Historic Park. It is open daily from 9am to 5pm and

admission is free. Streets are blocked off to all but foot traffic and an occasional stagecoach. A museum introduces visitors to the town's history, and related exhibits are scattered among the many restored historic buildings.

In fact, the whole town is basically a living museum. Private concessionaires operate modern versions of businesses one would have found here in the 1800s. Cold mugs of beer and old-fashioned rootbeer-like sarsaparilla are poured in the town saloon, and classic melodrama is performed on a subterranean stage in what used to be a "palace of pleasure." A blacksmith ekes out a living practicing his craft in a ramshackle shed, and a candy kitchen uses 100-year-old recipes and antique equipment to turn out such old-time favorites as horehound, rocky road, and almond bark. Customers in the photography studio dress in Gold Rush era clothing for portraits taken with vintage camera equipment using modern quick-develop processes. And what is reputed to be the oldest barbershop in the state is still giving haircuts. Visitors may even tour a still-operating gold mine and learn to pan for gold in a salted sluice.

In case Columbia looks familiar to you, *High Noon* and episodes of *Little House on the Prairie* were filmed here.

■ *WHERE TO STAY*

City Hotel, *Main St. (P.O. Box 1870), 95310, 209/532-1479; 2/$$; no private baths; cribs; continental breakfast; dining facilities.* This 1856 hotel provides overnight lodging in keeping with the town's flavor. The restored rooms are furnished with Victorian antiques from the collection of the California State Parks Department. Eager-to-please students from the Columbia College Hospitality Management program dress in period clothing and supplement the full-time staff by performing such esoteric duties as fluffing pillows and, in the beautifully appointed French restaurant downstairs, de-crumbing tables. Guests are encouraged to congregate in the parlor in the evening for sherry and to entertain each other with conversation and games. And to make their trek down the hall to the bath more civilized, guests are loaned a wicker basket packed with shower cap, slippers, robe, soap, and shampoo. A former chef at Ernie's in San Francisco runs the dining room and prepares elegant cuisine for lunch and dinner. Reservations are suggested and children are welcome. The cozy **What Cheer Saloon** adjoins.

Columbia Gem Motel, *22131 Parrotts Ferry Rd. (P.O. Box 874), 95310, 209/532-4508; 2-4/$; closed Jan; TVs; cribs.* Motel room decor greets guests inside the tiny cottages scattered in an attractive pine tree setting.

■ *WHAT TO DO*

Fallon House Theatre, *209/532-4644; summer performances only; reservations advised.* Recently refurbished, this historic theatre has been in operation since the 1880s. Plays have been performed here by the University of Pacific repertory theatre company since 1949. Call for current schedule.

MURPHYS

■ *A LITTLE BACKGROUND*

A map to the town's buildings and sights is available from merchants and at the check-in desk in the hotel. Across the street from the hotel the oldest stone building in town, circa 1856, houses memorabilia from the past.

■ *WHERE TO STAY*

Murphys Hotel, *457 Main St. (P.O. Box 329), 95247, 209/728-3444;*
2/$-$$, 4/$-$$$; some shared baths; TVs; cribs; dining facilities;
children under 12 stay free in parents' room. The rooms in this old
hotel, built in 1856, are said to have provided lodging for such Gold
Rush era luminaries as U. S. Grant, J. P. Morgan, Mark Twain, Horatio
Alger, John Muir, and Black Bart. It is now a National Historical
Monument. Modern motel rooms, with no legends attached, are avail-
able adjacent to the hotel. I have stayed in both and find the hotel
rooms immeasurably more interesting but with a big drawback. The
noisy hotel bar, reputed to be the best in the Mother Lode, is kept
jumping until the wee hours by townspeople and travelers alike. If
you want to sleep, opt for a less interesting but quiet motel room. In
the winter, inquire about special skier rates. The restaurant located
on the main floor of the hotel serves breakfast, lunch, and dinner
daily and is popular with locals. The meals tend to be large and con-
sist of hearty American country fare like fried chicken, steaks, and
hamburgers. Complete facilities are available for children.

■ *WHERE TO EAT*

The Peppermint Stick, *454 Main St., 209/728-3570; daily 10am–5:30pm;*
booster seats, children's portions; $; no cards. Stop into this cheerful
ice cream parlor for an old-fashioned soda or sundae and perhaps a

Calaveras Big Trees State Park.

homemade candy treat. Sandwiches and soups are also available, and everything can be packed to go.

■ WHAT TO DO

Black Bart Players, *P.O. Box 104, 95247, 209/728-2213; weekend performances in April & Nov, 8:30pm; reservations suggested; $5.* This little theatre group does musicals, melodramas, mysteries, comedies, and classics. Call for current schedule.

Calaveras Big Trees State Park, *on Hwy 4 fifteen miles east of town, Arnold, 209/795-2334; daily dawn to dusk; $2/car.* This ancient forest houses the mammoth and now rare sequoia variety of redwood. The Big Trees nature trail is choice. Other trails are available as are campsites and picnic and barbecue facilities. In warm weather, the Beaver Creek Picnic Area has a good wading area for children. Picnic provisions can be picked up in Arnold, where there are delis, markets, and restaurants. Ranger-led snowshoe walks and cross-country ski tours are scheduled in winter (see p. 201).

Mercer Caverns, *one mile north of town off Hwy 4, 209/728-2101; June–Sept daily 9am–5pm, rest of year weekends 11am–4pm; adults $3.50, 5–11 $1.75.* Discovered in 1885, this well-lit 55° cavern takes about a half-hour to tour.

Moaning Cavern, *north of town on Parrotts Ferry Rd., Vallecito, 209/736-2708; daily 10am–5pm; adults $3.95, 6–12 $1.95.* The 40-minute tour descends a 100 ft. spiral staircase into the largest public cavern chamber in California. The cavern was first discovered by Indians who used it as a burial site; 13,000-year-old human remains have been found here.

ANGELS CAMP

■ ANNUAL EVENTS

The third weekend in May brings the annual Calaveras County **Jumping Frog Jubilee** a la Mark Twain. Champion frogs have recorded jumps of over 20 ft. and have earned as much as $1,200. The area is mobbed for this event. If you're still interested, contact the Calaveras Fairgrounds Office, P.O. Box 96, Angels Camp 95222, 209/736-2561 for current information. Entry fee to jump a frog is $3. Rental frogs are available. Gate admission is $5–$7.50/adults, $3–$5.50/children.

■ *WHERE TO EAT*

Emporium Ice Creme Parlor,
*1262 S. Main St., 209/736-
0630; lunch daily; children's
portions; $; no cards.* Lo-
cated inside a converted
bank building, this cheerful
spot dispenses sarsaparilla,
ice cream sundaes, sand-
wiches, hot dogs, and water-
melon freezes as "big as an
ore car."

Picnic. Informal picnic areas
may be found by the river.
Scenic **Utica Park** has picnic
tables and a play area. **Angels Bakery** at 1277 Main
has cheese and salt bread-
sticks, garlic bread, and fruit
bars among its baked goods.
The **Pickle Barrel Deli** at
1225 Main will pack you
picnic supplies to go, and has
tables in case you want to stay.

■ *WHAT TO DO*

Angels Camp Museum, *753 Main St., 209/736-2181; weekends, call for
schedule; adults 50¢.* Of special interest here is the extensive rock
collection and the assemblage of old wagons and buggies.

SAN ANDREAS

Calaveras County Chamber of Commerce
P.O. Box 177
(30 Main St.)
San Andreas 95249
209/754-3391

■ *WHERE TO STAY*

Black Bart Inn and Motel, *55 St. Charles St. (P.O. Box 576), 95249,
209/754-3808; 2-4/$; some shared baths; pool; TVs; cribs; dining*

facilities. Guests may reserve a room in the old hotel or in the more modern motel located adjacent. All rooms in the hotel have shared baths.

■ *WHAT TO DO*

Calaveras County Historical Museum, *30 Main St., 209/754-4203; M-Sat 10am-4pm; adults 50¢, under 13 25¢.* Items on display upstairs in this restored 1867 courthouse include Indian and Gold Rush artifacts. The nicely organized exhibits include life-size room displays of a Gold Rush era general store and miner's cabin. Downstairs, in a rustic courtyard planted with native California flora, is a jail exhibit.

California Caverns at Cave City, *10 miles east of town off Mountain Ranch Rd., 209/736-2708; June-Oct daily 10am-4pm, in Nov Sat & Sun only; adults $4, 6-12 $2.* This cavern was first opened to the public in 1850. The lighted, nearly level trail follows the footsteps of John Muir, Mark Twain, and Bret Harte. The tour runs 1¼ hour. Another more strenuous spelunking tour through the unlighted portion of the cavern is available by reservation only. The $49 tour "involves climbing rocks and a 60 ft. ladder, squeezing through small passages, crossing 200 ft. deep lakes on rafts, and viewing breathtaking formations unequalled in any other cavern in the West." Participants must be in good health, not pregnant, and at least 12 years old.

MOKELUMNE HILL

Hotel Leger, *P.O. Box 50, 95245, 209/286-1401; 2-4/$-$$; some shared baths; some fireplaces; pool; cribs; dining facilities.* Once considered among the most luxurious of Gold Rush hotels, the 1879 Hotel Leger still has comfortable rooms, many with sitting areas and fireplaces and all with tasteful period furniture. The dining room serves French country dinners Thursday through Sunday (closed Dec-Feb) and has highchairs and booster seats for children. An old-time saloon adjoins. Sometimes plays are scheduled in the **Garden Courthouse Theatre.** Call for current schedule.

JACKSON

Amador County Chamber of Commerce
P.O. Box 596
Jackson 95642
209/223-0350

▪ *ANNUAL EVENTS*

Gold Dust Days, *first part of April.* Participate in free gold panning lessons and field trips.

Italian Picnic, *first weekend in June, at Italian Picnic Grounds at the Amador County Fair Grounds in Plymouth.* For over 100 years the public has been invited to this festive event. There are kiddie rides for the children, dancing for the adults, and a parade (in Sutter Creek) and barbecue for everyone.

Kennedy Mine Tour, *September, 209/267-0255.*

▪ *WHERE TO STAY*

Country Squire Motel, *1105 N. Main St., 95642, 209/223-1657; 2–4/$; cribs; continental breakfast.* Located out in the country adjacent to the old Kennedy Gold Mine site, this comfortable motel was one of the last private gambling casinos in California until it was closed in 1952. Some of the units are restored and some have been more recently constructed. Goldpanning may be practiced year-round in the backyard "crick," and ducks and sheep roam freely across the way. There is plenty of grass for children to romp on.

National Hotel, *2 Water St., 95642, 209/267-5632, 223-0500; 2–4/$; dining facilities; Saturday night reservations must include dinner reservations in the dining room.* This hotel claims to be the oldest in continuous operation (since 1862) in California. The cozy cellar dining room serves dinner Thursday through Sunday and breakfast on Sunday. Lunch is served daily in the bar.

Roaring Camp Mining Co., *P.O. Box 278, Pine Grove 95665, 209/296-4100; $265/week for a prospector's cabin, each extra person $60–$95; closed Oct–April; modern bath house; dining facilities.* A four-hour trip into a remote canyon is made via truck; cars are left behind. Guests stay in rustic cabins without electricity and must bring all their own gear and food. Recreation consists of swimming, fishing, and panning for gold in the Mokelumne River as well as hiking and perhaps collecting rocks. Guests may keep up to one ounce of found gold; anything over one ounce per cabin must be split with Roaring Camp. A saloon, short order restaurant, and general store are available when guests get tired of roughing it. On Wednesdays another group of guests is trucked in for a riverside cook-out. Weekly guests are invited to join this event at no charge. For stays of less than a week, call the Monday before you wish to go. Weekly stays run Sunday to Sunday.

▪ *WHERE TO EAT*

Jackson Sandwich & Ice Cream Emporium, *134 Main, 209/223-0611; lunch daily; highchairs, booster seats; $; no cards.* This old-fashioned ice cream parlor/candy store has been serving up sweet confections since the turn of the century. Nowadays you can also get soup, sandwiches, and freshly ground coffee.

Wells Fargo Restaurant, *Water St., 209/223-9956; breakfast, lunch, and dinner daily; highchairs, booster seats; $; MC, V.* Daily dinner specials include such all-American items as baked shortribs, roast lamb, roast pork, baked ham, and breaded veal. The restaurant is known for its steaks, chicken, and ribs. Well-prepared, generous portions keep even the locals coming back. Hot and cold sandwiches and hamburgers are also available at dinner.

▪ WHAT TO DO

Amador County Museum, *225 Church St., 209/223-2884; W–M 10am–4pm; adults $1, 6–12 50¢.* This museum is located inside an 1859 red brick house with a brightly painted wooden train engine permanently parked in front (it was formerly used as a prop on TV's *Petticoat Junction*). Scale models of the Kennedy Mine tailing wheels and head frame and the North Star Mine stamp mill are on display and are sometimes operated. Call for schedule.

Kennedy Mine Tailing Wheels, *on Jackson Gate Rd.; dawn to dusk; free.* Four huge 58 ft. diameter wheels, originally built in 1912 to carry waste gravel from the nearby mine, may be viewed by taking a short walk on well-marked trails on either side of the road. Two of the wheels have already collapsed. Better hurry to see this site before time takes its toll on the other two. The abandoned Kennedy Mine may be seen from the site of wheels 1 & 2. Picnic tables are available.

Pardee Lake, *take Hoffman Lane/Stony Creek Rd. west for 10 miles, 209/772-1472; closed Feb–Nov, open daily rest of year; $2.50/car.* Boat rentals, a pool, and a playground are available here. There are also picnic facilities and campsites.

South Camanche Shore, *about 28 miles from Jackson off Hwy 88, Wallace, 209/763-5178; day use $6/car.* This is where to go for fishing, goldpanning, swimming, picnicking, water-skiing, tennis, horseback riding, and boating. Waterslides are open in the summer, and cottages and campsites are available.

SUTTER CREEK

▪ A LITTLE BACKGROUND

Seven gold mines were once located on this quiet Main Street. Now it is lined with antique shops.

■ *WHERE TO STAY*

♥ **Sutter Creek Inn,** *75 Main St. (P.O. Box 385), 95685, 209/267-5606; 2/$–$$$; some fireplaces; full breakfast; two-night minimum on weekends; no children under 16.* Have you been longing to spend the night in a bed suspended from the ceiling by chains? You can fulfill that and other yearnings here. In the morning brandy and coffee are served by the fireplace, before a big country breakfast in the kitchen. Spontaneous entertainment, in the form of lectures and concerts, sometimes occurs in the parlor. When things get slow, the owner has been known to entertain her guests by reading palms and interpreting handwriting. The more expensive rooms are in the adjacent carriage house.

■ *WHERE TO EAT*

Bellotti Inn, *53 Main St., 209/267-5211; lunch and dinner daily; highchairs, booster seats, children's portions; reservations suggested; $$; no cards.* Huge Italian family-style dinners with veal, chicken, and steak entrees are served in this well-established restaurant located inside a historic building. A la carte items and a hamburger are also on the menu. Inexpensive rooms are available in the hotel.

Sutter Creek Palace, *76 Main St., 209/267-9852; lunch and dinner daily; highchairs, booster seats, children's portions; reservations suggested; $$; no cards.* Entry to this western-style saloon, dominated by a huge bar, is through old-time swinging corner doors. The menu fare is interesting, and sometimes on the weekends there is live entertainment.

VOLCANO

■ *A LITTLE BACKGROUND*

The scenic, rural drive here from Sutter Creek is also ill-marked and poorly paved and is best maneuvered during daylight. And it's been my experience that directions and information obtained around here can often be vague or misleading, leaving plenty of room for error.

Because this tiny town is built in a depression on top of limestone caves, it is green year-round. Sleepy and quiet now, during the Gold Rush it was well-known for its boisterous dance halls and saloons.

■ *WHERE TO STAY*

St. George Hotel, *P.O. Box 9, 95689, 209/296-4458; 2/$, on weekends*

$$$ but includes breakfast and dinner; closed M & Tu and Jan & Feb; some private baths; dining facilities. This solidly constructed hotel offers a choice of rooms in either the main hotel, built in 1862, or in an annex built almost a hundred years later in 1961. For safety reasons families with children under 12 must stay in the newer and charmless annex located around the corner, their consolation being that they get a private bathroom. In the hotel, there is a cozy memorabilia-crammed bar and parlour area, with fireplace and games, to relax in. Breakfast and dinner are served downstairs in the hotel each day and reservations are necessary except on Sunday when a special chicken dinner is served from 1 to 6pm.

■ WHERE TO EAT

Jug and Rose Confectionery, *Main St., 209/296-4696; breakfast and lunch W–Sun, breakfast only M, closed M–F in Jan & Feb; highchairs, children's portions; reservations suggested; $; no cards.* Famous for their all-you-can-eat sourdough pancake breakfasts, this charming spot has been in business since 1855 (in the Gold Rush days it was The Stone Jug Saloon). Pancakes are served with warm spice syrup, strawberries and sour cream, and blackberry topping. The breakfast special includes fresh fruit compote, scrambled eggs, ham, and beverage. Children's pancakes are made in animal shapes. Lunch brings homemade sandwiches, soups, and pie to the menu. Teatime and exotic sundaes lure afternoon customers. How about a moss rose sundae (homemade rose petal syrup on vanilla ice cream topped in season with a real rose), a Sierra split (three flavors of ice cream, wild blackberry topping, and banana), or a plain Jane for scaredy cats? All items are served with flower garnishes. A scaled-down table and chairs are available for kids, along with a basket full of toys to entertain them.

■ WHAT TO DO

Daffodil Hill, *3 miles north of town; mid-March through April; by donation.* Originally planted in the 1850s, this four-acre garden boasts more than 250 varieties of daffodils. Barnyard animals are penned for viewing, and there is a picnic area with tables.

Indian Grinding Rock State Historic Park, *on Pine Grove Rd. southwest of town, 209/296-7488; W–Sun, hours vary, closed Jan–March; $2/car.* The largest of the grinding rocks, a huge flat bedrock limestone measuring 175 x 82 ft., has over 1,158 mortar holes and 363 rock carvings (petroglyphs). All were made by Indians who ground their seed here with pestles. Also on display are a Miwok village complete with ceremonial roundhouse, a handgame house, a cultural center, several cedar bark tepees, a grain storage center, an Indian football field, an

Indian Grinding Rock.

Indian tepee village, and a nature trail. Special celebrations are scheduled each September. Campsites and picnicking facilities are available.

"Old Abe" Volcano Blues Cannon. Located in the center of town in a
protected shelter, this cannon—without firing a shot—helped win the
Civil War. Cast of bronze and brass in Boston in 1837 and weighing
737 pounds, it somehow reached San Francisco and was smuggled to
Volcano in 1863. It was used by the town to control renegades who
were drawn there in search of quick wealth. For the complete story,
ask around town. And don't believe everything you hear.

Park. Scenic stone ruins, rocky terrain, and a gurgling stream provide a
fantastic backdrop against which to enjoy a picnic or just a few mo-
ments of quiet contemplation. This spot is one of the most picturesque I've ever seen.

Sing Kee's Store. Built in 1857 and formerly a general store, this building is now a gift shop.

Volcano Pioneers Community Theatre Group, *209/223/0587; April–Oct,
F & Sat at 8pm, occasionally Thur & Sun; tickets $5; reservations
necessary.* The first little theater group to form in California was the
Volcano Thespian Society in 1854. Children are welcome at performances in the intimate 50-seat theater.

AMADOR CITY

■ *WHERE TO STAY*

Mine House Inn, *P.O. Box 245, 95601, 209/267-5900; 2–4/$$; pool; continental breakfast.* Gold Rush era antiques furnish the unusual rooms in this restored brick building, which was once a mine office. Each room in the attractive motel-like structure is named for its original function: the Mill Grinding Room, the Vault Room, the Retort Room. In the morning, just push the buzzer and coffee is delivered to the door. One Easter when my family was staying here, we arranged for an Easter basket to arrive in this same mysterious manner. Our son still hasn't figured out how that one was pulled off.

■ *WHERE TO EAT*

Buffalo Chips Emporium, *Hwy 49, 209/267-0570; breakfast and lunch daily, closed M & Tu in winter; highchairs; $; no cards.* Some folks just buy a cone here and then sit outside on one of the old benches to leisurely watch the busy world drive by. Others prefer to sit inside what was once the town's Wells Fargo Bank and indulge in a fancy fountain item.

The Cellar, *10 Main St., 209/267-0384; lunch and dinner daily, closed Sun–W in winter; highchairs; $$; MC, V.* Located in the stone-wall cellar of an old bakery, this unusual restaurant serves fondue, sandwiches prepared with homemade sourdough bread, and homemade soups and desserts. Children may be interested to know there is a peanut butter and jelly sandwich and chocolate fondue on the menu.

DRYTOWN

■ *A LITTLE BACKGROUND*

Once the home of 27 saloons, Drytown is now known for its equally abundant antique shops.

■ *WHAT TO DO*

The Great Western and Pacific Wagon Train Co. Ltd., *P.O. Box 12, Fiddletown 95629, 209/296-5577; operates May–Sept; $150/adult, special children's prices.* The wagons used on these 3-day, 2-night trips are authentic reproductions of the ones used by the pioneers. They are built and maintained in a shop at Red Mule Ranch. At night the wagons form a wagon circle. Participants eat chuck wagon food around a campfire and then retire to their sleeping bags for the night. Side trips are taken on horseback. This trip is not recommended for children under 5.

Piper Playhouse, *209/245-3812; May–Sept, Sat at 8:30pm; tickets $9; reservations necessary.* Raucous melodramas are the bill of fare. Call for current schedule.

SHINGLE SPRINGS

■ *WHERE TO EAT*

Sam's Town, *Hwy 50/Cameron Park, 95682, 916/677-2273, 933-1662; daily 6am–2am.* This is a funky combination restaurant/honky-tonk piano bar/general store/memorabilia museum/pinball arcade. The outside is littered with covered wagons and the inside floors are littered with peanut shells discarded by happy revelers. For snacks you can choose a hamburger, fried chicken, or prime rib and champagne.

■ *WHERE TO STAY*

Crazy Horse Campgrounds, *P.O. Box 388, 95682, 916/677-2258; $9–$12.50/campsite.* During the summer something special always seems to be happening here: aloha weekend, bathtub regatta, Oktoberfest, wagon train days. Call for the current special events schedule. Children should be thrilled about taking the raft to Tom Sawyer Island, hitching a ride on the firetruck, and playing in the two tree forts. These facilities, as well as gold panning, a 350 ft. water slide, swimming, boating, fishing, kiddie rides, miniature golf, and horseback riding, are available June–Sept. Campsites are available year-round.

EL DORADO

■ *WHERE TO EAT*

Poor Red's, *Hwy 49, 916/622-2901; lunch and dinner M–F, dinner Sat & Sun; highchairs, booster seats; no reservations; $; AE, V.* Judging just from the outside, which looks for all the world like an unsavory bar, I would easily have passed this spot by. But then I would have missed the experience of dining on exquisite ham, ribs, chicken, and steak—all cooked over an open oakwood pit and served in generous portions. Because the restaurant is very popular and also very small, weekend dinner waits can run over an hour. Some patrons pass that time downing Gold Cadillacs at the old-time horseshoe bar, some pass it staring at the mural behind the bar which depicts the town as it appeared in the late 1800s, and some pass it feeding the jukebox. Others beat the wait by getting a take-out order.

PLACERVILLE

El Dorado County Chamber of Commerce
P.O. Box 268
(542 Main St.)
Placerville 95667
916/626-2344

■ *ANNUAL EVENTS*

Reenactment of Pony Express, *July in Pollock Pines, 916/644-3970.*

■ *A LITTLE BACKGROUND*

Placerville was once known as Hangtown, because hangings here were so common. This is where the Hangtown Fry (eggs, bacon, and oysters) originated. Mark Hopkins, Philip Armour, and John Studebaker all got their financial starts here as well.

■ *WHERE TO EAT*

John Pearson Soda Works & Bottling Room, *594 Main St., 916/626-8272; breakfast, lunch, and dinner daily.* Limestone cooling caves are still in use in the back providing natural air-conditioning and making this a good place to cool off on a hot day. The old-time soda fountain, circa 1850, has swivel stools and there are also some wooden booths. Diners reach the second floor via a water-powered elevator or old iron staircase. At press time, this historic spot was going through a change of ownership. Call for further details about the facilities and menu.

■ *WHAT TO DO*

Apple Hill. Located on a mountain ridge east of town, the route for the Apple Hill tour follows a historic path originally blazed out in 1857 by Pony Express riders. In the fall (Sept–Dec), various farms along this route sell tree-fresh apples at bargain prices as well as homemade apple goodies like apple cider, spicy apple butter and caramel apples. Many of the farms offer picnic facilities; some also have hiking trails, fishing ponds, pony rides, and train rides. A number of Christmas tree farms are also located here. For a free map to the farms, send a legal-size stamped, self-addressed envelope to: Apple Hill, P.O. Box 494, Camino 95709.

Boeger Winery, *1709 Carson Rd. (at Schnell School Rd. off Hwy 50), 916/622-8094; tasting and tours W–Sun 10am–5pm.* The old stone cellar tasting room is part of the original winery which was operated from the 1860s through the 1920s. Stream-side picnic tables beckon.

Gold Bug Mine, *in Bedford Park on Bedford Ave., 1 mile from center of town, 916/622-0832; daily 8:30am–dusk; free.* Visitors can walk through the ¼-mile long lighted mine shaft, picnic at stream-side tables, and hike in this rugged 68-acre park.

El Dorado County Historical Museum, *360 Fairlane, off Placerville Dr. 2 miles west of town in the El Dorado County Fairgrounds, 916/626-2250; W–Sat 10am–4pm; free.* Historic exhibits include an old stagecoach and a wheelbarrow made by John Studebaker in the days before he manufactured cars.

Mama's Llamas. See p. 218.

COLOMA

■ *A LITTLE BACKGROUND*

This is where James Marshall discovered gold in California in 1848.

■ *WHERE TO STAY*

Sierra Nevada House III, *on Hwy 49 (P.O. Box 268), 95613, 916/622-5856, 933-0547; 2/$$, 4/$$$; continental breakfast; dining facilities.* This is an authentic reconstruction built near the ruins of two former hotels of the same name which burned in 1907 and 1926. Some rooms are in the older hotel and some are in the newer motel addition. A soda fountain dispenses short order items as well as a special soda made from a turn-of-the-century recipe. Delicious homemade dinners with all the trimmings are available in the casual dining room. If food was this good here during the Gold Rush, the miners must have lost plenty of gold while they sat here eating instead of panning.

♥ **The Vineyard House,** *on Cold Springs Rd. (P.O. Box 176), 95613, 916/622-2217; 2/$–$$; all shared baths; continental breakfasts; dining facilities; no children under 17.* Rumored to be haunted, this old inn's wine cellar dates from the 1840s and now serves as a bar with live music on Friday and Saturday nights. Daily homemade dinners and a Sunday brunch are served in the five dining rooms.

Menu items include chicken and dumplings, beef stroganoff, fish, and prime rib. Children's portions are available as are highchairs and booster seats.

■ WHAT TO DO

Marshall Gold Discovery State Historic Park, *on Hwy 49, 916/622-3470;*

Where the Gold Rush began: reconstruction of the original Sutter sawmill.

park: daily 10am–sunset, $2/car; museum: daily 10am–5pm, adults 50¢, 6–17 25¢. This lovely 245-acre park encompasses 70% of the town. It contains a reconstruction of the original Sutter sawmill (where the Gold Rush began) as well as picnic facilities, nature trails, Gold Rush era buildings and artifacts, and a museum. An exact replica of the piece of gold Marshall found is on display in the museum (the original is at the Smithsonian in Washington D.C.). The mill is operated on weekends at 2pm.

AUBURN

Auburn Chamber of Commerce
1101 High St.
Auburn 95603
916/885-5616

■ *WHERE TO EAT*

Auburn Hotel, *853 Lincoln Way, 916/885-8132; dinner daily; highchairs, booster seats, children's portions; reservations suggested; $$; MC, V.* The 7-course family-style Basque dinners are popular with both locals and travelers. Call for the current menu. A coffee shop is also on the premises and is open for breakfast and lunch.

■ *WHAT TO DO*

Gold Rush Plaza Old Opera House Dinner Theater, *111 Sacramento St., 916/885-7708; F & Sat, dinner served at 7:30pm, curtain at 8:30pm; adults $7/dinner, $6/entertainment, children ½ price for dinner only.* The dinner of soup, salad, roast beef, baked potato, dessert, and coffee is served family-style at long rows of tables. The well-done melodramas are original productions with titles like *East Lynne, or The Feckless Father's Fatal Furnace.* Wine cocktails with names like the Dirty Sally Phizz (a Sunrise) and the Miner's Dilemma (a Bloody Mary) and sangria, beer, and fancy non-alcoholic drinks are available to sip during the show. At intermission the audience dismisses outside for some fresh air and to mingle with the actors.

Placer County Historic Museum Complex, *museum: 1273 High St. in the Gold Country Fairgrounds, house: 291 Auburn–Folsom Rd., 916/885-9570; daily 10am–4pm; adults $1, 6–16 50¢, fee good for both locations.* This old-time museum exhibits local Maidu Indian and gold mining artifacts as well as an extensive doll collection. Docent-led tours are available of the nearby Greek Revival-style Bernhard House, built in 1851 and furnished with Victorian antiques.

GRASS VALLEY

Grass Valley Chamber of Commerce
151 Mill St.
Grass Valley 95945
916/273-4667

It's worth visiting this office in person because of its location inside the historic home of the well-known Gold Rush personality Lola Montez.

- **ANNUAL EVENTS**

  Bluegrass Festival, *in June and September.*
  Cornish Christmas Street Faire, *December.*

- **A LITTLE BACKGROUND**

  This was once the richest gold mining region in the state.

- **WHERE TO STAY**

  Alta Sierra Motel, *135 Tammy Way, 95945, 916/273-9102; 2–4/$; pool access; TVs; cribs.* Finding this rustic modern motel, located down a winding country road, is a little like going on a treasure hunt. Just keep following those signs and when you finally find it, you'll probably agree it is somewhat of a treasure. The woodsy spacious rooms overlook a small lake and picturesque grounds. A country club across the street provides access to a pool, golf course, and inexpensive dining.

  Sivananda Ashram Vrindavan Yoga Farm, *McCourtney Rd. (P.O. Box 2742), 95945, 916/272-9322; 2/$–$$; all shared baths; meals included.* The bell rings at 5:30 each morning to wake guests. Attendance at the scheduled meditation and yoga disciplines is mandatory. In-between, guests are fed vegetarian meals and given plenty of free time to enjoy the natural surroundings of the 60-acre farm. Guests bring their own sleeping bags and are assigned to the separate men's or women's dorms. Small huts are available for couples and families.

- **WHERE TO EAT**

  King Richard's Pasties, *251 S. Auburn, 916/273-0286; M–Sat 9:30am–6pm; $; no cards.* Located inside a pristine white Victorian home, this unusual takeout eatery specializes in pasties. These meat and potato turnovers were once popular lunch fare among the area's Cornish miners, who were said to carry them down into the mines in their pockets. At lunchtime the miners reheated their pasties on a shovel held over their hat's candle. Fruit turnovers and drinks are also available. How about a tasty pasty picnic?

Scheidel's Old European Restaurant, *10140 Alta Sierra Dr., 6 miles south of town, 916/273-5553; dinner W-Sun, closed Jan; booster seats, children's portions; reservations suggested; $$; MC, V.* Wienerschnitzel, sauerbraten, and veal Oscar are featured fare at this popular spot.

Tofanelli's, *302 W. Main St., 916/273-9927; breakfast and lunch daily, dinner M-F; highchairs, booster seats, children's portions; $; MC, V.* Every kind of breakfast item you can imagine is on this menu—including design-your-own omelettes, whole wheat pancakes and waffles, and a huge selection of teas. Salads, sandwiches, and a variety of hamburgers—including a tofuburger and a veggieburger—join the menu at lunch. All this and an attractive brick and oak decor, too.

■ *WHAT TO DO*

Bridgeport Bridge, *take Hwy 20 west about 8 miles to Pleasant Valley, turn right (north) and follow the south fork of the Yuba River 5-6 miles.* Built in 1862 and in use until 1971, this is the longest (233 ft.) single-span wood-covered bridge in the world. It is now a State Historical Landmark. It is not currently maintained and its condition is shaky, so be careful should you decide to walk across it.

Empire Mine State Historic Park, *10791 E. Empire St., 916/273-8522; daily 9am-dusk; guided tours available daily in summer at 1:30 and*

3:30 pm; adults 50¢, 12-17 25¢. The Empire Mine was once the largest and richest hard rock mine in the state and was operated for over a century from 1850 to 1956. Now it is a 784-acre State Park. Of special interest are the stone **Bourn Mansion** (open weekends and holidays noon–4pm), designed by Willis Polk in the style of an English country lodge, and the formal gardens and fountains which surround it. The mining area illustrates many facets of mining and allows visitors to look down a lit mine shaft. With the aid of the park's 50¢ brochure, 22 miles of self-guided back-country hiking trails may be enjoyed.

Memorial Park, *Colfax/Central Aves., 916/273-3171.* This is a good spot to picnic, get in a game of tennis, swim in the public pool, wade in the creek, or let the kids romp at the well-equipped playground.

Pelton Wheel Mining Museum, *Allison Ranch Rd./McCourtney Rd., 916/273-6752; May–Oct daily 11am–5pm, Nov–April Sat & Sun 10am–4pm; adults 50¢, under 18 free.* This rustic stone building, which was once the North Star Mine Power House, houses a collection of old photographs, mining dioramas and models, and 30 ft. Pelton waterwheels weighing ten tons each. A grassy picnic area is located across adjacent Wolf Creek.

NEVADA CITY

Nevada City Chamber of Commerce
132 Main St.
Nevada City 95959
916/265-2692

■ *ANNUAL EVENTS*

Home Tour, *May and October.*

4th of July Parade.

Constitution Day Parade, *September.*

Fall Colors, *trees change colors mid-Oct through mid-Nov.*

Victorian Christmas, *the four Wednesday evenings before Christmas.*

■ *A LITTLE BACKGROUND*

This picturesque mining town is one of the best-preserved in the Gold Country. Scenically situated on seven hills, the town boasts many lovely gingerbread-style Victorian homes. It makes a convenient rest stop off Hwy 80 when traveling to or from North Lake Tahoe.

■ *WHERE TO STAY IN TOWN*

National Hotel, *211 Broad St., 95959, 916/265-4551; 2/$-$$, 4/$$; some private baths; pool; cribs; dining facilities.* Located on the town's main street, this claims to be the oldest continuously operating hotel in the West. Built in 1856, the hotel is solid and features high ceilings, cozy floral wallpapers, and old-time furniture. Families of four can be accommodated with two separate rooms with a bath between. The plush, old-fashioned dining room offers moderately priced lunches and Sunday brunch and expensive steak and lobster dinners.

Northern Queen Motel, *400 Railroad Ave., 95959, 916/265-5824; 2-4/ $-$$$; some kitchens; pool, whirlpool; TVs.* Located on the outskirts of town, this pleasant motel has some cottages as well as picnic tables, grills, and a stocked trout pond.

♥ **Red Castle Inn,** *109 Prospect, 95959, 916/265-5135; 2/$-$$$; some shared baths; continental breakfast; no children under 13.* This beautifully restored and comfortably furnished Gothic Revival home, featuring gingerbread and icicle trim, was built in the 1860s. Its hilltop location affords good views of the town, making it a prime spot to be staying on parade days. Old-fashioned double brick walls provide insulation.

■ *WHERE TO STAY NEARBY*

Herrington's Sierra Pines, *P.O. Box 235, Sierra City 96125, 916/862-1151; 2/$-$$, 4/$$; some kitchens and fireplaces; TVs; cribs; dining facilities.* Located on the north fork of the Yuba River, this lodging is mostly motel units but has a few cottages too. It also has a trout pond and a restaurant (closed Nov–Mar) known for its fresh rainbow trout and baked goods.

Kenton Mine Lodge, *off Hwy 49, 45 miles north of town in a quiet canyon at the end of a 3-mile dirt road (P.O. Box 942), Alleghany 95910, 916/287-3212; $60/person/night, special rates for children; some shared baths; some kitchens and wood-burning stoves; cribs; includes three meals; children under 3 stay free in parents' room.* In case you haven't heard, there's a gold rush on. Miners are heading for the hills again, and one of the most favored areas surrounds the tiny Sierra town of Alleghany. City-slickers are advised to be careful around here, though, as many miners camp on top of their claims and some have been known to get mean when confronted with trespassers. To assure your safety and warmth while trying your luck at panning for gold, consider spending a weekend at this remote, semi-refurbished mining camp dating from the 30s. Though vivid imaginations have been known to run wild here (several guests have commented that the winding forest road from Nevada City is not unlike the one seen at the beginning of the movie *The Shining*), once the freaked-out city traveler relaxes and acclimates to the unaccustomed peace and tranquility, apprehensions dissolve. Guests sleep in old miners' cabins or bunkhouse rooms and are fed home-cooked meals, served family-style at long tables in the Cookhouse. Gold panning equipment may be borrowed for use in gurgling Kanaka Creek, which runs through the camp. An abandoned gold mine and stamp mill, also on the site, provide for some interesting exploring.

Packer Lake Lodge, *P.O. Box 237, Sierra City 96125, 916/862-1221; 2-4/$-$$; closed Nov-May; some shared baths; cribs; one week minimum in housekeeping cabins during summer; dining facilities.* Rustic cabins here have sundecks overlooking Packer Lake. Cabin rental includes the use of a rowboat. Sleeping cabins are available by the night.

Salmon Lake Lodge, *P.O. Box 121, Sierra City 96125, 415/771-0150 (reservations phone is in San Francisco); 2-4/$; closed Oct-May; all shared baths; some kitchens and fireplaces; one week minimum in July and Aug.* This remote resort, located in the glaciated high country of Sierra County, has been in continuous operation for almost a century. Guests park their cars at the east end of Salmon Lake and are then transported by barge across the lake. Guests sleep in rustic tent-cabins and must provide their own bedding, kitchen utensils, and supplies. Cabin rates include use of an assortment of boats. Catered barbecue dinners on the lake's island are occasionally scheduled.

Sierra Shangri-La, *P.O. Box 285, Downieville 95936, 916/289-3455; 2/$-$$, 4/$$-$$$; some kitchens and woodburning stoves; cribs; two-night minimum.* There is little to do here except commune with nature. Guests can relax, do some fishing and hiking, and enjoy the sight and sound of the Yuba River rushing past their cottage door.

■ *WHERE TO EAT*

American Victorian Museum Restaurant, *325 Spring St., 916/265-5804; dinner F & Sat, Sunday brunch, closed Feb; highchairs, children's portions; reservations essential; $$; MC, V.* Located in the historic Miners Foundry, where machine parts and architectural iron were once manufactured for use throughout the world, this is the only museum in the United States devoted to collecting, preserving, and exhibiting art and artifacts from the Victorian period (1840-1900). Acting as a cultural center for the community, the museum hosts theater productions, concerts, and lectures in its huge Old Stone Hall (1856), one of the largest free-span rooms in the area. The interesting meals served here are an unexpected bonus. Call for current menu and performance schedule.

Cafe Les Stace, *311 Broad St., 916/265-6440; breakfast Sat & Sun, lunch and dinner daily; highchairs, booster seats; $; MC, V.* The eclectic menu in this mellow spot consists of tasty, fresh food like hamburgers, fried chicken, spaghetti, steaks, and Mexican items.

Friar Tuck's, *111 N. Pine St., 916/265-9093; dinner Tu–Sun; highchairs, booster seats, children's portions; reservations suggested; $$; AE, MC, V.* A large variety of casual fondue items (even chocolate dessert fondue) share the menu with grilled fresh fish, chicken, and steak. The extensive wine list, stocked by the restaurant's adjacent wine shop, runs the gamut from inexpensive local labels to expensive rare vintages. Relaxing live guitar music is piped throughout the catacomb-like interior furnished with comfortable, large wooden booths.

Nevada City Cafe, *236 Broad, 916/265-5504; breakfast and lunch daily; highchairs, booster seats; $; no cards.* At this old-time ice cream parlor patrons choose from a variety of soda flavors and a plethora of ice cream concoctions.

■ WHAT TO DO IN TOWN

Brass Rubbings, *at Freeman and Swig, 108 N. Pine St., 916/265-6111; W–M 10am–5pm.* This claims to be the first shop in the United States to specialize in brass rubbings. Some are already done and ready to purchase; others are waiting for you to do yourself. A child's kit (good for beginning adults too) includes waxes, scissors, and papers. The proprietor is eager to help and answer any questions you might have about this old art form.

Firehouse Museum, *214 Main St., 916/265-9941; daily 11am–4pm; 50¢.* Located inside an 1861 firehouse, this museum is said to be haunted. Visitors can see a Chinese altar and snowshoes made for a horse. More pioneer memorabilia is found in the annex **Bicentennial Museum.**

Nevada City Winery, *321 Spring St., 916/265-WINE; tours and tasting daily noon–sunset.*

NEVADA COUNTY HISTORICAL SOCIETY MUSEUMS:

American Victorian Museum. See p. 160.

Martin Luther Marsh House, *254 Boulder St., 916/265-6716; tours by appointment; by donation.* The tour of this completely restored and authentically furnished Victorian Italianate house, built in 1873, allows viewing of all the rooms.

Mt. Wesley House, *431 Broad St., 916/265-5804; tours by appointment.* This Gothic Revival Folly house is made of spare pieces and parts and now holds the Museum's collection of Gothic Revival furniture and an art and architecture library.

Nevada Theatre, *401 Broad St., 916/265-6161; live theatre on most F & Sat evenings; tickets $4–$7.50.* Opened in September of 1865, this claims to be the oldest theater building in California. It has been refurbished to appear as it did when it first opened. The theatre is very small and all seats are close to the stage, making it an excellent spot to expose children to a live production. The audience is usually filled with locals, and they bring their children when the production is appropriate. Movies are often scheduled for Sunday afternoons. Call for current production information.

■ *WHAT TO DO NEARBY*

Campbell Hot Springs/Consciousness Village, *Sierraville, off Hwy 89, 26 miles north of Truckee, 916/994-8984; baths open M-F 8am-10pm; adults $5, children by donation.* Swimsuits are optional in the hot tubs at this secluded spa which has been in operation since the 1850s. A cool natural mineral water swimming pool rounds out the facilities. Rebirthing and conscious breathing seminars are sometimes scheduled, and a vegetarian restaurant serves breakfast and dinner. Rooms in a 1909 hotel are available.

Independence Trail, *5 miles north of town off Hwy 49, 916/265-3650; free.* Basically level and easy for baby strollers and children, this one-mile nature trail passes Transitional Zone vegetation.

Malakoff Diggins State Historic Park, *23579 North Bloomfield/Graniteville Rd., North Bloomfield, off Hwy 49, 17 miles northeast of town, 916/265-2740; museum: daily April–Oct 10am–5pm, weekends rest of year; $2/car.* Inhabited by over 1,500 people in the 1800s, when it was the biggest hydraulic mining operation in the world, **North Bloomfield** is now a ghost town. Several buildings have been restored and a supplies shop features a clerk in period dress, but there are no commercial stores. The park Historic Center has an interpretive display on hydraulic mining. On weekends at 2pm a demonstration of an old hydraulic mining monitor is followed by a tour of the town. Old logging roads are now hiking trails, a small lake is stocked with fish, and picnic facilities are available. Campsites may be reserved through Ticketron (see p. 224) and two primitive cabins may be inexpensively rented through the park.

Oregon Creek Swimming Hole, *18 miles north of town on Hwy 49.* Located in the middle fork of the Yuba River, this popular area has sandy beaches, deep swimming and shallow wading spots, and picnic facilities. A Tahoe National Forest campground is also located here.

Sierra County Historical Park and Museum, *on Hwy 49, Sierra City, 916/862-1310; W–Sun 10am–5pm June–Aug, Sat & Sun Sept–Oct, closed Nov–May; adults $1/tour, 50¢/museum, under 13 free.* Take a guided tour through the reconstructed 1850s Kentucky Mine and Stamp Mill, where all the machinery is still intact.

LAKE TAHOE

SOUTH LAKE TAHOE

South Lake Tahoe Visitors Bureau
P.O. Box 17727
South Lake Tahoe 95706
916/544-5050
800/822-5922, reservations service
916/577-3550, winter road and weather conditions

■ *A LITTLE BACKGROUND*

> ". . . At last the Lake burst upon us—a noble sheet of
> blue water lifted six thousand three hundred feet above
> the level of the sea, and walled in by a rim of snowclad
> mountain peaks that towered aloft full three thousand
> feet higher still!
> "It was a vast oval. As it lay there with the shadows
> of the great mountains brilliantly photographed upon its
> surface, I thought it must surely be the fairest picture
> the whole earth affords . . ."
>
> —*Mark Twain*

Lake Tahoe lies half in California and half in Nevada. It is the largest (193 sq. miles surface) and deepest (1645 ft.) lake in North America and the second largest Alpine lake in the world. At 6,225 ft. above sea level, its summer waters are a crystal clear deep blue—providing a striking contrast with the extensive green forests and majestic mountains encircling it.

Once a remote Sierra lake, Tahoe is now a popular and well-equipped vacation area offering a wide range of recreational activities as well as spectacular scenery. Swimming, hiking, boating, tennis, bicycling, horseback riding, river rafting, camping, fishing, water-skiing, and backpacking are some of the summer outdoor activities you can look forward to. In winter there is excellent skiing.

On the Nevada side gambling is another big attraction. Children may go into a casino with adults but are not allowed to "loiter" (not even babies in backpacks) or play the slot machines. Most lodgings offer transportation to the casinos and have discount casino coupons for their guests. Inquire at the desk.

Childcare is relatively easy to find in this area. Lodging facilities often maintain a list of local sitters. Inquire at the desk. The yellow pages list a number of childcare centers that take drop-ins. **Tender Loving Care** (916/541-5197) provides sitters over the age of 35 for a minimum of 4 hours at $5/hour. Harrah's Casino has a recreation center for children 6-14. It operates year-round from 9am–11:30pm, admission is $2.50, and there is a 5 hour maximum. The lounge has ping-pong, pool tables, bowling, jukeboxes, a movie theater, kiddie rides, TV, and a snack bar. Children will need extra money for some of the facilities. Sure beats sitting on the curb reading comic books like I did when I was a kid. For further information and current schedule call 800/648-3773 or 702/588-6611 x447.

- *ROUTE*
Located approximately 200 miles north of San Francisco. Take Hwy 80 to Hwy 50 to the lake.

- *STOPS ALONG THE WAY*
The Nut Tree. See page 115.
Placerville. See page 152.

Poor Red's. See page 151.

Sacramento. See page 113.

Sam's Town. See page 151.

■ *WHERE TO STAY*
LAKEFRONT:

Inn by the Lake, *3300 Lake Tahoe Blvd. (P.O. Box 849), 95705, 800/228-2828, 916/542-0330; 2/$$-$$$+; some kitchens and lake views; pool, 2 hot tubs, sauna; TVs; cribs; continental breakfast; children under 18 stay free in their parents' room.* Located in a grove of pine trees across the street from the lake, this attractive new motel offers comfortable, quiet rooms.

Royal Valhalla, *4104 Lakeshore Blvd. (Drawer GG), 95729, 916/544-2233; 2/$-$$$+, 4/$$-$$$+; some kitchens and lake views; pool; TVs; cribs.* This motel also has suites and townhouses and a private beach.

Sail-In Motel Apartments, *861 Lakeview Ave. (P.O. Box 653), 95705, 916/544-8615; 2/$-$$, 4/$$; some kitchens and lake views; TVs.* Located off the beaten path, this attractive and comfortable motel is right on the beach and close to a park.

Tahoe Marina Inn, *P.O. Box 871, 95705, 800/822-5922, 916/541-2180; 2-4/$$-$$$; some kitchens, fireplaces, and lake views; pool, sauna; TVs; cribs.* These motel units are located right on the edge of the lake. Some beachside condominiums are also available.

Timber Cove Lodge, *Hwy 50/Johnson Blvd. (P.O. Box AC), 95705, 800/528-1234, 916/541-6722; 2/$-$$, 4/$$-$$$; some lake views; pool; TVs; cribs; dining facilities.* This motel has a private beach, marina, and pier.

CONDOS AND HOMES:

Accommodation Station, *2540 Hwy 50 (P.O. Box 14441), 95702, 916/541-2355; $$-$$$+; all have kitchens and fireplaces; some TVs; two-night minimum, five-night minimum during holidays.* Privately-owned condominiums, cabins, and homes may be rented through this agency. Price is determined by the number of bedrooms and type of accommodation. **Lake Tahoe Accommodations** *(P.O. Box 7722, 95731, call collect 916/544-3234; four-night minimum)* is very similar to Accommodation Station.

Lakeland Village, *P.O. Box A, 95705, 800/822-5969, 916/541-7711; 2-4/$-$$$+; packages; some kitchens, fireplaces, and lake views; 2 pools, wading pool, jacuzzi, 2 saunas; 2 tennis courts (fee); TVs; cribs; usually two-night minimum.* Though located on bustling Hwy 50, this condominium complex manages to retain a secluded, restive feeling. Many of the units are located right on the lake; all are within a few minutes walk. A recreation room and playground are also available.

OTHERS:

Casinos. The major casinos offer large numbers of hotel rooms. Call for details. **Caesars** 800/648-3353, **Harrah's** 800/648-5070, **Harvey's** 800/648-3361, **High Sierra** 800/648-3322.

Motel Row. Hwy 50 into town is littered with more motels than is to be believed.

Motel 6, *2375 Lake Tahoe Blvd., 916/541-6272; 2-4/$; pool; cribs.*

Zephyr Cove Resort, *on Hwy 50, 4 miles north of Stateline (P.O. Box 830), Zephyr Cove, Nevada 89448, 702/588-6644; some private baths; 2-4/$-$$; some kitchens; cribs; dining facilities.* Located in a lovely forested area by the lake, these rustic cabins and lodge rooms are run by the Forest Service and provide a convenient yet out-of-the-way spot to stay. Facilities include a beach, marina with boat rentals, stables, and arcade. Campsites are also available.

■ *WHERE TO EAT*

Cantina Los Tres Hombres, *Hwy 89/10th St., ¼ mile north of the Y, 916/544-1233; lunch and dinner daily; highchairs, booster seats, children's portions; no reservations; $$; AE, MC, V.* There is almost always a wait to be seated in this popular spot, but don't let that keep you away. My family often passes the wait sitting in the bar. We order a pitcher of Margaritas for the adults, some soft drinks for the kids (the niña colada is excellent), and some nachos (tortilla chips heated with green chiles, melted cheese, chorizo, and topped with sour cream and guacamole) for all of us. Then we settle into the noisy, happy surroundings and munch and sip. We have found that sometimes our hunger is satisfied by this tactic, and we are ready to leave before we are even called to a table. When we do stick around to dine, we've been overwhelmed by the wonderful menu which includes chimichangas, "grande" tacos and tostadas, crab enchiladas, steak picado, a large variety of huge burritos, and fresh fish on Fridays. The menu has changed a lot over the years, but it just keeps getting better. Children are given a box of crayons and their own menu to order from (taco, enchilada, or hot dog) and color.

Casinos. For some of the best and least expensive food in this area, try the casino restaurants and buffets. Most offer bargain prices and family amenities. My favorites are:

Caesar's Aspen Room, *702/588-3515; breakfast, lunch, and dinner daily; highchairs and booster seats.* The $1.99 breakfast special includes eggs, hash browns, sausage, toast, and coffee.

Harrah's Forest Buffet, *702/588-6611; breakfast, lunch, and dinner daily; children's portions.* Located on the 18th floor, diners are treated to spectacular views and excellent food.

Harvey's Garden Restaurant, *702/588-2411; breakfast, lunch, and dinner daily; highchairs and booster seats.* Don't miss the delicious, bargain-priced fried chicken and ribs at dinner. Harvey's also has an ice cream parlor and video arcade/shooting gallery to entertain children.

Cook Book, *787 Emerald Bay Rd., 916/541-8400; breakfast, lunch, and dinner daily, no dinner Oct–Nov; highchairs, booster seats; no reservations; $$; MC, V.* Claiming to have the largest omelette menu on earth, this restaurant also has what at times may be the longest wait. While waiting, get a copy of the menu and begin to decide which omelette to try from among the almost 500 possibilities. For those who are hard to please, the usual breakfast, lunch, and dinner items are also available.

Top of the Tram, *top of Ski Run Blvd., Heavenly Valley, 916/544-6263; reservations suggested; $$.* A bright red aerial tram lifts diners 2,000 ft. above Lake Tahoe to enjoy magnificent views while dining. The meal times vary from season to season and year to year, as does the menu. Call for the current offering.

■ WHAT TO DO

Amusement Centers. These spots are open daily in summer, and in winter as the weather permits.

Magic Carpet Golf, *2455 Hwy 50, 916/541-3787.* 19- & 28-hole miniature golf courses.

Stateline Amusement, *4050 Hwy 50, 916/544-3833.* Arcade and 19-hole miniature golf course.

Tahoe Amusement Park, *2401 Hwy 50, 916/541-1300.* Kiddie rides and a giant slide.

Angora Lakes. Take the road to Fallen Leaf (visit the lake there to see the falls) and then turn left at the sign to Angora Lakes. It is a mile hike from the end of the road to the lakes, where you should be able to find a quiet spot to picnic and swim.

Beaches/Biking. The **Pope-Baldwin Recreation Area,** on Hwy 89 between the Y and Emerald Bay, is lined with good beaches. A small fee is collected for parking. This same stretch of highway has a number of bike rental facilities and a nice bike trail.

BOATING:

Lake Tahoe Cruises, *at foot of Ski Run Blvd., 916/541-3364; call for schedule; adults $9, children $4.50.* The big new Tahoe Queen paddlewheeler offers two-hour cruises to Emerald Bay. The boat

has a large window area in the floor for underwater viewing. Call for information on the sunset dinner dance cruise and winter ski shuttle to Squaw Valley.

M.S. Dixie, *on Hwy 50, 4 miles north of Stateline, Zephyr Cove, Nevada, 702/588-3508; May–Oct, call for schedule; adults $8, 3–11 $4; reservations required.* Cruises to Emerald Bay take about 2½ hours on this paddlewheel steamer which was used on the Mississippi River in the 1920s. Dinner cruises are also available.

Rentals of various kinds of boats are available at **Ski Run Marina** 916/544-0200 and **South Shore Marina** in Tahoe Keys 916/541-1137, 541-2155, and **Timber Cove Marina** 916/544-2942.

Waterskiing/Windsurf Lessons and Rentals are available at Ski Run Marina 916/544-0200.

Woodwind, *on Hwy 50, 4 miles north of Stateline, Zephyr Cove, Nevada, 702/588-3000; May–Oct, call for schedule; adults $8, 2–12 $4; reservations advised.* Only 24 passengers fit on this 41 ft. trimaran with glass bottom viewing window. A sunset champagne cruise is also available. Small boats and yachts may be rented.

Camp Richardson Corral and Pack Station, *Emerald Bay Rd./Fallen Leaf Rd., 916/541-3113; daily, closed Nov–May; guided rides $8/hour; no children under 6.* Breakfast rides are scheduled at 8am ($18); for later risers, brunch rides leave at 10 ($20). Barbecue steak dinner rides ($17.50) are also available. Fishing trips, overnight pack trips, and spot pack trips may all be arranged. Reservations are necessary.

Casino Shows. Big name entertainment is always booked into these showrooms. Be sure to call ahead for reservations to the dinner or cocktail shows. Seats are unassigned and the rumor goes that you must tip the maitre d' (the person who greets you, not the captain— who takes you to your seat). A $5 tip per person along with a request for a seat facing the stage should do it. If you are a couple and the room isn't crowded or if you are a group of four, ask for a booth. When the room is crowded, couples are doubled up at tables, so part of the fun is sharing dinner or drinks with someone you've never seen before and probably will never see again. The best seats are held for late arrivals, so plan to arrive about 15 minutes before a cocktail show and about an hour and a half before a dinner show.

Caesars, Cascade Showroom, *800/648-SHOW, 702/588-3515.*

Harrah's, South Shore Room, *800/648-3773, 702/588-6606.*

High Sierra, High Sierra Theatre, *800/648-3322, 702/588-6211.*

Drive Around the Lake. A leisurely drive around the 72 mile perimeter of Lake Tahoe can be accomplished in about 3 hours. Allow all day, though, as there are many tempting places to stop for picnicking, resting, swimming, and exploring. Call the Visitors Bureau for a free informative brochure.

Grover Hot Springs, *20 miles southeast of town in Grover Hot Springs State Park, 916/694-2248; daily 10am–9pm; adults $1, children 50¢.* Beautifully situated in a valley meadow ringed by pine-covered slopes, these nonsulphurous springs fill two pools. A small one is 102° and a larger one is 80°. They are well-maintained, clean, safe, and lifeguards are on duty. In winter this is a popular après ski destination. Campsites are available.

Lake Tahoe Historical Society Museum, *3058 Hwy 50, 916/541-5458, 544-2312; daily in summer 10am–4pm, rest of year call for current schedule; free.* See interesting memorabilia on the history of Lake Tahoe's south shore.

Lake Tahoe Visitor Center, *on Hwy 89 north of Camp Richardson, 916/ 544-6420; July & Aug daily 8am–6pm; June, Sept, Oct call for schedule; closed Nov–May; free.* Enjoy campfire programs, guided nature tours, self-guided trails, and underground viewing of mountain stream life at the **Taylor Creek Stream Profile Chamber.** Call for a free brochure listing the area's campgrounds.

Tahoe Trout Farm, *1203 Blue Lake Ave. off Hwy 50, 916/541-1491; daily 10am–7pm, closed mid-Oct to mid-May; charged by the size of fish caught, $1 (7″) and up.* Though there is, of course, no challenge to catching trout here, there are some compelling reasons to give it a try. No license is required, bait and tackle are furnished free, and there is no limit. You are virtually guaranteed to go home with tasty dinner fare. Young children, who frustrate easily, are fairly sure to succeed at catching a fish. Do bear in mind, however, that some children will be appalled at the idea of eating the fish they catch.

Vikingsholm, *reached by a scenic one-mile walk from the parking area on Hwy 89 in Emerald Bay, 916/525-7232; tours July & Aug daily 10am–4:30pm; 50¢.* Butterflies, waterfalls, and wildflowers await you on the steep, dry trail which descends to this magnificent Swedish home. It was built completely by hand using native materials and was completed in one summer. Picnic tables are available, and there is a sandy beach where swimming is permitted.

Winter Activities. See p. 194.

SIDE TRIP:

VIRGINIA CITY

After the quiet, scenic, hour-long drive through the hills from Lake Tahoe (take Hwy 50 east through Carson City then Hwy 17 north), arrival in Virginia City—with its noisy beerhalls and gaudy advertising signs—can be shocking to the senses. Touted as "the liveliest ghost town in the west," it certainly does exude a honky-tonk atmosphere.

Established in 1859, Virginia City became the richest mining town in the world due to its rich deposits of gold and silver known as the Comstock Lode. At one time it was the largest city between St. Louis and San Francisco.

This is where Samuel Clemens got his first writing job. He worked on Nevada's first newspaper, *The Territorial Enterprise,* from 1862 to 1864. It was during this time he took the pseudonym Mark Twain. His first book, *Roughing It,* documents his adventures in Virginia City.

An authentic western mining town, Virginia City's main street is now lined with shops, museums, and saloons. One-armed bandits are everywhere. You can have your fortune told, purchase authentic cowboy attire, and have your photo taken in antique garb. And when you get tired, you can take a tram tour of the town.

Some of the lavish Victorian mansions have been restored and are open to the public for tours daily June–October. The Castle, built in 1868, has a three-story tower and some of the original furnishings. It has not been restored but is seen as it originally was used. For further information call 702/847-0275. The Mackay Mansion, built in 1860, also features original furnishings. The Savage Mansion, built in 1861, also offers bed and breakfast on its third floor. For information and reservations call 702/847-0574.

An interesting graveyard is located on the outskirts of town. Take time to read the epitaphs, and be sure to bring your camera.

Outlaw's Gulch is six blocks down the hill from the Bucket of Blood Saloon. A re-creation of Chinatown, it features 12 miniature buildings and is open daily.

The Chollar Mine, a combination gold and silver mine on South F Street (702/847-0155) has daily tours April–October. A tour of the Best & Belcher begins in back of the Ponderosa Saloon on Main Street.

Historic Piper's Opera House, dating from 1885, presents periodic performances and a Chamber Music Festival each July. For information call 702/847-0433. Tours operate daily 10am–4pm, mid-May to September.

The Virginia and Truckee Railroad, located between D & F Streets, runs daily May–September. Built in 1869, this railroad originally carried miners into Carson City and ran as many as 45 trains a day. Now the steam engine carries passengers on a 1½ mile trip through the scenic desert hills to Gold Hill. The train operates daily from 10:30am to 6pm, June–September. Adult fare is $2.50, children $1.25. Call 702/847-0380 for exact schedule.

The favored cuisine in town is jumbo hot dogs and cold beer. Kids should try the sarsaparilla. Dessert is best in an ice cream parlor or candy shop. If you hanker for something fancier, try the Sharon House on Taylor/C Streets (702/847-0133). Located inside the old Bank of California building, it serves Chinese and American dinners daily and mixes up drinks at an antique bar.

If you're interested in visiting for the **Camel Races** held each September, contact the Reno Chamber of Commerce for details (see p. 183).

For more information contact the Virginia City Visitors Bureau, 18 South C Street, Virginia City, Nevada 89440, 702/847-0177. Each day in its office, the Bureau continuously shows a short film on the city's history.

NORTH LAKE TAHOE

North Lake Tahoe Chamber of Commerce
P.O. Box 884
(950 N. Lake Blvd.)
Tahoe City 95730
916/583-2371

Tahoe North Visitors & Convention Bureau
P.O. Box 5578
Tahoe City 95730
800/822-5959, reservations service
916/583-3494

■ *ROUTE*
Located approximately 210 miles north of San Francisco.
Take Hwy 80 to Truckee, then Hwy 267 south to the lake.

■ *STOPS ALONG THE WAY*
Auburn. See page 155.
Grass Valley. See page 156.
Nevada City. See page 158.

■ *GETTING THERE*
You can also get there **by train.** The Chicago-bound Amtrak
train leaves Oakland daily at 11:25am and arrives in Truckee
at 4:58pm. Call 800/872-7245 for fare and schedule information and to make reservations.

■ *WHERE TO STAY*
CONDOS ON THE LAKE:
Rates quoted are for a one bedroom unit for one week, from a low for
off-season to a high for in-season. Many resorts require one-week minimum stays during peak summer season and winter holidays.
Brockway Springs, *P.O. Box 276, Kings Beach 95719, 916/546-4201;*
$420-$525; two-night minimum; lakefront beach club and recreation
center, tennis courts, pool, children's wading pool, sauna, hot springs,
private beach. All units have massive stone fireplaces and balconies
overlooking the lake.
Chinquapin, *P.O. Box RR, Tahoe City 95730, 916/583-6991; $475–*
$675; two-night minimum; 3 private beaches, 7 tennis courts, pool
and sauna, boating facilities, fishing pier, 1-mile paved beachfront
path.
Coeur du Lac, *P.O. Box 7107, Incline Village, Nevada 89450, 702/831-*
3318; $560; no minimum; recreation center, pool, jacuzzi, saunas,
private beach. This attractive complex is actually located one block
from the lake.
Star Harbor, *P.O. Box 1740, Tahoe City, 95730, 916/583-5594, 583-*
3625; $400-$650/three-bedroom unit is smallest; three-night mini-
mum; sandy beach, lagoon, pier, 2 tennis courts, pool.

CONDOS FURTHER OUT:
Carnelian Woods, *P.O. Box 62, Carnelian Bay 95711, 916/546-5924*
(call collect for reservations); ¼ mile from lake; $240-$360; two-night
minimum; access to private lakefront beach club, recreation center

with pool, jacuzzi, sauna, sports facilities, tennis courts, bicycles, 1-mile parcourse, 2-mile cross-country ski course, snow play area.

Granlibakken, *P.O. Box 6329, Tahoe City 95730, 800/543-3221, 916/ 583-4242; 1 mile from lake; $350–$910; two-night minimum; pool, spa, sauna, tennis courts, ski and snow play area, jogging trail.* See also p. 197.

Northstar.

Kingswood Village, *P.O. Box 1919, Kings Beach 95719, 916/546-2501 (call collect for reservations); ¾ mile from lake; $290–$360/two-bedroom unit is smallest; two-night minimum; access to private lakefront beach club, recreational game area, tennis courts, pool, saunas.*

Northstar, *P.O. Box 2499, Truckee 95734, 800/822-5987, 916/562-1113; 6 miles from the lake; $420–$448; two-night minimum; 10 tennis courts, pool, jacuzzi, par course, exercise room, 8-hole golf course, stables, supervised children's recreation programs, childcare center in July & Aug for ages 2–8.* Northstar has been described by the Sierra Club as a "model development." Hotel rooms and homes are also available for rental. A complimentary on-site shuttle bus makes it unnecessary to use your car within the complex. See also p. 197.

LAKEFRONT MOTELS:

Beesley's Cottages, *6674 N. Lake Blvd. (P.O. Box 347), Tahoe Vista 95732, 916/546-2448, off-season 213/335-9891; 2/$, 4/$–$$; closed mid-Oct to mid-May; some kitchens and lake views; TVs; cribs.* A few motel units are also available, and facilities include a private beach and playground.

The Dunes Resort, *6780 N. Lake Blvd. (P.O. Box 34), Tahoe Vista 95732, 916/546-2196; 2/$–$$$, 4/$$–$$$; kitchens, lake views; TVs; cribs; two-night minimum in cottages.* Both motel units and cottages are available here, as well as a private beach and recreational facilities. Weekly rates are discounted.

Mourelatos' Lakeshore Resort, *6834 N. Lake Blvd. (P.O. Box 77), Tahoe Vista 95732, 916/583-5334; 2/$–$$, 4/$–$$$; some kitchens and lake views; TVs; cribs.* These woodsy cottages and motel units are situated in a pine forest that opens to a private beach on the lake.

Trading Post Resort, *5240 N. Lake Blvd. (P.O. Box 209), Carnelian Bay 95711, 916/546-2652; 2/$$–$$$, 4/$$$; kitchens, fireplaces; some lake views; TVs; cribs.* Facilities include a pier and sundeck.

Villa Vista Resort, *6750 N. Lake Blvd. (P.O. Box 199), Tahoe Vista 95732, 916/546-3518; 2/$–$$$, 4/$$–$$$; closed part of the year, call for schedule; some kitchens, fireplaces, and lake views; pool; TVs; cribs; two-night minimum in cottages.* Motel units and cottages are available. Facilities include a sandy beach and a deck overlooking the lake.

OTHER:

Hyatt Lake Tahoe Casino, *P.O. Box 3239, Incline Village, Nevada 89450, 800/228-9000, 702/831-1111.* A special mid-week package costs just $99.90/couple and includes two nights' lodging in the modern hotel, 2 lucky bucks, and 2 breakfasts, 1 dinner, and 4 cocktails per person.

Children under 18 stay free in the same room with their parents. Now that's a bargain! Price and content of the package sometimes varies slightly.

Motel Row. Last-minute lodging can often be found among the numerous motels and cabins lining the lake in Kings Beach and Tahoe Vista. Your chances are best, of course, on weekdays.

The Tahoe Escape, *3000 N. Lake Blvd. (P.O. Drawer UU), Tahoe City 95730, 916/583-0223; two-night minimum.* This service handles over 150 private condominium properties located on the north and west shores. Another service, **Incline Village Sales Co.,** *940 Tahoe Blvd. (P.O. Box 3033), Incline Village, Nevada 89450, 702/831-3349,* handles properties on the northeast shore.

■ *WHERE TO EAT*

Cantina Los Tres Hombres, *8791 N. Lake Blvd., Kings Beach, 916/546-4052.* For description see p. 168.

Clementine's Kitchen and Tavern, *2255 W. Lake Blvd., Tahoe City, 916/583-3134; dinner daily, Sun brunch; highchairs, booster seats, children's portions; reservations suggested; $$; AE, MC, V.* This cozy, casual restaurant has an unpretentious old-fashioned decor and serves tasty American-style fare.

Granite Chief Restaurant, *Olympic Valley, 916/583-0985; July to mid-Sept 10am–5pm, adults $6, under 17 $3; Dec–April 9am–4pm, adults $6, under 13 $4.* This restaurant is located on the slopes of the Squaw Valley ski area and is reached via a tram ride. Call the restaurant for dining details.

Lake House Pizza, *600 N. Lake Blvd., Tahoe City, 916/583-2222; lunch and dinner daily; highchairs, booster seats; no reservations; $; AE, MC, V.* This casual pizza house offers a stunning view of the lake and a choice of sitting inside or outside on the deck. Menu choices include pizza, sandwiches, salads, steaks, and exceptionally good homemade potato chips. **The Great American Omelette Company** (916/583-2225) is located upstairs and serves a breakfast menu daily until 2pm.

The Squirrel's Nest, *Homewood, 916/525-7944; lunch daily July–Sept; highchairs, booster seats; reservations suggested; $; no cards.* Dine outdoors on tasty homemade soups, salads, sandwiches, and desserts. An interesting, well-stocked gift shop adjoins.

Sunnyside Resort, *1850 W. Lake Blvd., Sunnyside, 916/583-4226.* In the past it has been hard to beat a summer meal here outside on the huge deck, watching the sailboats on the lake or enjoying live jazz on Sunday afternoons. At press time the management had changed but was promising even better food. The restaurant was being remodeled, and menu details were not available. If you're in the area, you may want to check it out.

Tahoe City Bakery, *in the Lighthouse Center, Tahoe City, 916/583-8918; M-Sat 7am-6pm, Sun to 4.* Fresh donuts, cinnamon bread, and other bakery goods may be enjoyed on the premises or taken out.

Water Wheel, *115 W. Lake Blvd., Tahoe City, 916/583-4404; dinner daily, lunch also in summer, closed Mar-May and Sept-Nov; booster seats; reservations necessary; $$; MC, V.* Diners here are treated to a river view and some of the tastiest and spiciest Chinese Szechwan, Hunan, and Mandarin cuisine in Northern California. The beef Hunan (beef with noodles and chiles), kung pao chicken (chicken with red peppers and peanuts), and pork Szechwan (pork with water chestnuts, mushrooms, garlic, and peppers served on a pancake) are all highly recommended. Indeed the whole menu seems promising.

■ *WHAT TO DO*

BEST BEACHES:

Across from 510 N. Lake Blvd., Tahoe City. This family beach has a lakefront playground.

Moondunes Beach, *at the end of National Ave., Tahoe Vista.* Shallow water makes this a nice spot for young children.

Sand Harbor Beach, *in Nevada 4 miles south of Incline; $2/car.* This is a perfect beach. The sand is clean and fine, lifeguards are on duty, and there is usually plenty of parking. Arrive early on weekends to assure getting in.

William Kent Beach, *south of Tahoe City.* This is a small, rocky beach. Parking is difficult, but it's worth it.

Bike Trails begin in Tahoe City and follow the north shore to Tahoe Pines. Rentals are available in Tahoe City.

Boreal Alpine Slide, *off Hwy 80 at the Castle Peak exit, 10 miles west of Truckee, 916/426-3666; daily mid-June to mid-Sept 10am-10pm; adults $3, 7-11 $2, no pregnant women or children under age 2 may ride.* Imported from Germany, the Boreal slide is the only one of its kind in northern California. Riders take a chair ski life to the top of the mountain and then sled 3,000 ft. (more than ½ mile)

down to the bottom. Sleds are well-spaced at the top, and speeds can be controlled. The average descent takes 5 minutes and can be described as either exhilarating or relaxing—depending on whom you talk to. Racing cars and bumper boats are also available.

Donner Memorial State Park, *2 miles west of Truckee on Hwy 40, 916/ 587-3841; open June–Aug; $2/car; museum daily 10am–4pm; 50¢.* Located on Donner Lake, this park is a monument to the Donner Party which was stranded here by blizzards in 1846. Picnic facilities, lake swimming, hiking trails, nature programs, and campsites are available. The **Emigrant Trail Museum** has exhibits on the history of the area.

Fishing Charters. Get the names of captains, and your fishing license, at one of the local sporting goods shops. Captains usually supply bait and tackle.

Gatekeeper's Museum, *130 W. Lake Blvd., Tahoe City, 916/583-1762; daily 11am–5pm, closed mid-Oct through April; by donation.* Operated by the North Lake Tahoe Historical Society, this museum is located inside a replica of a 1910 log cabin. The 3½ acre lakeside park is equipped with picnic tables and barbecue facilities.

Miniature Golf. Boberg's Mini Golf, *8685 N. Lake Blvd., Kings Beach, 916/546-3196,* and **Magic Carpet,** *5167 N. Lake Blvd., Carnelian Bay, 916/546-4279,* are open long hours during the summer season and the rest of the year as weather permits.

Ponderosa Ranch, *on Tahoe Blvd., Incline Village, Nevada, 702/831- 0691; daily 10am–6pm Apr–Oct; adults $4.50, 5–12 $3.50.* Created especially for filming scenes for the TV show *Bonanza,* the Ponderosa Ranch is now open to the public for tours. Visitors get a bumpy ride from the parking lot up the hill to the ranch and then a guided tour. After the tour, there is time to explore and visit the petting farm and outdoor barbecue restaurant. The tin cups in which beer and soft drinks are served make great souvenirs. An adjacent stable offers rides over dusty trails featuring spectacular views of the lake. Call 702/831-2154 for reservations and information about the breakfast ride.

River Rafting/Inner Tubing/Truckin' on the Truckee, *begins at the Y in Tahoe City; daily 9:30am–3:30pm June to mid-Oct; approximately $7.50/person.* What better way to spend a sunny summer Alpine day then floating down the peaceful Truckee River a la Huckleberry Finn? All you need is a swimsuit, waterproof shoes, some suntan lotion, and a raft. White-water enthusiasts stay away—this trip is so civilized that there are even portable toilets strategically placed along the riverbank. The three-hour trip ends at **River Ranch,** a restaurant featuring outdoor barbecue dining. Tahoe City concessionaires rent a package which includes raft, life jacket, paddles, and return ride. It is first-come, first-served so get here before 11am to avoid crowds. Children must be at least four.

Sugar Pine Point State Park, *on west shore, 916/525-7982, 525-7232 (winter).* The Visitors Center is located in the huge 1902 three-story Queen Anne Ehrman Mansion. Also on the property near the water is the General Phipps Cabin, built in 1870 of hand-split logs. Hiking trails are available, and campsites are open year-round. In winter, cross-country skiing and snowshoe walks (some ranger-led tours are scheduled) and snow camping lessons join the agenda.

Truckee River Bridge/Fanny Bridge, *junction of Hwys 89 and 28 (the Y), Tahoe City.* You'll know you're here when you see all the fannies lined up. Spectators gather here to view the large trout that congregate beneath the bridge. This dam is the only outlet from the lake.

Winter Activities. See p. 197.

SIDE TRIP:

RENO

"The biggest little city in the world" is located just 35 scenic miles from Lake Tahoe (take Hwy 267 north then Hwy 80 east). Its famous Arch was built in 1927 to commemorate the transcontinental Highway Exposition.

If you want to make Reno your total destination, consider the **Reno Fun Train.** It leaves the Oakland Amtrak terminal Friday evenings February through May and the $115–$140/person fare (adults 21 and older only) includes train transportation complete with a dance band to help people get happy, two nights lodging, and coupons for drink, food, and assorted surprises in Reno. For information and reservations call 415/568-6780.

Of course, most people come to Reno to gamble, and many of the restaurants and attractions are in the casinos. Bargain buffets are available at both **Cal Neva** and **Circus Circus. Harold's Club** is known for the **Prime Rib Room** which serves a filling prime rib dinner each night (adults 21 and older only); reservations are suggested (702/329-0881).

Harold's Club has a huge collection of antique weapons, **Harvey's** a spectacular coin collection, and the **Liberty Belle Saloon** a large collection of antique, commemorative, and just

plain unusual slot machines. **Harrah's Automobile Collection** can be reached via free vintage shuttle buses which leave the casino regularly. The collection is open daily from 9am to 6pm and contains over 1,000 classic restored antique cars which fill three huge showrooms. Admission is $5, 6-15 $3. For further information call 702/788-3242.

Fleischmann Atmospherium-Planetarium at the University of Reno campus features exciting architecture and spectacular shows. Hours and programs vary. Call 702/784-4811 for current show schedule.

Interesting places to stay include the gaudy **Circus Circus** (800/648-5010) which specializes in inexpensive rooms. Free continuous circus acts occur daily from 11am to midnight and children are welcome. The **Comstock Hotel** (800/648-4866), located a few blocks from Casino Row, has a turn-of-the-century decor and an elevator which operates through an imitation mine shaft complete with sound effects. The **MGM Grand** (800/648-5080, 702/789-2000), which claims to be the world's largest casino, is located on the outskirts of town. Inside this gigantic, glittery casino are 7 restaurants, over 40

MGM Grand, Reno.

shops, a 50-lane bowling alley, a pinball parlor, a jai alai court,
2 movie theaters, and a wedding chapel—not to mention plenty
of slot machines and 2,001 rooms. Hotel guests have access to
a pool, tennis courts, and health club. Outside, Camperland
accommodates RVs.

For more information contact the Reno-Sparks Chamber
of Commerce at P.O. Box 3499, Reno, Nevada 89505,
702/329-3558.

MT. SHASTA
AND VICINITY

Shasta-Cascade Wonderland Association
1250 Parkview Ave.
Redding 96099
916/243-2643

■ *ROUTE*

Located approximately 235 miles north of San Francisco.
Take Hwy 80 north to Hwy 5 north.

LAKE SHASTA

Houseboats. See p. 214.

Lake Shasta Caverns, *O'Brien, off Hwy 5, 15 miles north of Redding,
916/238-2341, 238-2386; tours on the hour daily 9am–4pm, Oct–
Apr 10am & noon, closed Jan; adults $7, 4-12 $3.* Discovered in
1878, these caverns didn't open for tours until 1964. The 2½ hour
tour begins with a 15-minute catamaran cruise across the McCloud
arm of Lake Shasta. Then visitors board a bus for a scenic, winding
ride up the mountainside to where the caverns are located. In this
case, getting there really is half the fun.

Mount Shasta Hostel, *200 Sheldon Ave., Mt. Shasta 96067, 916/926-
4896.* This lodging consists of a small cluster of cabins located at the
base of the great mountain. See also p. 219.

Shasta Llamas. See p. 218.

LASSEN VOLCANIC NATIONAL PARK

Mineral 96063
916/595-4444

- ## A LITTLE BACKGROUND

  Imposing 10,457 ft. Lassen Peak is a dormant volcano and is thought to be the largest plug dome volcano in the world. Visitors may enjoy self-guided nature walks and, in the summer, guided hikes and campfire talks. Wooden catwalks guide visitors through popular **Bumpass Hell**, an area featuring geological oddities like boiling springs and mud pots, pyrite pools, and noisy fumaroles. The trail covers three miles and takes about three hours round-trip. The park also offers over 150 miles of backcountry trails including a 17-mile section of the **Pacific Crest Trail**. A free newsletter orients visitors and lists daily activities. The park has four campgrounds (no reservations are taken) but no lodging facilities. It is best to visit July through October, when the 30-mile road through is least likely to be closed by snow. For skiing information, see p. 194.

NORTH

- ## WHERE TO STAY

  Hat Creek Resort, *on Hwy 89 just north of Hwy 44, 11 miles from Lassen Park (P.O. Box 15), Old Station 96071, 916/335-2359; 2–4/$; some kitchens; cribs; two-night minimum in cabins.* These motel units and old-time housekeeping cabins are located on rushing Hat Creek. The cabins are available only May–Oct.

  Little other lodging is available in this area, but many forest **campsites** are available on a first-come, first-served basis. Visitors must bear in mind that this area is remote and does not offer big-city facilities like supermarkets.

- ## WHERE TO EAT

  Uncle Runt's Place, *Hwy 44, Old Station, 916/335-2832; lunch and dinner Tu–Sun; highchairs, booster seats; $; no cards.* This cozy restaurant caters to locals and has a short order menu of sandwiches, hamburgers, and dinner specials.

- ## WHAT TO DO

  McArthur-Burney Falls Memorial State Park, *30 miles north of Old*

Station on Hwy 44; $2/car. A lovely nature trail winds past the soothing rush of the 129 ft. falls, allowing for closer inspection of the volcanic terrain for which this area is known. Also in the park is man-made **Lake Britton,** with picnic tables and a sandy beach and wading area for children. Paddle boats may be rented. Swimming is allowed only in designated areas as the lake has a steep drop-off. Five miles away, the town of Burney offers modern motels and supermarkets.

Spattercone Crest Trail, *½ mile west of Old Station across the street from Hat Creek Campground; free.* This two-mile self-interpretive trail winds past a number of volcanic spattercones, lava tubes, domes, and blowholes. It takes about two hours to walk and is best hiked in early morning or late afternoon.

Subway Cave, *one mile north of Old Station near junction of Hwys 44 & 89; free.* Lava tubes were formed here about 2,000 years ago when the surface of the lava flow cooled and hardened while the liquid lava beneath the hard crust flowed away. This cave, actually a lava tube, winds 1,300 ft. (about ¼ mile) and is completely unlit. Always a cool 46°, it makes a good place to visit on a hot afternoon. However, it is pitch black inside so you must take along a powerful lantern. Even chickens can enjoy the cave—by making a furtive entry and then picnicking in the lovely surrounding woods.

SOUTH

■ *WHERE TO STAY*

Childs Meadows Resort, *on Hwy 36, 9 miles from Lassen Park (Route 5, Box 3000), Mill Creek 96061, 916/595-4411; 2–4/$–$$$; open week- ends only in winter; some kitchens; pool; tennis courts; cribs; dining facilities.* Motel units and cabins are available here. Lawn games, a recreation room, and horseback rentals round out the facilities.

Drakesbad Guest Ranch, *4 Mineral Ave. (P.O. Box 75), Mineral 96063; location: in Warner Valley, 18 miles from Chester; 916/529-1512; 2/$$$, 4/$$$+; closed mid-Sept to mid-June; some shared baths; natural hot springs pool; cribs; all meals included; two-night mini- mum; dining facilities.* In the mid-1800s, Drakesbad was a hot springs spa. Since the turn-of-the-century it has been a guest ranch. Located in a secluded scenic mountain valley in Lassen National Park, most of the rustic cabins, bungalows, and lodge rooms have no electricity and depend on kerosene lanterns for light. The ranch is close to some of Lassen's thermal sights: one mile from the steaming fumaroles at **Boiling Springs Lake** and two miles from the bubbling sulphurous mud pots at the **Devil's Kitchen.** Guests may rent horses from the ranch stables (others should call ahead for reservations; meal reserva- tions may also be made) and take guided rides into these areas. Pack trips may also be arranged. All this and a good trout-fishing stream too!

LAVA BEDS NATIONAL MONUMENT

You can continue north of Lassen Park to Hwy 299 and then head north on Hwy 139 to Lava Beds National Monument. A good stop on this drive through sparsely populated forest and farmland is the **Fort Crook Museum** in Fall River Mills. It is open daily from 1 to 5pm and displays six rooms of antique furniture, a blacksmith's shop, and the old Fall River jail, as well as a collection of early farm implements and Indian artifacts.

It doesn't hurt to be warned ahead of time that Lava Beds is located in the middle of nowhere. Some people might even go so far as to call it a wasteland. The Monument has a camp- ground, but the nearest motels and restaurants are in Tulelake. Perhaps you've heard of the expression "out in the toolies." This could be where the expression originated. It's a good idea to pack in picnic supplies as there is no where to buy food within many miles of the Monument. The area also buzzes with insects, is a haven for rattlesnakes, and, when I visited, had posted plague warnings. But it is still an unusual place and, in my opinion, worth the visit.

The Visitors Center at the southern entrance offers a good orientation. Historically this area is known as the site of the 1872 Modoc War—the only major Indian war to be fought in California. Geologically the area is of interest because of its concentration of caves—approximately 300.

Mushpot Cave, located in the Visitors Center parking lot, is the only lighted cave and has interpretive displays. A loop road provides access to most of the other 19 caves which are open without passes. They have such descriptive names as Blue Grotto, Sunshine, Natural Bridge, and Catacombs—one which must be crawled through. All are unlit and require a good lantern, which may be borrowed free from the Visitors Center. To visit some of the other caves, it is required to register at the Visitors Center . . . just in case. The gravel road north out of the Monument passes through **Tulelake National Wildlife Refuge,** a welcome sight and home to a variety of interesting wildlife which can be easily viewed from the car.

TRINITY ALPS

This is wonderful country to camp in. There really isn't much to do here except relax and perhaps fish, boat, or hike.

■ *WHERE TO STAY*

Cedar Stock Resort and Marina, *on Hwy 3, 15 miles north of Weaverville, Star Route Box 510, Lewiston 96052, 916/286-2225; 2-4/$-$$$; closed Dec-Feb; kitchens; dining facilities; one-week minimum mid-June through mid-Sept.* This quiet spot offers a cabin in the woods or a houseboat on Trinity Lake. Guests provide their own bedding and linens. The marina also rents boats and slips, and the bar and restaurant offer a terrific view of the lake.

Coffee Creek Guest Ranch, *(Star Route 2 Box 4940), Trinity Center 96091, off Hwy 3, 40 miles north of Weaverville, 916/266-3343; $269-$309/person/week, includes 3 meals/day, special rates for children; closed Nov-Apr; some fireplaces; pool; cribs; two-night minimum in spring and fall, one-week minimum June-Aug.* Cabins here are private and located in the woods. Planned activities include hayrides, movies, steak-frys, outdoor games, square dancing, archery, goldpanning, and a kiddie korral with supervised activities for children 2-9. Horseback riding is available at additional charge.

Trinity Alps Resort, *(Star Route Box 490), Lewiston 96052, on Hwy 3, 12 miles north of Weaverville, phone: ask operator for area code 916, Weaverville Exchange, Minersville 332; $195-$290/cabin/week, one-week minimum June–Aug, spring and fall prices by the day, 2-4/$; kitchens; 1 tennis court, dining facilities.* Totally set up to please families, this 90-acre resort offers 40 rustic 1920s brown shingle cabins with sleeping verandas, all scattered along the rushing Stuart Fork River. Guests provide their own linens. They cross the river via a suspension bridge, hang out at the General Store, or gather for theme meals in the dining room which has a patio over the river. Scheduled activities include square dancing and evening movies. Horseback riding is available at additional cost, and kids can ride their bikes endlessly.

■ *WHAT TO DO*

Joss House State Historic Park, *Main/Oregon St., Weaverville, 916/623-5284; tours M–F on the hour 10am–4pm, Sat & Sun on the half-hour; adults 50¢, 6-17 25¢.* Located in a shaded area beside a creek, this Chinese Taoist temple is still in use and makes a cool respite on a summer day.

J. J. Jackson Memorial Museum, *next door to Joss House, 916/623-5211; daily 10am–5pm May–Nov; by donation.* Trinity County's history is traced through mining equipment, old bottles, and photographs. A reconstructed blacksmith's shop and miner's cabin are also on display. Outside a creekside picnic area beckons.

WINTER
SNOW FUN

DOWNHILL SKIING

Ski areas are plentiful in northern California. The season runs
from the first snow, usually in late November, through the
spring thaw in April. A few resorts are known for staying
open longer.

Lifts usually operate daily from 9am to 4pm. Rates for an
all-day lift ticket vary from a low of $5 (rope tow) to a high
of $22; many resorts offer weekday discounts. To avoid park-
ing problems and long lines for lift tickets and rentals, plan
to arrive early. On-site equipment rentals run $11–$14/day.
Group downhill lessons range from $10 to $18 and average
two hours. Childcare runs $2–$3/hour; many resorts have an
all-day fee ranging from $14 to $34. Many resorts offer lodg-
ing/lift, learn-to-ski, and bargain midweek packages.

The least crowded times at the resorts are the three weeks
after Thanksgiving, the first two weeks in January, and late in
the season. The two weeks around Christmas are ridiculous.

CROSS-COUNTRY SKIING

Cross-country skiing is becoming more popular each year. One
reason for this surging popularity is the advantages it has over

191

downhill skiing: there are no lift tickets to purchase; the equipment is less expensive; the sport is considered safer, can be enjoyed in groups, and allows you to get away from crowds. But cross-country also requires more stamina and is less exhilarating.

Specialized cross-country centers offer equipment rentals, lessons (average cost is $6–$10 and reservations are usually required), maintained trails, and warming huts. Trail maps are usually available at the center headquarters, and use fees range from free to $5. Some centers also offer lodging, guided tours, the option of downhill facilities, and reduced rates for children.

Children age 4 and older are usually taught in classes with their parents; but some centers have special children's classes. If you have the strength, younger children can be carried in a backpack.

It is a good idea for beginners to rent equipment and take a few lessons to learn safety guidelines and basic skiing techniques. Once the basics are learned, this sport can be practiced just about anywhere there's a foot of snow.

SNOW PLAY

Toboggans, saucers, inner tubes (the most fun), and sometimes sleds (the most dangerous) are the equipment found in snow play areas. They are inexpensive to buy but bulky to store. Many commercial areas will let you use your own equipment, but some require that you rent their equipment.

Snow play can be dangerous when people do not pay attention to safety rules. I once had the wind knocked out of me by an antsy bear of a man who didn't wait for me and my young child to come to a stop before he pushed down the same hill in his saucer. He said, "Sorry. But you shouldn't have been there." I'm sure worse stories are waiting to be told.

Dress for cold, wet weather. Wear wool when possible, and pack a change of clothes. Protect feet with boots. If you don't have boots, a cheap improvisation is to wrap feet in newspapers and then in plastic bags and then put shoes on. Also large plastic garbage bags can improvise as a raincoat if need be. Always wear gloves to protect hands from sharp, packed snow.

DRESSING KIDS FOR THE SNOW

Until you know what you want or need, borrow clothing from friends.

I have found the following to be a comfortable, warm way to dress children for the snow. Most of the ideas carry over and work for adults as well. Many of the items you will have on hand already. Others make excellent presents for Christmas or Hanukkah—which comes just at the beginning of the season.

Dress children in thermal underwear (available at Sears, REI Co-op 800/426-4840) which can afterwards be used for pajamas. Then put on a cotton turtleneck to keep out drafts. On top of that put a wool or wool-blend pullover sweater and insulated bib-front water-repellent pants (Sears) or regular overalls treated with a water-repellent spray. Top it off with their regular winter jacket. For insulation use two layers of socks: a thin cotton liner and a thicker wool pair—unribbed to avoid blisters. If you have them, legwarmers can add an extra layer of warmth worn over or under pants.

To avoid loss of children's gloves or mittens, thread a length of elastic or thick yarn through their jacket sleeves and pin mittens to the ends. A wool hat that can be pulled down over their ears is essential (20–30% of body heat is lost through uncovered heads); some convert to face masks for windy days. Avoid long neck scarves as they have been known to become entangled in lift equipment, and we all know what happened to Isadora Duncan. Sunglasses with a safety strap or cuter, more expensive goggles are necessary to cut the glare. A warm pair of waterproof boots for after-skiing are useful; avoid rubber as it gets very cold. Good-looking, popular, and warm "moon boots" can be purchased inexpensively.

Zip into pockets: sun-block cream, chapstick, loose change for a snack, kleenex, an identification slip (with name and address or location of parents) and perhaps a box of raisins or a candy bar treat.

Information about ice skating, snowcat rides, snowshoe walks, and miscellaneous other winter facilities are also included in this section.

WAY UP NORTH

Lassen Volcanic National Park Ski Area, *Mineral 96063, 916/595-3376; 49 miles east of Red Bluff; downhill and cross-country; 1 triple chair, 2 rope tows; lift $5–$12, children under 6 ski free; children's program; lodging nearby 916/529-1512, packages available; free beginning ski lessons; free snowshoe walks on weekends 916/595-4444; free snow play area.* California's "undiscovered National Park" is an excellent area for families and beginners. The scenery includes hot steam vents and mud pots, allowing for an unusual and interesting cross-country ski tour. See also p. 186.

SOUTH LAKE TAHOE

Echo Summit, *P.O. Box 8955, South Lake Tahoe 95731, 916/659-7154; on Hwy 50, 42 miles east of Placerville; downhill and cross-country;*

*2 double chairs, 1 rope tow; lift $10-$12.75; lodging nearby 800/
822-5922.* This area is especially good for families and beginners to
low intermediates.

Heavenly Valley, *P.O. Box 2180, Stateline, NV 89449, 916/541-1330;
downhill only; 5 triple chairs, 11 double chairs, 10 rope tows; lift
$22; lodging nearby 800/822-5922, adjacent townhouses 800/822-
5967, packages available; children's ski school (5-12), private classes
for younger children.* This is one of the largest, and possibly most
scenic, ski areas in the country. Situated in two states, the runs on
the California side offer breathtaking views of Lake Tahoe. Heavenly
has been rated as having the best intermediate skiing in California. It
has exhilarating expert slopes, and now it even offers helicopter skiing.

Kirkwood Ski Resort, *P.O. Box 1, Kirkwood 95646, 209/258-6000; on
Hwy 88, 30 miles south of Lake Tahoe; downhill only; 1 triple chair,
7 double chairs, 1 rope tow; lift $20; childcare center (3-8), children's
ski school (4-12); lodging on premises in condominiums (209/258-
7247) and nearby housekeeping cabins at* **Kays Resort** *209/258-8598
and* **Sorenson's** *916/694-2203.* This is an uncrowded family area and
is famous for its snow. It is said to snow here when it is raining at
other Tahoe ski areas. Located adjacent is the **Kirkwood Cross Country Ski Area** (P.O. Box 77, 209/258-8864) which offers guided overnight trips including lodging and meals.

Sierra Ski Ranch, *Twin Bridges 95735, 916/659-7475; 3 miles west of
Echo Summit; downhill only; 8 double chairs, 1 triple chair; lift $16;
lodging nearby 800/822-5922.* This family-run ski area is popular
with families and teenagers.

Strawberry Ski Touring, *Hwy 50, Kyburz 95720, 916/659-7200; 15
miles west of South Lake Tahoe; cross-country only; lodging nearby.*
Snow camping and courses in survival are offered.

■ *SNOW PLAY*

Borges' Sleigh Rides, *on Hwy 50 across from the High Sierra casino,
916/541-2953; daily 10am-dark; adults $5, under 12 $4, family
rates.* Take a 45-minute ride around a meadow in an old-fashioned
"one-horse open sleigh."

Hansen's Resort, *1360 Ski Run Blvd./Needle Peak Rd. near Heavenly
Valley, South Lake Tahoe, 916/544-3361; daily 9am-noon, 1-4pm;
3 hour toboggan rental/$5 M-F, $9 Sat & Sun, saucer rental $3.*
Facilities include a saucer hill and a packed toboggan run with banked
turns and a mechanical toboggan return (return operates only on
weekends). Equipment must be rented on the premises. Lodging
facilities are available.

Snowshoe Walks. *Sierra State Parks, P.O. Drawer D., Tahoma 95733,*

916/525-7232. Request a schedule of ranger-led snowshoe and cross-country hikes in Lake Tahoe area state parks by sending a stamped, self-addressed legal size envelope to the above address. Hikes are scheduled January–April.

Taylor Creek Ski Tour and Snow Play Area, *off Hwy 89 west of Camp Richardson at the end of Cathedral Rd.* This is an informal, small area good for younger children.

Winter Carnival, *916/541-5255.* Three days of theme sports and special snow activities are scheduled for late in January. Call for details.

Winter Wonderland, *3672 Verdon, So. Lake Tahoe 95705, 916/544-7903;*

daily; free. This snow play area is an open field located behind the Winter Wonderland ski rental shop. Saucers may be rented in the shop for $4/day.

NORTH LAKE TAHOE

Alpine Meadows, *P.O. Box AM, Tahoe City 95730, 916/583-4232; 4 miles north of Tahoe City; downhill only; 10 double chairs, 1 T-bar, 2 poma; lift $22; childcare snow school (3–6), children's ski school (6–12); lodging nearby, 916/583-1045; packages available.* Alpine is usually open through Memorial Day and some years is open into July—giving it the longest ski season at Lake Tahoe. Ask about their five day learn-to-ski program which begins each Monday. Reservations are necessary for the free on-hour guided tours offered on Saturdays and Sundays beginning at 9:30am. Tours show participants the main runs and how to avoid crowds. Alpine also hosts a free ski clinic for amputees; call for details.

Granlibakken, *(see p. 176), 916/583-9896; 1 mile south of Tahoe City; 1 rope tow, 1 poma; lift $8, lodging guests free.* This small ski area has beginner and intermediate slopes and a snow play area.

Homewood, *P.O. Box 165, Homewood 95718, 916/525-7256; on Hwy 89 six miles south of Tahoe City; downhill only; 1 quadruple, 1 triple, 1 double chair, 1 T-bar, 3 platter, 2 beginner lifts; lift $16; children's ski school (4–6); lodging nearby 916/583-3494.* The slopes here are ideal for intermediates.

Northstar, *P.O. Box 129, Truckee 95734, 916/562-1010; off Hwy 267*

six miles south of Truckee; downhill and cross-country; 6 double, 3 triple chairs, 2 rope tows; lift $21; childcare center (2–6), children's ski school (5–12); lodging in modern condos on premises 800/822-5987, 916/562-1113, packages available. Lift ticket sales are limited to assure the slopes don't get overcrowded. This area is said to be the least windy at Tahoe and is good for beginners and excellent for intermediates. It offers organized activities throughout the week and caters especially to families. Free two-hour introductory tours, in which participants are shown the best runs and given a history of the area, are available on Fridays and Sundays beginning at 11am. See also p. 177.

Squaw Valley, *P.O. Box 2007, Olympic Valley 95730, 916/583-6985; off Hwy 89 five miles north of Tahoe City; downhill only; aerial tramway, 6 passenger gondola, 5 triple, 17 double chairs, 2 rope tows; lift $22; childcare snow school (2–5), children's ski school (5–14); lodging on premises, 800/545-4350 or 916/583-5585 collect, packages available.* Squaw Valley made its name in 1960 as the home of the VIII Winter Olympic Games. Today it is a world-class ski area known internationally for its open slopes and predictably generous snowfall, which usually allows Squaw to stay open into May. Many avid skiers consider it to be the best ski resort in the state because it has the steepest, most challenging expert slopes. Indeed, there are good slopes for every ability level. The old Papoose ski area is now Squaw Valley's Children's World, a special area for children under 12 equipped with 2 platter pulls and a poma lift. Senior citizens over age 70 ski free; children 12 and under ski for $5. A free 1–2 hour introductory tour is scheduled each day at 1pm.

Tahoe Nordic Ski Center, *925 Country Club Dr. (P.O. Box 1632), Tahoe City 95730, 916/583-9858, 583-0484; on Hwy 28, 3 miles east of Tahoe City; cross-country only; children's lessons (4–10), weekends only; lodging nearby.* Ask about the moonlight tours.

Tahoe Ski Bowl, *P.O. Box 305, Homewood 95718, 800/822-5910, 916/525-5224; on Hwy 89 seven miles south of Tahoe City; downhill only; 1 double, 1 triple chair, 1 T-bar, 2 rope tows; lift $14; childcare center, children's ski lessons (4–6); lodging nearby 916/583-3494.* Forest ski runs and excellent views of the lake make this medium-sized family resort special.

■ SNOW PLAY

Carnelian Woods Condominiums. See p. 175.

North Lake Tahoe Regional Park, *off Hwy 28 at the end of National Ave., Tahoe Vista, 916/546-7248; daily; free.* This 108-acre park has a snow play area for toboggans and saucers. Snowmobile rentals are available on weekends to use on a quarter-mile oval racing track and

2½ miles of trails. Cross-country trails and picnic tables round out the facilities.

Snow Shoe Walks, *(Sierra State Parks).* See p. 195.

Sugar Pine Point State Park. See p. 181.

DONNER SUMMIT

Big Chief Guides Nordic Center, *P.O. Box AE, Truckee 95734, 916/587-4723; on Hwy 89 two miles north of Squaw Valley; cross-country only; housekeeping cabins on premises.*

Boreal, *P.O. Box 39, Truckee 95734, 916/426-3666; Castle Peak exit off Hwy 80 ten miles west of Truckee; downhill only; 8 double chairs, 1 triple chair; lift $14; children's ski school (3–12); motel lodging on premises (916/426-3668), packages available.* Facilities are especially good for beginners and low-intermediates. This area is known for being relatively inexpensive and convenient to the Bay Area. Night skiing is available.

Donner Ski Ranch, *P.O. Box 66, Norden 95724, 916/426-3635; on Hwy 40, 3½ miles from the Norden/Soda Springs exit off Hwy 80; downhill only; 4 double chairs, 1 poma; lift $15; lodging on premises, packages available.* This area offers no frills and is best for beginners and intermediates.

Royal Gorge Nordic Ski Resort, *P.O. Box 178, Soda Springs 95728, 916/426-3871; at Soda Springs/Norden exit off Hwy 80 near Donner Pass; cross-country only; lodging on premises, packages available; children's ski school (3–10).* Modeled after Scandinavian ski resorts, Royal Gorge is not easily accessible. Guests are brought in by snowcat-drawn sleigh (sorry, no reindeer or horses yet) and leave by skiing the two miles back out. Lodging is primitive. In the old 1920s hunting lodge, everyone shares the same toilet area. Bathing facilities are a choice of steaming in a sauna or soaking in an outdoor hot tub, both of which are reached by a short trek through the snow. Sleeping facilities are dormitory-style bunk beds and your own sleeping bag, making this a place to avoid for a romantic weekend. The food, however, is remarkably civilized. A chef works full-time in the kitchen preparing attractive, tasty, and bountiful French repasts. Oh, yes. The skiing. Guests may cross-country ski whenever they wish, and the capable staff gives lessons each morning and afternoon. A two-night weekend runs $148/person (children under 15 $110) and includes everything except equipment, which may be rented on the premises. Special midweek rates are available. Royal Gorge also operates a more accessible cross-country center for day skiers.

Soda Springs, *P.O. Box 67, Soda Springs 95728, 916/426-3666; at Soda Springs exit off Hwy 80, 4 miles west of Donner Summit; downhill only; 1 double, 2 triple chairs; lift $10; open F–Sun; children's ski school (4–12); lodging nearby.* This relatively new resort is built on the former site of one of the very first Sierra ski resorts. Slopes are best for beginners and intermediates. Ask about the learn-to-ski packages.

Sugar Bowl, *P.O. Box 5, Norden 95724, 916/426-3651; on Hwy 40 three miles from the Soda Springs exit off Hwy 80; downhill only; 7 double chairs; lift $20; lodging on premises, packages.* This is one of the oldest Sierra ski resorts and is known for having short lift lines and good runs at all ability levels. Skiers park their cars carefully (to avoid tickets) and then ride a gondola or chair lift up to the resort. Night skiing is available. The **Norden Ski Inn Hostel** (916/426-3079) is situated just 200 yards from Sugar Bowl. It is open year-round and offers homecooked meals. See also p. 219.

Tahoe Donner, *P.O. Box TDR45, Truckee 95734, 916/587-6046; on Hwy 40, ½ mile from the Truckee/Donner Lake exit off Hwy 80; downhill and cross-country; 2 double chairs, 1 rope tow; lift $12; children's ski lessons (4–6), lodging in modern condos and homes on premises.* This small resort is good for beginners and intermediates. The cross-country ski center, located at Tahoe Donner Northwoods

Clubhouse, schedules special tours like Ski With Santa, a Morning Nature Tour, a Sauna Tour, and an annual Donner Trail Tour. For information call 916/587-9821.

EAST

Bear Valley Nordic, *P.O. Box 5005, Bear Valley 95223, 209/753-2834, 753-2844; on Hwy 4, 45 miles from Angels Camp; cross-country only; lodging nearby.* Overnight tours, complete with lodging and food, are available.

Cottage Springs, *P.O. Box 4338, Camp Connell 95223, 209/795-1401, 795-1803, 795-1209; on Hwy 4 eight miles east of Arnold; 1 double chair, 1 platter, 2 rope tows; lift $5–$12; lodging nearby; snow play area.* Beginner and intermediate slopes only are available here.

Dodge Ridge, *P.O. Box 1188, Pinecrest 95364, 209/965-3474, 415/345-7763; 32 miles east of Sonora off Hwy 108; downhill only; 1 triple, 5 double chairs, 3 rope tows; lift $15; childcare center (2–8), children's ski lessons (3–12); lodging nearby.* This low-key, family-oriented ski area is good for beginners and intermediates and is known for its short lift lines. Classes are available in ballet skiing.

Mt. Reba/Bear Valley, *P.O. Box 5038, Bear Valley 95223, 209/753-2301; on Hwy 4, 55 miles east of Angels Camp; downhill only; 2 triple, 7 double chairs, 2 beginners; lift $19; childcare center, children's ski school (4–7); lodging in condos, homes, and lodges on premises, 209/753-6222.* If you stay in this secluded resort village, you can ski home at the end of the day. Visitors park at the edge of the village and then walk. Skiers take a bus to the slopes. Bear is one of the biggest ski areas in the state, with runs for all ability levels and short lift lines. It is popular with families and especially good for beginners and intermediates. More condos and lodge rooms are available through 800/247-9346. Inexpensive rooms with bathrooms down the hall are available at nearby **Red Dog Lodge** 209/753-2344.

■ *SNOW PLAY*

Bear River Lake Resort, *on Bear River Reservoir, 20 miles east of Pioneer, 3 miles off Hwy 88, 209/295-4868; daily 8am–10pm; free.* Visitors may use their own equipment in this groomed snow play area. Snowmobiles, cross-country equipment, snow shoes, saucers, and tubes are available for rental, and back-country cross-country trips may be arranged.

Calaveras Big Trees State Park, *see p. 142.* Bring your own snowshoes or cross-country skis for the free ranger-led walks. Reservations must be made at least one week in advance (209/795-2334).

Cottage Springs, *(see ski area on p. 201), open daily; tube rentals $3–*
$5/day. You must rent their equipment to use the tube hill.

Crystal Springs Ski Touring, *2640 Crystal Springs Ct., Camino 95709,*
916/644-3608; cross-country only; children's lessons; lodging nearby.
Call for schedule of full-moon wiener roast tours.

Leland Meadows, *P.O. Box 1498, Pinecrest 95364, 209/965-3745; 36*
miles east of Sonora off Hwy 108; daily 9am–4:30pm; admission $4,
under 5 free, rentals $3–$8, visitors may bring own equipment. Tubes
give the best ride on these supervised, groomed slopes but toboggans
and saucers may also be used. Bring a picnic and plan to spend the
day. Guests staying in the adjacent townhouses may use the facilities
for half-price. Snowcat tours and rentals and a cross-country ski area
are also available.

Long Barn Lodge Ice Rink, *23 miles east of Sonora off Hwy 108, Long*
Barn, 209/586-3533; adults $3, 12 and under $2, skate rental $1.
The top of this rink is covered, but two sides are left open. The rink
is located behind an old bar and restaurant built in 1925. Call for
current schedule.

SOUTH

Badger Pass, *Yosemite National Park (see p. 123), 209/372-1330; off*
Hwy 41, 20 miles from the valley; downhill and cross-country; 4
double chairs, 1 T-bar, 1 rope tow; lift $15.50; childcare center (3
and older), children's ski school (7 and older); lodging nearby, pack-
ages available; snow play area. Badger Pass opened in 1935, making
it California's oldest organized ski area. It is a prime spot for beginners and intermediates and is especially popular with families. Its
natural bowl has gentle slopes and provides shelter from wind. A
free shuttle bus delivers valley guests to the slopes. Tickets must be
picked up the day before at any lodging reservations desk. A snow
play area is located several miles from the slopes, but it is not always
accessible and there are no equipment rentals. Cross-country skiing
is arranged through the Mountaineering School (209/372-1244), the
oldest cross-country ski school on the west coast. Survival courses
and snow camping and overnight tours including lodging and meals
are available. Ask about the bargain "midweek ski special."

Grant Grove Ski Touring Center, *Kings Canyon National Park 93633,*
209/335-2314; in Grant Grove Village; children's lessons; lodging
nearby. Moonlight and guided overnight tours are available. Snow
play areas are located at Azalea campground and Big Stump picnic
areas. See also p. 131.

The old days.

June Mountain, *P.O. Box 146, June Lake 93529, 619/648-7733; 4 miles south of Hwy 395, 58 miles north of Bishop; downhill only; 5 double chairs, 1 T-bar; lift $20; childcare center (4–5), children's ski school (6–12); lodging nearby.* This compact, uncrowded area is excellent for beginners and popular with families. For lodging try the June Lodge (714/648-7713). A former hunting lodge, it was once a popular retreat for movie stars like Clark Gable and Humphrey Bogart.

Mammoth Mountain, *P.O. Box 24, Mammoth Lakes 93546, 619/934-2571; 50 miles north of Bishop; downhill only; 2 gondolas, 6 triple, 17 double chairs, 2 T-bars, 1 poma, 1 beginners; lift $21; infant care, childcare center (2–8), children's ski school (6–12); lodging nearby.* One of the three largest ski areas in the country, Mammoth has the highest elevation of any California ski area. It also has some of the longest lift lines and one of the longest seasons, usually staying open through June and sometimes into July. A 7-hour drive from the Bay Area, it is actually more popular with southern Californians. Lodging reservations may be made through Mammoth Realty and Reservations Bureau 619/934-2528 and Mammoth Reservation Service 619/934-2522.

Mammoth Ski Touring Center, *P.O. Box 69, Mammoth Lakes 93546, 619/934-2442; at Tamarack Lodge on Twin Lakes, 2½ miles from Mammoth Lakes Village; cross-country only; lodging nearby.* For the hearty, expedition tours are scheduled in which the night is spent in a snow cave or tent.

Montecito-Sequoia Nordic Ski Center, *1485 Redwood Dr., Los Altos 94022, 415/967-8612; on Hwy 180 between Kings Canyon and Sequoia National Parks; cross-country only; lodging on premises (see pp. 132 and 210), packages; natural lake ice skating rink.* Here you can enjoy breath-taking ski tours and snow-shoe walks through groves of giant sequoias.

Sequoia Ski Touring Center, *Sequoia National Park 93262, 209/565-3373; in Giant Forest Village; cross-country only; children's lessons; lodging nearby (see p. 132).* Moonlight and overnight guided tours are available.

Wilsonia Ski Touring, *Kings Canyon National Park, 93633, 209/335-2404; cross-country only; lodging on premises (see p. 132).* Inexsive overnight hut tours may be arranged.

Wolverton Ski Bowl, *Sequoia National Park 93262, 209/565-3373; on Hwy 198, 52 miles east of Visalia; 2 rope tows, 1 T-bar; lift $12; open weekends and holidays; lodging nearby; snow play area.* This is a beginner and intermediate area. See also p. 131.

■ *SNOW PLAY*

Yosemite, *(see p. 123).* Ice skate in the shadows of Glacier Point and Half Dome at the scenic outdoor rink in Curry Village.Lessons are available. Call 209/372-1442 for schedule; admission $3.50, rentals $1. Open-air snowcat rides leave from Badger Pass daily 10am–3pm. Call 209/372-1330 for reservations; tickets are $5. Free ranger-led snowshoe walks are available at Badger Pass (209/372-4461). A good place to snowshoe on your own is the Sequoia Forest Trail in Mariposa Grove.

FAMILY CAMPS

Remember the good old days when you were a kid and got to go away to summer camp? Bet you thought those days were gone for good. Well, they're not. Now you can go to a family camp.

Family camps provide a reasonably-priced, organized vacation experience. They are sponsored by city recreation departments, university alumni organizations, and private enterprise. The city and private camps are open to anyone, but some university camps require a campus affiliation.

And you don't have to have children to attend. One year when I was at Santa Barbara, a couple was actually honeymooning! Elderly couples whose children have grown sometimes attend, and family reunions are sometimes held at a camp. Whole clubs have been known to book in at the same time.

Housing varies from primitive platform tents or cabins without electricity, plumbing, or bedding to comfortable campus dormitory apartments with daily maid service. Predictably, cost varies with the type of accommodations and facilities. The average charge per adult ranges from $16 to $22/day, $90–$495/week. Children are usually charged at a lesser rate according to their age.

Most family camps operate during the summer months only and include special programs for children, meal preparation

and clean-up, an informal atmosphere where guests can unwind, and recreation programs complete with campfires and
sports tournaments.

Locations vary from the mountains to the sea. Activities
can include river or pool swimming, hikes, fishing, volleyball,
ping pong, badminton, hayrides, tournaments, campfires, crafts
programs, songfests, tennis, and horseback riding.

Each camp has its own special appeal, and usually over half
the guests return. Repeat guests and their camp friends often
choose the same week each year.

For detailed rate information, an itemization of facilities,
session dates, and route directions contact the camp reservation offices for a free brochure. And to avoid disappointment,
make your reservations early.

■ CITY/GROUP CAMPS

Camp Concord, *Concord Department of Leisure Services, Civic Center,
2974 Salvio St., Concord 94519, 415/671-3273; daily rates; located
near Camp Richardson at South Lake Tahoe; cabins with electricity,
provide own bedding, community bathrooms; cafeteria-style meals;
special program for ages 3–6, and 7–16; horseback riding and river
rafting available at extra charge.*

Camp Sacramento, *Department of Community Services, 3520 5th Ave.,
Sacramento 95817, 916/449-5195; daily rates; located in the El
Dorado National Forest 17 miles south of Lake Tahoe; cabins with
electricity, provide own bedding, community bathrooms; cafeteria-
style meals; program for age 3 and older, babysitting available at
extra charge.*

Camp Sierra, *Associated Cooperatives, Inc., 4801 Central Ave., Rich-
mond 94804, 415/526-0440; weekly rates; located in a pine forest
between Huntington and Shaver Lakes about 65 miles east of Fresno;
some cabins with electricity, lodge rooms, or bring own tent; provide
own bedding, community bathrooms; family-style meals; special activities for teens, playground and crafts program for younger children;
special programs on consumer topics.*

Cazadero Family Music Camp, *CAMPS Inc., 1744 University Ave., room
208, Berkeley 94703, 415/549-2396; weekly rates; located in Russian
River area; platform tents with electricity, dormitories; provide own
bedding, community bathrooms; family-style meals; daycare for toddlers, program for ages 2–6.* The music classes are open to everyone
regardless of ability or experience. Campers may learn anything from
beginning musical theory to advanced steel drums. Private lessons are

available on all instruments. Dance and art classes are also available.

Echo Lake Family Camp, *CAMPS Inc., 1744 University Ave., room 208, Berkeley 94703, 415/549-2396; weekly rates; located on the western rim of the Lake Tahoe basin near the Desolation Wilderness Area; tent cabins without electricity, provide own bedding, community bathrooms; family-style meals; infant care, program for toddlers and older children; swimming pool, seminars on nature exploration and survival techniques.*

Feather River Family Camp, *Office of Parks and Recreation, 1520 Lakeside Dr., Oakland 94612, 415/273-3791; daily rates; located in the Plumas National Forest near Lake Tahoe; cabins and platform tents without electricity, provide own bedding, community bathrooms; family-style meals; play area and activities for ages 2–6, program for age 6 and older; three theme weeks: nature, square dancing, folk dance.*

Mather Family Camp, *San Francisco Recreation and Park Department, McLaren Lodge, Golden Gate Park, San Francisco 94117, 415/558-4870; daily rates; located on the rim of the Tuolumne River gorge near Yosemite National Park; cabins with electricity; provide own bedding, community bathrooms; cafeteria-style meals; playground area, program for age 6 and older; pool, horseback riding.*

San Jose Family Camp, *San Jose Parks and Recreation Department, 151 W. Mission St., room 203, San Jose 95110, 408/277-4661; daily rates; located in the Stanislaus National Forest 30 miles from Yosemite National Park; platform tents without electricity, provide own bedding, community bathrooms; buffet and family-style meals; play area, program for age 3 and older; pool.*

Silver Lake Family Camp, *Department of Parks and Recreation, City Hall, room 301, Stockton 95202, 209/944-8371; daily rates; located 40 miles south of Lake Tahoe; platform tents without electricity, cabins with electricity; provide own bedding, community bathrooms; cafeteria-style meals; program for toddlers and older; swimming in lake, horseback riding.*

Tuolumne Family Camp, *Berkeley Camps Office, 2180 Milvia St., Berkeley 94704, 415/644-6520; daily rates; located on south fork of Tuolumne River near Yosemite National Park; platform tents without electricity, provide own bedding, community bathrooms; family-style meals; programs for toddlers–6, 6–12, teens; swimming instruction in river, cookout and breakfast hikes.*

■ *PRIVATE ENTERPRISE CAMPS*

Coffee Creek Guest Ranch. See p. 189.

Emandal. See p. 75.

Greenhorn Creek Guest Ranch, *P.O. Box 11, Spring Garden 95971, 916/283-0930; weekly rates; located 70 miles north of Lake Tahoe in Feather River country; modern cabins and hotel units with maid service, private bathrooms; family-style meals; female wrangler cares for children 2-5 from 8am-4:30pm daily, babysitting available at additional charge; pool, swimming hole, horseback riding, hayrides, fishing, hiking, golf and tennis nearby.* All activities are included in the price. A special Thanksgiving weekend is available, and in the spring and fall daily and weekend rates may be secured on a space-available basis. This is where you go to rough it in comfort.

Highland Ranch. See p. 70.

Kennolyn's Family Camp, *8205 Glen Haven Rd., Soquel 95073, 408/ 475-1430; weekly rates; located four miles from Soquel in the Santa Cruz mountains; cabins with electricity, provide own bedding, some private bathrooms; family-style meals; infant care, programs for all ages; 3 tennis courts, pool, darkroom access for photographers, and instruction in horseback riding, riflery, archery, gymnastics, crafts, sailing, and soccer.*

Montecito-Sequoia Lodge Family Camp Program, *1485 Redwood Dr., Los Altos 94022, 415/967-8612; weekly rates; located in Sequoia National Forest between Kings Canyon and Sequoia National Parks; lodge, bedding provided, private baths; also open cabins, provide own bedding, community bathrooms; buffet meals; programs for age 3 and older; 2 tennis courts, lake swimming, pool, sailing, canoeing, boating, archery, photography darkroom, fishing, riflery, waterskiing, horseback riding.* See also pp. 132 and 204.

Skylake Yosemite Camp, *summer: P.O. Box 25, Wishon 93669, 209/ 642-3720, rest of year: P.O. Box 11163, Palo Alto 94306, 415/493- 4075; weekly rates; located on Bass Lake 20 miles from Yosemite National Park; screened cabins without electricity, provide own bedding, community bathrooms; buffet and family-style meals; no special children's programs; 2 tennis courts, canoes, sailboats, archery, riflery, crafts, waterskiing, horseback riding.*

■ *UNIVERSITY CAMPS*

Alumni Vacation Center, *University of California, Santa Barbara 93106, 805/961-3123; weekly rates; located on U.C. campus in Santa Barbara; dormitory suites with private bathrooms, refrigerators, and daily maid service; bedding provided; cafeteria-style meals; infant care, eight hours of programs daily for all ages; 10 tennis courts, pool, swimming and tennis lessons, bicycle rentals.*

Lair of the Bear, *Lair Reservations, Alumni House, University of California, Berkeley 94720, 415/642-0221; weekly rates; located in the*

Stanislaus National Forest near Pinecrest; tent cabins with electricity, provide own bedding, community bathrooms; family-style meals; supervised play for ages 2–6, program for 6 and older; two camps (Camp Blue and Camp Gold), pool, 3 tennis courts, swimming and tennis lessons.

■ *AND THEN THERE'S . . .*

OZ. See p. 66.

HOUSEBOATS

Living in a houseboat for a few days is an unusual way to get away from it all. You can dive off your boat for a refreshing swim, fish for dinner while you sunbathe, and dock in a sheltered, quiet cove for the night.

Houseboats are equipped with kitchens and flush toilets. Most rental agencies require that you provide your own bedding, linens, and groceries. Almost everything else is on your floating hotel—including lifejackets. Rates vary quite dramatically depending on the time of year (summer rentals are the highest) and how many people are in your party (a group of six to ten people gets the best rates). Weekly rates for 6 average $500–$700 and can go as high as $1,300, depending on the size and quality of the boat. Fuel is additional. Some rental facilities have enough boats to offer midweek specials and three-day weekends; some offer a Thanksgiving special which includes the turkey and pumpkin pie. During the off-season, some will even rent their boats for just a day. Contact rental facilities directly for their current stock and rates.

LAKE OROVILLE

Lime Saddle Marina, *P.O. Box 1088, Paradise 95969, 916/534-6950.*

For more information on this area contact:

Oroville Chamber of Commerce
1789 Montgomery
Oroville 95965
916/533-2542

LAKE SHASTA

Bridge Bay Resort & Marina, *10300 Bridge Bay Rd., Redding 96003, 916/275-3021.*

Holiday Flotels, *P.O. Box 336, Redding 96099, 916/246-1283.*

For more information on houseboating on Lake Shasta contact Shasta-Cascade Wonderland Association (see p. 185) or:

Shasta Dam Area Chamber of Commerce
P.O. Box 1368
Central Valley 96019
916/275-8862

SACRAMENTO DELTA

Herman & Helen's Marina, *Venice Island Ferry, Stockton 95209, 209/951-4634.* Inquire about the special RV barge.

Holiday Flotels, *11540 W. 8 Mile Rd., Stockton 95209, 209/477–9544.*

Paradise Point Marina, *8095 Rio Blanco Rd., Stockton 95209, 209/952-1000.*

For more information on houseboating on the Delta contact:

Stockton Chamber of Commerce
1105 N. El Dorado
Stockton 95202
209/466-7066

Rio Vista Chamber of Commerce
60 Main St.
Rio Vista 94571
707/374-2700

RIVER TRIPS

The adventure of rafting down a changing and unpredictable river offers a real escape for the harried, city-weary participant. But don't expect it to be relaxing. Participants are expected to help with setting up and breaking camp and are sometimes mercilessly exposed to the elements. While not dangerous when done with experienced guides, an element of

risk is involved. Still, most participants walk away ecstatic and addicted to the experience.

The outfitter will provide shelter, food, and equipment for the trip. You need only bring sleeping gear and personal items. Costs range from $130–$200/person for an overnight run. Some one-day trips are available. Seasons and rivers vary with each company. The minimum age for children ranges from 6 to 10. For details contact the tour operators.

American River Touring Association, *445 High St., Oakland 94601, 415/465-9355.*

ECHO: The Wilderness Company Inc., *6529 Telegraph Ave., Oakland 94609, 415/652-1600.*

Mariah Wilderness Expeditions, *P.O. Box 1384, El Cerrito 94530, 415/ 527-5544.* This is California's only woman-owned and operated whitewater raft and wilderness company. Special mother/daughter trips are scheduled, as well as father/son trips (with male guides).

Whitewater Voyages/River Exploration Ltd., *P.O. Box 906, El Sobrante 94530, 415/222-5994.*

PACK TRIPS

Packing your equipment onto horses or mules allows for a much easier and luxurious trek into the wilderness than does backpacking. All necessary equipment, food, and paraphernalia can be packed onto these beasts of burden. You need simply to make the choice as to the type of pack trip you desire.

On a spot pack trip the packers will load the animals with your gear, take them to your prearranged campsite, unload your gear, and return to the pack station with the pack animals. They will return to repack your gear on the day you are to leave. You may either hike or ride on horses to your campsite. If you ride, you will usually have a choice of keeping the horses at your campsite or of having the packers take them back out. If you wish to keep them, you will need to arrange in advance for a corral and feed, and you should be experienced with horses. Do not bring along small children who haven't had at least basic riding instruction.

A more rugged trip (where you move your campsite each day) or an easier trip (with all expenses and a guide included) can also usually be arranged with the packer.

This is not an inexpensive vacation. Prices will vary according to which of the above options you choose. For example: all-inclusive guided trips average $90–$120/day/person, spot pack trips average $215–$390/person plus a daily fee for the stock. Trips are usually available only in the summer. Special rates are usually available for children, who must be at least five years old. For general information and a list of packers contact:

Eastern High Sierra Packers Association, *690 N. Main St., Bishop 93514, 619/873-8405.*

High Sierra Packers Association, Western Division, *P.O. Box 1362, Clovis 93613.*

Guided pack trips can also be taken with llamas. They're used to this chore, having been used for it for over 2,000 years in the Andes. And they are so gentle even a four-year-old can lead one. For details contact the following outfitters:

Mama's Llamas, *P.O. Box 655, El Dorado 95623, 916/622-2566.*

Shasta Llamas, *P.O. Box 5160, Oakland 94605, 415/635-0286 and P.O. Box 1137, Mt. Shasta 96067, 916/926-3959.*

MISCELLANEOUS ADVENTURES

American Youth Hostels, *Golden Gate Council, 680 Beach St. #363, San Francisco 94109, 415/771-4646.* The idea behind hosteling is to save money, so accommodations are simple. Women bunk in one dormitory-style room and men in the other. Some hostels have separate rooms for couples and families. Bathrooms and kitchens are shared. All guests are expected to do a chore, and lights are out at 11pm. Hostels are closed during the day, usually from 9:30am to 4:30pm. Fees are low, ranging from $2 to $10/person/night. Hostel members receive a $2 discount at most hostels as well as a newsletter and handbook of U.S. hostels. Call for further information and a brochure listing all the hostels in northern California. Hostels listed in this book are: Arcata Crewhouse (p. 80), Midpines (p. 126), Montara Lighthouse (p. 19), Mount Shasta (p. 185), Norden Ski Inn (p. 200), Pigeon Point Lighthouse (p. 19), Point Reyes (p. 65), and Saratoga (p. 14).

Audubon Canyon Ranch, *4900 Hwy 1, Stinson Beach 94970, 415/383-1644.* Past weekend programs have included From Branches to Baskets, a weekend of weaving, and Small Animal Safari, especially for families. Lodging is in a bunkhouse featuring solar-heated water and toilets operated by wind power. Participants provide their own bedding and meals. Inquire if you are interested in trading your labor for a reduction in the seminar fee.

Backroads Bicycle Touring Co., *P.O. Box 5534, Berkeley 94705, 415/652-0786.* Bicycle tours include the Wine Country, Russian River, Coast, Solvang, and Death Valley as well as areas outside of California including the Colorado and Canadian Rockies, Yellowstone, and the Grand Canyon. The emphasis is not on endurance but on getting some exercise. Two tour guides accompany bikers and a support vehicle transports equipment (and cyclists if they get tired). To allow for different ability levels, several routes are available on each trip. Accommodations are in either interesting hotels or comfortable campgrounds, and meals are included.

Bed & Breakfast International, *151 Ardmore Rd., Kensington 94707, 415/525-4569, 527-8836.* Lodging and full breakfast are provided in private homes throughout northern California. There is a two-night minimum.

California Adventures, *Department of Recreational Sports, University of California, 2400 Durant, Berkeley 94720, 415/642-4000.* Adventure trips include rock climbing, backpacking, snow camping, cross-country skiing, river rafting, kayaking and canoeing, bike tours, sailing and wind surfing.

Marin Adventures, *Marin Community College, Kentfield 94904, 415/485-9581.* Overnight trips are varied and in the past have included a backpacking trip for parents with babies, a whale-watching trip to Monterey, and a ski tour of the Tahoe rim.

Nature Explorations—Tuleyome, *2253 Park Blvd., Palo Alto 94306, 415/324-8737.* These teacher-led trips are mostly camping and backpacking—some specifically aimed at families and/or single parent families. For example, in the winter there might be a snow camping trip and a cross-country ski weekend, in the spring a backpacking trip to the Sierras or a photography trip to Yosemite. The program also offers many daytrips. The organization's objective is to foster in residents attachment to their environment.

Point Reyes Field Seminars, *Point Reyes 94956, 415/663-1200.* These interpretive programs held at Point Reyes National Seashore are co-sponsored by the National Park Service and the Coastal Park Association. Instructors are experts in their fields and courses include both day trips and overnight trips—some designed especially for families. Subjects include art, photography, horseback riding, cooking, whale and bird watching, and Indian culture.

Stone Witch Expeditions, *Pier 33, San Francisco 94111, 415/431-4590.* This 70 ft. square rigged schooner was launched in 1975. She has been chartered by Greenpeace for whale watching trips and has sailed to Central America and Micronesia. May–December she is available for sail training day trips on the Bay. Two-night weekend trips include meals and berths for $200/person. Longer expeditions are scheduled in the winter.

University Extension. Contact your local State College or University about their travel/study extension program. San Jose State offers a program of family vacations (408/277-3736). The University of California sponsors a program of research expeditions (415/642-6586).

Volunteer Vacations. Get a job as a volunteer in a state park or forest. Host a campground, improve trails, collect data on wildlife, explain an area's history to visitors. Only a very few of these jobs reimburse travel and food costs or provide accommodations. For a copy of the booklet *Helping Out in the Outdoors* ($3) contact 16812 36th Ave. West, Lynnwood, Washington 98036, 206/743-3947. You may also be able to find it in your library.

Wildlife Weekend, *S.F. Zoological Society, Sloat Blvd., San Francisco 94132, 415/661-2023.* This weekend trip is usually scheduled in early June and includes nature seminars and evening campfires. Participants provide their own transportation and camping equipment. Meals are included in the nominal fee. This special program is for members of the Zoological Society only. A $35 family membership allows unlimited free admission to the Zoo, a subscription to Animal Kingdom Magazine, invitations to other member-only events, discounts at the Zoo Shop, and free admission to 50 other U.S. zoos and aquariums.

CAMPING

Because there are excellent resources available for information on campgrounds, I have mentioned only a few unusual ones which otherwise might be missed. For more complete information, consult the following references:

California-Nevada Camping (a book) and *Camping, California-North* (a map) list camping facilities and fees and are available free to AAA members.

The California State Park System (available by mail for $2: Department of Parks and Recreation, P.O. Box 2390, Sacramento 95811). This informative brochure contains a map which pinpoints all state parks, reserves, recreation areas, historic parks, and campgrounds.

Western Campsites, a Sunset Book, is updated annually. It is the *complete* camping guide. Everything you need to know is here.

■ *TICKETRON CAMPSITE RESERVATIONS*

Reservations are advisable at most state park campgrounds and can be made through Ticketron for a small service fee. This may be done in person (bring cash) or by mail. Reservations may be made as early as eight weeks in advance. For general information on state park campgrounds and for the location of the Ticketron outlet nearest you call 800/952-5580 or 916/445-8828.

ABOUT THE AUTHOR

Carole Terwilliger Meyers, a native San Franciscan, holds a B.A. degree in anthropology from San Francisco State University and an elementary teaching credential from Fresno State College. Currently she is a columnist for *California* magazine and a contributing editor for *Parents' Press.* In the past she has been a columnist for the *San Jose Mercury News* and *California Travel Report* and an editor for *Goodlife* magazine and the San Francisco Bay Area *ASPO* (Lamaze Natural Childbirth) *Newsletter.* Her articles have been published in *California Living, San Francisco* magazine, and *New West* as well as numerous other magazines and newspapers. Ms. Meyers resides in Berkeley with her husband and two children.

INDEX

Northstar, 177, 197
Northwood Lodge, 110
Nut Tree, 115

O
Oak Meadow Park, 15
Oakville Grocery, 96
Oakwood Lake Resort, 125
Occidental, 111
Ocean Echo Motel & Cottages, 21
Ocean View Lodging, 74
Octagon Santa Cruz County Historical
  Museum, 22
"Old Abe" Volcano Blues Cannon, 148
Old Bath House, 36
Old Eagle Theatre, 119
Old Faithful Geyser, 102
Old Milano Hotel, 67
Old Sacramento, 118
Old Theatre Cafe, 21
Old Town, Eureka, 82
Old Town, Los Gatos, 15
Orr Hot Springs, 75
Outrigger, 29
Oz, 66

P
PG&E Energy Information Center, 58
Pacheteau's Original Calistoga Hot
  Springs, 100
Pacific Garden Mall, 23
Pacific Grove Museum of Natural History,
  36
Pacific Lumber Company, 85
Packer Lake Lodge, 160
Pajaro Dunes, 21
Pardee Lake, 146
Patisserie Boissiere, 41
Pebble Beach Equestrian Center, 44
Pedro's, 15
Pelican Inn, 64
Pelton Wheel Mining Museum, 158
Peppermint Stick, 141
Petrified Forest, 102
Pfeiffer-Big Sur State Park, 46
Piedmont Hotel, 75
Pine Beach Inn, 74
Pioneer History Center, 128
Piper Playhouse, 151
Point Lobos State Reserve, 44
Point Motel, 55
Point Piños Lighthouse, 37
Point Reyes National Seashore, 65
Ponderosa Ranch, 180
Poor Red's, 151
Presidio of Monterey Museum, 33
Pygmy Forest, 74

R
Red Castle Inn, 159
Ricochet Ridge Ranch, 74
Ridenhour Ranch House Inn, 110
Ripplewood Resort, 47
River Galley, 116
Riverlane Resort, 111
Roaring Camp Mining Co., 145
rock climbing, 128
Rocky Point, 41

Rose's Landing, 56
Rosicrucian Egyptian Museum, 17
Royal Copenhagen, 59
Royal Gorge Nordic Ski Resort, 199
Royal Valhalla, 167

S
Sacramento Delta, 213
Sacramento Science Center and Junior
  Museum, 119
Sail-In Motel Apartments, 167
Salmon Lake Lodge, 160
Samoa Cookhouse, 81
Sam's Town, 151
San Antonio House, 39
San Benito House, 19
San Jose Family Camp, 209
San Simeon Pines Resort Motel, 51
Sancho Panza, 29
Santa Cruz City Museum, 23
Santa Cruz Municipal Wharf, 22
Santa Cruz Yacht Harbor, 24
Santa Cruz Boardwalk, 22
Sardine Factory, 29
Scheidel's Old European Restaurant, 157
Scopazzi's Inn, 12
Sea Gull Inn, 70, 72
Sea Ranch, 66
Sea Rock, 70
Sea View Inn, 39
Sebastian's General Store, 53
Sequoia Park and Zoo, 82
Sequoia Ski Touring Center, 204
Serenisea, 67
Seven Gables Inn, 35
17-Mile Drive, 37, 44
Shadowbrook, 26
Sharpsteen Museum and Sam Brannan
  Cottage, 102
Sierra County Historical Park and
  Museum, 163
Sierra Nevada House III, 153
Sierra Shangri-La, 160
Sierra Ski Ranch, 195
Silver Lake Family Camp, 209
Silverado Country Club, 93
Silverado Museum, 97
Silverado Restaurant, 101
Sivananda Ashram Vrindavan Yoga Farm,
  156
Skippy's Hacienda Inn, 111
Skylake Yosemite Camp, 210
Skylark Motel, 106
Smoke Cafe, 136
Snowline Lodge, 132
Soda Springs, 200
Soldier Factory, 53
Sonoma Cheese Factory, 89
Sonoma French Bakery, 89
Sonoma Hotel, 88
Sonoma Mission Inn, 88
Sonoma Sausage Company, 90
Sonoma State Historic Park, 90
Sonoma Town Square Park, 90
Sonora County Museum, 138
South Camanche Shore, 146
Southside Resort, 111
Spaghetti Warehouse, 29

ORDER FORM

_____Weekend Adventures for City-Weary People: Overnight
Trips in Northern California, Meyers @ $7.95 . . . $_____

_____How to Organize a Babysitting Cooperative and Get Some
Free Time Away From the Kids, Meyers @ $3.95 . . . $_____

_____   hardcover $8.95 . . . $_____

_____What to Do Between Here & There (_260 travel activities
designed to stimulate discussion_), Kirsch @ $4.95 . . . $_____

_____Family Bike Rides: A Guide to Over 40 Specially
Selected Bicycle Routes in Northern California,
Grossberg @ $5.95 . . . . $_____

_____Offbeat Oregon: Connoisseur's Collection of Travel
Discovery in Oregon, Bell @ $6.95 . . . . $_____

_____Places to Go With Children in Southern California,
Kegan @ $6.95 . . . . $_____

_____The Best Places: Restaurants, Lodging, and Tourism in
Washington, Oregon & British Columbia, 1984 ed.
Brewster @ $11.95 . . . . $_____

_____Private Schools of the East Bay (_Alameda and Contra
Costa Counties_), Parents' Press @ $6.95 . . . . . . $_____

TRAVEL PAPERS: Short travel articles by
Carole Terwilliger Meyers

_____A Weekend In Ensenada, Mexico @ $2.00 . . . . . $_____

_____Oregon: Camping Favorites, Shakespeare Festival in
Ashland, Coast Attractions, Eugene, Stops Along Hwy
5 @ $3.00 . . . . $_____

_____Washington State: Mount St. Helens/Northwest Trek,
Seattle With Children @ $2.00 . . . . $_____

_____The English Side of Victoria, British Columbia @ $2.00 . $_____

_____Los Angeles: Disneyland, Going Hollywood @ $3.00 . . $_____

☐ Please send fund-raising brochure   subtotal $_____

6½% sales tax (Calif. residents only) $_____

postage/handling $___1.50___

total amount enclosed $_____

SEND TO (please print):

name_____ phone_____

address_____

city, state, zip_____

ALL ORDERS MUST BE PREPAID. Make check or money order payable to
Carousel Press and mail to: **Carousel Press**, P.O. Box 6061, Albany, CA 94706